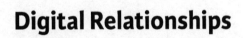

Digital Relationships

Digital Relationships

NETWORK AGENCY THEORY AND BIG TECH

Jason Davis

STANFORD BUSINESS BOOKS
An Imprint of Stanford University Press
Stanford, California

Stanford University Press

Stanford, California

©2023 by the Board of Trustees of the Leland Stanford Junior University. All rights reserved.

Special discounts for bulk quantities of Stanford Business Books are available to corporations, professional associations, and other organizations. For details and discount information, contact the special sales department of Stanford University Press. Tel: (650) 725-0820, Fax: (650) 725-3457.

Printed in the United States of America on acid-free, archival-quality paper

ISBN 9780804791106 (cloth)
ISBN 9781503634176 (electronic)

Library of Congress Control Number: 2022015730

Library of Congress Cataloging-in-Publication Data available upon request.

Cover design: Kevin Barrett Kane

Cover illustration: Adobe Stock

Typeset by Newgen in Minion Pro 10.5/14.5

For my family

CONTENTS

PART II

Theory of the Firm: Network Agency
Problems in the Organizational Context

PREFACE

Why do so many organizations fail to utilize the social networks of individual members to respond to disruptions, innovate, and change? In this book, I develop a new perspective on this fundamental question in the study of networks and organizations that I call network agency theory. The central idea is that individual and organizational interests in networking can come out of alignment such that the network ties that individuals form are organizationally suboptimal, thereby reducing the organization's capacity to achieve its most ambitious goals. The theory explains how network agency problems emerge, the role of digital technology adoption by organizations in amplifying misalignment, and the capacity of managers and the function of the executive to resolve agency problems and mitigate their impact. This book builds upon two decades of qualitative research in American, Asian, and European big-tech companies and new analytical and computational modeling to develop theory about network agency problems in organizational environments where digital technologies are prevalent.

The first half of the book describes four pathologies that emerge from seemingly prosocial networking behaviors pursued by individuals to enhance their social capital that are nonetheless organizationally detrimental, such as too many ties, ties that are too weak, entrenched brokers, and networks with high social capital inequality. My argument is not merely that organizational networks occasionally fall into these maladaptive states, but rather that they inevitably do so if individuals pursue their networking interests in modern organizational contexts without intervention. A central idea is that digital technologies including both enterprise software tools (e.g., email, Slack, Yammer, Zoom) and consumer and social media platforms (e.g., Twitter, Facebook, LinkedIn)—have decreased networking costs but increased networking incentives to such an extent that the creation and maintenance of maladaptive networks is likely. The overriding metaphor is that digital technologies produce "digital relationships," where mere affiliations and brief contacts are reified and members collaborate on critical organizational projects without sufficient relational quality in network structures and with pernicious social capital distributions.

In the second half of the book, I discuss the organizational implications of network agency theory, including the persistence of social capital pathologies in the face of managerial interventions and its implications for organization design and governance. I describe a critical equilibrium in which organizations reconstitute disrupted networks to explain why managerial interventions in networks often fail—that is, networks often "snap back" to maladaptive states without continued managerial attention. I also offer a new interpretation of classical problems in organizational design (silos and bottlenecks) and strategic management (exploration failure and the prominence of inorganic growth modes) as a manifestation of network agency problems. To address these problems, a new function of the executive that focuses on strategic social capital practices in human resource management—hiring, socialization, and role formation—can be used to minimize future network agency costs. Finally, I argue that an inductive research agenda focused on theory building with cases, models, and experiments is best able to advance network agency theory.

Two types of readers may be interested in this book. For scholarly readers, who are the primary audience, I suggest beginning with Chapter 1, where I sketch the basic arguments and implications of the network agency theory I develop. The later chapters in Part I accumulate evidence for network agency problems; extend this evidence with arguments that generalize the theoretical mechanisms, typically culminating in analytic or computational models where these are formalized; and draw implications. Citations are kept to a minimum in the main text in order to avoid excessive interruptions, although numerous connections to the literature are made in the chapter endnotes and in the references. As the arguments are developed, it may be useful to follow along in Table 1, which summarizes the main predictions, mechanisms, and outcomes of the theory. In Part II, I unpack implications of network agency theory for organizational theory and strategic management. Chapter 6 presents evidence for the persistence of network agency problems in organizations and the impact of managerial interventions, which helps to clarify central agentic mechanisms and so might be generally interesting. Yet depending on their scholarly subfield, readers may wish to jump to chapters on strategic social capital and the work-from-home experiment, where I draw implications for human resource management, work, and technology; organizational design and boundaries; or entrepreneurship and innovation. Those interested in further developing or testing network agency theories may be interested in the Chapter 10, on research agendas.

I am hopeful that some practicing managers may find the book useful. For practitioners, I suggest skimming Chapter 1 and reading the other chapters in Part I with an eye to the resemblance of network agency problems to issues in their own organization. Short summaries at the beginning of chapters may aid in chapter selection. Practitioners may be particularly interested in Chapter 6, on the short- and long-run effectiveness of managerial interventions, while Chapter 7, on strategic social capital practices and organizational design may be useful for executives who have responsibility for policies to mitigate network agency problems. The science of network agency problems is in its infancy. Further research may generate diagnostic tools and interventional frameworks that help organizations overcome these persistent network sources of failure.

Digital Relationships

PART I
PRINCIPAL-AGENT PROBLEMS IN NETWORKS

Conflicting Interests in Networking and Their Effects

Networks Are the Problem

CONFRONTING THE SOCIAL CAPITAL CONSENSUS

This chapter introduces network agency theory and outlines the book. The central idea is that individual and organizational interests about networking can come out of alignment such that the network ties that individuals form are organizationally suboptimal, thereby reducing the organization's capacity to respond to disruptions, innovate, and change. The theory explains how network agency problems emerge, the role of digital technology adoption by organizations in amplifying this misalignment, and the capacity of managers and function of the executive to resolve agency problems and mitigate their impact.

Organizations hold great promise to solve many of society's biggest problems, provide a livelihood for their members, and create wealth for their owners. A key characteristic of an organization is that it brings together people to work toward a common purpose with higher goals than any one individual can achieve alone. To do so, leaders of large modern organizations must align interests and coordinate the work of different groups of people, often enduring and adapting to changes in organizational conditions and the environment.

Organizations may not always have the most noble purposes (to be sure, exploitation and war have been the stated aims of some organizations); however, they often create the tools—innovative products and services—that can be used to meet humanity's highest aspirations, such as improving human life, exploring the world and outer space, and alleviating poverty and suffering. In fact, there is evidence that organizations may play an outsized positive role in changing public opinion to support more fair, equitable, and just outcomes in society. Many of society's greatest achievements stem from organizations, even if most organizations do not achieve greatness.

Although organizations may hold great promise, they are also rife with failure. Despite ambitious goals and strong purposes, they routinely fail to achieve the objectives that are essential for their well-being and survival. They fail to respond to technological disruptions and create innovations that meet evolving customer needs. They fail to encourage collaboration either within or across boundaries. They also fail to explore new options and identify new models for doing business. Most important, they fail to change at a fundamental level when faced with large environmental or industry discontinuities such as the current revolutions in digital technologies and corporate social responsibility.

These failures rarely occur because organizational leaders do not see these discontinuities on the horizon. Rather, their responses lack urgency, are ineffective, or are limited to window-dressing meant to capture the public relations value of their stances without fundamentally transforming the organization.

Consider the example of Multibank—the pseudonym for a global financial services conglomerate I studied—which operates in the retail, commercial, and investment banking sectors. Multibank's leaders identified digital banking as the single most important disruption they faced. This recognition was matched by a strong commitment by Multibank's board and top managers, with a CEO who staked his reputation on transforming Multibank into a "true digital bank."

In fact, Multibank was well positioned to go digital, having spent more than its peers on computing technology, and it was known to have strong technical capabilities in its award-winning R&D group. "In many ways, we are already a high-tech company," an executive at the company told me, referring to the various digital initiatives that were already in place.

However, despite seemingly ideal conditions, informants recounted several examples of disorganized projects, ineffective initiatives, and internal resistance, with years of effort spent just to reach industry parity with a basic mobile banking app. Higher-value fintech initiatives such as open banking, back-end automation, and branch virtualization failed despite extensive internal efforts including bootcamps, hackathons, and partnerships with startups. The bank even implemented "agile" and "Lean Startup" methods to breathe entrepreneurial spirit into its change efforts, yet, after three painful years, the CEO found himself retrenching and reorganizing these efforts in a massive organizational restructuring exercise.

Every organizational scholar can recount similar examples of organizational failure that occur despite seemingly ideal strategic, financial, and technical conditions. Indeed, it is the persistence of these company-wide failures—and associated internal dysfunction—that justifies the mandate for organizationally focused explanations of performance. Why do organizations fail to innovate, grow, and change?

At the time of its founding, the modern field of organizational theory was shaped by a passionate debate about whether organizational change was even possible, with some insisting that unresponsiveness was a necessary price to pay for the reliability, accountability, and reproducibility expected from organizations.[1] These theories suggested that organizations had a sort of inertia that insulated them from overly risky change.

A subsequent generation of organizational scholarship focused on understanding the rare examples of successful innovation and change that did occur, against great odds. Typically, this literature focused on managerial practices or organizational arrangements that enabled organizations to explore new opportunities while maintaining sufficient stability. Researchers developed these organizational ideas in the contexts of breakthrough product development, adoption of cutting-edge technologies and practices, and strategic reorientation and renewal, among others. Their studies noted the improvisational, temporary, and informal character of such adaptive activities, along with the uncertainty, risk, and anxiety involved in implementing them.[2] A surprisingly common finding was that long-standing relationships among organizational members provided a strong foundation for risky organizational change. These relationships often preceded successful innovation, collaboration, and reorganization efforts because of the stability they provided.[3]

THE SOCIAL CAPITAL CONSENSUS

In line with the themes just described, organizational scholars began examining a more fundamental driver of organizational failure and success—social networks themselves. Here, social networks are defined as sets of relationships among individuals that form a basis for future interactions.

Sociologists and psychologists have long found that preexisting relation-ships, or "ties," among individuals are a good foundation for new collabo-rations grounded in trust, good will, and common understanding of each other's preferences and capabilities.[4] These ties are said to provide valuable "social capital" that supplements the financial, political, and human capital required by individuals and groups to achieve goals.[5]

On the basis of these foundational ideas, social capital researchers con-vincingly demonstrated that network features such as the number, charac-ter, structure, and topology of interpersonal relationships can explain dif-ferences in individual outcomes, for instance job attainment, income, and even happiness.[6] Several canonical theories have emerged. For example, it is well established that a larger network is more useful for an individual than a smaller one, as additional ties increase the likelihood of accessing vital resources (centrality theory). Strong ties characterized by emotional inten-sity, intimacy, and several prior interactions are thought to be particularly useful in getting things done. However, although strong ties are important, possessing an adequate number of weak ties—which enable individuals to access diverse information—can be more likely to reveal fresh opportunities (weak-tie theory). Individuals who occupy network positions bridging those who are otherwise disconnected have advantages related to information and control (brokerage and structural hole theory). Finally, individuals posi-tioned in a few network hubs with a high number of ties are likely to capture a disproportionately large share of value in that network (small-world and scale-free theory).

Organizational scholars were attracted to network theories because fea-tures of internal organizational networks seemed to provide a root-cause explanation as to why some organizations were able to initiate successful innovation, collaboration, and change while others were not. Armed with new tools for measuring networks, researchers began to apply them to the networks of employees and managers. Decades of empirical research ensued using statistical measures, such as centrality, betweenness, and constraint, which were meant to capture important intuitions regarding the advantages of network structures.

A consensus emerged in fits and starts. Scholars argued that various sources of network diversity—whether structural, relational, positional, or scale-based—were particularly useful for accessing the new knowl-edge, skills, or other resources necessary to achieve substantial change in organizations.[7] The ideal network, they argued, was dense in connections, with sufficient weak ties and brokers to bridge structural holes across many otherwise disconnected parts of the social space. In such a network, diverse knowledge diffused fast and far, good ideas were developed, and novel combinations of ideas from disparate domains were available for the organization to explore and exploit during innovation and change efforts. If members formed enough of the right relationships to bring together different ideas, people, and resources, it was concluded, then organizations could avoid many of the problems that plagued them, or so the story went.

Recently executive leaders at Multibank came to a similar conclusion: although their managers were some of the most internally and externally connected employees in the banking industry, executives felt that members lacked enough connectivity or the right linkages to collaborate effectively across Multibank's organizational silos or with external stakeholders such as regulators, retailers, and fintechs. Much effort was put into facilitating new connections between individuals with complementary expertise and launching new strategic alliances with other organizations. The initiatives were popular; employees were energized by the new collaborations. However, despite great promise, many of these intensive initiatives stalled. Managers remained undaunted, as they were hopeful that new linkages would eventually generate good outcomes, consistent with the claims discussed previously.

In fact, the evidence for social capital theories of organizational improvement is mainly inferential.[8] Because a large population of different organizational networks is rarely available for study, most empirical efforts rely on individual-level analyses in a single organization with regression models resembling those in social capital research. The dependent variables are individual outcomes. Therefore, only by inference can one conclude that positive network outcomes for individuals will aggregate to the organizational level. An assumption is that the individual benefits of networks should produce benefits for the broader collective. Putting these empirical difficulties aside, this effort must be viewed as a substantial scholarly success. Theory from another discipline had been adapted to the organizational case, generating a cottage industry of publications with a rich intellectual heritage.

In an ironic twist, some of the strongest evidence for individual social capital theories themselves emerged from organizational research sites because of the ease of collecting individual network data by managerial fiat.

Although social capital theories of organizational performance may have less supporting evidence than desired, it is clear that individual organizational members benefit from social capital in terms of promotions, wages, and leadership responsibilities. At a broader level, perhaps the largest contribution of this body of organizational theory is the development of a consensus view about how organizations, teams, and individuals can overcome pervasive failures to innovate, collaborate, and change with an extensive and diverse network of relationships.

TAKING AN ORGANIZATIONAL PERSPECTIVE ON INDIVIDUAL NETWORKING

In this book, I develop a different perspective. I argue that, rather than offering a true solution to organizational problems, networks—as conceptualized by organizational scholars and structured in modern organizations—are actually the source of these problems. Instead of enabling collaboration, innovation, and change at a broader organizational level, individual network dynamics often harm them. Based on extensive field research, I developed new models of organizational networking that account for these difficulties. The key insight is that network theories underlying the social capital consensus do not adequately explain organizational outcomes. This is because they do not fully embed networks in the modern organizational context in which networking is technologically enabled and mobilized toward specific organizational objectives.

Of course, the reality of networking in organizations is that it is primarily an individual affair, shaped by widely varying interests, capabilities, and positions of different organizational members. Yet networking interests may vary predictably across organizational roles and formal positions in the managerial hierarchy, especially as individual executives and managers are given responsibility to achieve organizational outcomes that stem from their span of control. This echoes the long dormant political view of organizational life,[9] in which conflicts of interest between employees, managers, and owners are treated as a common occurrence demanding managerial attention. We should expect that organizational social networks are no less fraught with conflict than other administrative structures, and are perhaps more so considering the "dual character" of interpersonal relationships in that they are critical for both individual and organizational ends.

It is useful to take the organizational perspective on individual networking since the difference in levels of analysis clarifies both normative and positive dimensions. For instance, while it is natural to ask about the optimal organizational network, this is a logically separate issue from the networks that individuals actually enact when they follow their own interests, which are in turn shaped by their own beliefs and expectations. Analysis may reveal effective organizational network designs, but this tells only part of the story if managers are unable to achieve them. For example, it has been argued that loosely coupled, centralized, and matrix networks are most useful under various conditions. Yet these designs may in fact be unachievable with the behavioral inclinations of a particular employee set.[10] According to one executive, when asked why he did not implement a particular network design, "We can't get there from here."

Networks may be the most difficult organizational features to design. Charles Perrow (1972) famously called organizations "recalcitrant tools" because of the manner in which individual employees can sometimes resist the dictates of management. In fact, networks may be the most recalcitrant organizational tool of all precisely because it is individual employees, not managers, who form, maintain, and work within most sets of relationships. Managers rarely participate in employees' ties, and hence they cannot observe or directly control these relationships, which individuals may use for different ends. In fact, we should not assume that individual networking will always generate positive organizational outcomes because the accumulation of even seemingly positive behavior can generate negative aggregate outcomes that thwart organizational designers. A truly organizational perspective on networks must be multilevel because individual networking behavior may generate surprising organizational outcomes. It is only by understanding the interplay of individual interests, networking behavior, and organizational outcomes that managers can design the most appropriate interventions.

SOCIAL CAPITAL PATHOLOGIES IN ORGANIZATIONS

Most of this book is concerned with difficulties that I refer to as "social capital pathologies" to indicate their problematic character for the organizational system, and the potential for diagnosing and solving them. These problems stem from individual networking behavior that may not be in the organization's interests. Each problem presents a challenge to existing social capital theorizing as it is applied to organizational science. Here, in Part I, I describe common network pathologies in which individuals develop too many ties (Chapter 2); ties that are too weak (Chapter 3); bridges that are too old, with ossified brokerage positions (Chapter 4); and networks with a scale that is too "free," with relationships that are distributed too unequally across individuals (Chapter 5).

I present evidence of unchecked network growth in organizations that results in overcommitment and excessive communication in large tie portfolios, relational quality insufficient to mobilize heterogeneous resources, entrenched positions that reduce diffusion and block innovation, and misallocated and underutilized human resources stemming from an unequal distribution of social capital. Table 1 summarizes the network agency theory that is developed here, including linkages between social mechanisms and outcomes. I show how the relationship between excessive ties, the weakness of ties, bridge age, scale dispersion, and negative organizational outcomes such as limited diffusion and innovation are a logical consequence of the shifting costs and risks of individual networking demonstrated in modern technologically enabled organizations.

These networking costs include the organizational attention required to form and maintain many ties, ensuring the effectiveness of interpersonal interactions without sufficient trust and mutual knowledge, management of the misaligned incentives and insufficient knowledge of brokers, and the negative spillovers of relational inequality. I argue that, although some features of networks are necessary for effective innovation, collaboration, and change, these advantages have been vastly overemphasized, especially in prescriptive articles for managers.[11] Well-meaning recommendations in the managerial literature to form more ties, broker alters, facilitate others' ties, span boundaries, embrace cross-functionality, and design matrix structures may actually be creating and amplifying organizational problems.

Although past research was nuanced in its treatment of organizational networking, in practice and managerial accounts this treatment was often interpreted as suggesting a simple positive relationship between the extent of networking and organizational performance. Some research recognized the downside of too much structural, relational, and position-based embeddedness in an individual's network.[12] Yet the downsides of networks were underrepresented in organizational studies, and most scholarship was about the organizational challenges of too little connectivity and insufficient weak ties or established brokers and hubs. Similarly, organizational research about tie formation was vastly overrepresented when compared with research about tie dissolution,[13] suggesting that one of the most critical relational challenges that organizations face is network growth.

By contrast, some foundational microsociological, anthropological, and psychological literature highlighted the disruptive, revolutionary, or dissonant conditions that disrupt networks. A common thread in this older literature was that individuals rarely require organizational support in order to form ties. That is, the capacity and motivation to form ties may be innate, routinely repurposed to specific cultural scripts, norms, or organizational routines.[14] Facilitation of new ties by third parties may stem only from a few close contacts. As I describe later, these older studies may have been an accurate depiction of networking prior to proliferation of the corporate organizational form. Yet modern organizational culture and corporate incentives seem to amplify pathological network growth dynamics by encouraging tie formation, with many organizations caught in an accelerating spiral of unchecked expansion in network connectivity, weakening of relational quality, and ossification and unequal dispersion of advantageous positions.

DIVERGENT INDIVIDUAL AND ORGANIZATIONAL INTERESTS IN NETWORKS

To be clear, I am not merely arguing that organizations occasionally possess too many ties, weak ties, entrenched brokers, and unequal scale. Instead, I maintain that organizations inevitably fall into these states if individual network dynamics unfold as they tend to in modern organizations. As individuals seek to improve their social capital, organizational network pathologies increase. In other words, employee networks are not always organizational social capital but often organizational liabilities. Like a debt spiral, network pathologies catalyze additional unaligned networking activity that becomes uncontrollable. In this book, I demonstrate the existence of unstable tipping points around which the dysfunctional growth of networks accelerates away from the healthy organizational optimum.

In the case of Multibank, individual network activity increased dramatically as it became clear that an increasing share of the rewards in terms of salary, bonuses, and promotions was accruing to the few individuals with the most ties. New managerial proclamations about the need for further collaboration only amplified this activity. In fact, even without managerial inducements, a self-reinforcing process took shape in which the individual benefits of pernicious networking begat more of it, with organizational inertia, exploitation, and failure as consequences.

A key puzzle is why networks can be a source of positive benefits for individuals and simultaneously cause some of the most significant organizational difficulties at the same time. The solution lies in recognizing that individual interests are not always aligned with organizational interests in networks. Individuals may have incentives that lead them to create more ties, many of which are weak, in order to "keep their options open." They occupy structural hole positions to maintain control for as long as possible, and support an arrangement in which they are one of the few hubs on which the organization relies. Dissemination of social capital theories in MBA courses, executive programs, and managerial publications accelerate these pernicious dynamics as individuals become more effective networkers.

In contrast, organizational goals require well-functioning teams and groups that depend on strong ties, a smaller set of weak ties, task-dependent reassignment of individuals to positions of power, and a distribution of ties of moderate scale across members. That is, the networks that individuals prefer are often misaligned with the organization's interests, suggesting a decoupling of social capital theories from networking logics that should be the object of study in organization scholarship.

In fact, it is a form of intellectual slippage and reductionism to assume that elements of individual social capital automatically aggregate to benefit organizations. Quite the contrary—as virtually any experienced manager can tell us—the organization can rely on individuals to leverage their most valuable social capital toward organizational objectives in only the most special circumstances. The social capital of organizations is completely owned by employees; rarely is it under direct managerial control. It takes only one more logical step to wonder when employees might *choose* to leverage their social capital to serve organizational objectives.

The key questions are why, when, and how individual and organizational networking interests come into and go out of alignment. Some prior theorizing points to negative motivations, such as shirking, malfeasance, and neglect, as key causes of misalignment. Yet these orientations are not necessary to induce network pathology—one can assume employee goodwill but still observe misalignments in networking if the individual costs and benefits of internal collaboration diverge from organizational economics. In fact, as I illustrate, promoting a prosocial orientation is associated with faster contagion of agency problems underlying network pathologies.

A variety of circumstances can lead to divergences in individual and organizational risk and exploration preferences for networking. In uncertain environments, administrative mandates may push individuals toward risky behavior that puts their employment in jeopardy. The organization easily absorbs the failure, but the individual does not. Forming "extra" connections in other units, organizations, and industries is a well-known social insurance policy against job disruption. While some organizations may attempt to develop relational contracts or "a culture of trust" to ensure against these outcomes (for example, "no one gets fired for doing the right thing here"), full assurance is rarely seen. Therefore, it is not surprising that employees act to protect themselves with a robust portfolio of ties.

Individual and organizational networking interests can also come out of alignment when employees possess higher aspirations and exploration preferences than the organization. Some employees develop connections while searching for better opportunities or as a source of leverage during promotion periods. In fact, the entrepreneurship literature is replete with examples of "frustrated" employees who cannot realize their ambitions in a company because of insufficient social support, and found a new venture as a response. The Silicon Valley ecosystem is a byproduct of these networking activities, as forming new network ties before quitting is a well-known step in the formation of a new firm. These are only a few of the reasons that networking interests diverge, although they all appear to have a common impact: leading individuals to form additional network ties that are not clearly in the organization's interest.

DIGITAL TECHNOLOGIES AND THE RISE OF THE MODERN MISALIGNED ORGANIZATION

It is natural to imagine that new digital technologies might play a role in resolving divergences by enhancing networking productivity. For example, when Multibank began its "collaboration surge," managers asked employees to leverage enterprise communication software (such as Slack, Yammer, and WhatsApp) and social media and networking sites (such as Facebook, Twitter, and LinkedIn). They hoped that these digital tools would improve the productivity of collaborative activities and lead to better performance. Of course, managers recognized that some technologies might amplify divergent interests. For instance, it was well known that LinkedIn could be used by other banks to poach employees, as Multibank's own HR department had done with new hires. However, managers believed that the increasing connectivity and collaborative activity generated by digital tools would overwhelm any effects on turnover and help the organization align with employee interests. Indeed, turnover rates did not change, although project performance continued to lag during this period.

A wider historical lens is useful here. Massive organizational networks characterized by many weak ties and stable holes and hubs are a departure from the social networks created by individuals prior to the rise of complex formal organizations, of which corporations are only the most prominent modern form. The families, guilds, and clans of premodern times often lacked large-scale formal social organization; networks were small and geographically constrained. A premodern individual's average number of acquaintances was presumably far below Dunbar's number, defined as the cognitive limit to the number of people with whom one can maintain social relationships. Dunbar's number is often used to note the natural number of ties that people formed before the advent of modern society. Anthropologists estimate Dunbar's number to be between fifty and one hundred and fifty based on the size of a typical Neolithic farming village.[15]

Yet over the course of a modern corporate career, most employees interact with significantly more than a hundred people—in some functions like sales, employees may interact with more than a hundred people in the course of a year. Many of these relationships might be assumed to be weak ties managed by a few brokers making referrals from hub-and-spoke–like networks. Yet every new interaction does entail some cost in terms of time and attention, which increase if the individual wishes to maintain the relationship in the future. These costs may be magnified in organizational collectives where there is an expectation of knowing some socially acceptable minimum number of contacts in order to get work done. These higher levels of time and effort spent maintaining large networks may be a historically bounded phenomenon.

Although such a proposition may be difficult to test, business historians have assembled sufficient evidence to indicate that the rise of the large, complex organization was likely dependent on the adoption of analog communication technologies, such as the telegraph (and later the telephone), which enabled individuals to connect for work with those outside of their circle of geographically proximate friends and family. One imagines a substantial increase in network reach for the few individuals fortunate enough to work in organizations like the railroads, where communication across distance was important.

However, something qualitatively different occurred with the introduction of IT-based communication systems and relational databases used to track activities in a proliferating number of jobs and functions. Digital technologies were adopted on a greater scale and scope than analog technologies. In particular, the introduction of email produced an explosion in communication and connectivity, allowing corporations to become truly multinational and multibusiness and capture the immense economies of scale and scope that the first scholars of the Industrial Revolution could have scarcely imagined. Social media is only the latest manifestation of this trend.

In this book, I put aside the issue of the potential historical boundedness of my arguments, which is difficult to settle in any case short of a surprise discovery of nineteenth-century network surveys. The seemingly irreversibility of corporate IT adoption provides a sufficient scope of application for my arguments.

FROM DIGITAL TECHNOLOGIES TO DIGITAL RELATIONSHIPS

Digital thinking plays a critical role in my efforts to understand these dynamics. In this book, I argue that digital technologies create "digital relationships," a type of interpersonal linkage resembling the digital representation of ones or zeros that enterprise software databases use to track employees and that network scholars often leverage to measure network ties. Digital relationships come into being whenever an introduction, contact, or referral is made, yet there is little effort to extend the relationship further. As one informant explained, "We have so many contacts these days that we don't invest in relationships—all that matters is whether we know each other." In this way, consideration of relational quality and content is neglected, and individuals act upon linkages in a way similar to an "on/off" switch that digital relationships represent. To be fair, these linkages may have some utility in a complex and bureaucratic context, if only to mark affiliation or simple information transfer. However, problems emerge when these mere affiliations and brief contacts are reified and network dynamics push the organization into an equilibrium where few strong ties remain. The greatest challenges emerge when members are forced to rely on digital relationships to achieve complex, risky, and uncertain organizational objectives. In a network of digital relationships, employees may have no choice.

As digital platforms such as email, instant messaging, and broadcast social media make it easier to form and maintain many ties, weak ties, stable holes, and hubs, employees increasingly form digital relationships with less relational content than before. In doing so, they neglect the hard work of establishing trust and shared experience that serves as a necessary foundation for mutual understanding and effective joint work. In a world of ever decreasing networking costs, forming new digital relationships can become a substitute for discernment and investment in existing relationships.

How do digital relationships arise? Organizational members often consider key trade-offs between forming new ties and maintaining existing ones. They may ask: Is this relationship appropriate for the task at hand? Does it require further investment? In modern organizations, the calculus has been shifting. As I document later, forming a new relationship is thought to mitigate the risks of prior ties and becomes a substitute for investing in current relationships. This results in a larger network of weaker relationships. The problem emerges when new tie formation through introduction, referral, or casual interaction—or a large portfolio of such ties—is thought to be a sufficient basis for difficult joint work. Acting on this assumption has obvious negative consequences in terms of opportunism, lack of commitment, and perfunctory performance.

In my view, digital relationships are the proximate cause of most modern organizational dysfunction. Hidden in full view for decades, the impact of digital relationships has only recently caught the attention of the popular press as the adoption of digital technologies has increased dramatically since the turn of the millennium. At the least, they are such a pervasive enabler of negative dynamics that it has become nearly impossible to test whether most dysfunctions would endure without them. Digital technologies are foundational to modern corporate activity, and the basic business functions of many organizations would cease to exist without them. Yet their functional value is offset by negative spillovers of digital relationships that predominate in a world of low-cost networking. In many large organizations, these negative externalities are absorbed by the organization as the damaging effects cascade through the organizational network.

In this theory, digital technologies amplify agency problems that underlie network pathologies. In the language of causation, technology is more likely to be a contingent factor or moderator of network agency problems rather than their antecedent cause. Although many such problems may only become apparent after the adoption of new IT tools, their actual cause is a combination of misaligned incentives and social capital inducements for individuals to network in ways that are not in the organization's interests. That is, the ultimate cause of network agency problems is motivational—digital technologies enhance misaligned incentives and enable individuals to act on them.

In this book, I rely on qualitative evidence and elaborative modeling to develop ideas about network agency problems in organizational contexts where digital technologies are used. To develop my theories, I leverage data that I collected at American, Asian, and European "big-tech" companies. Why big tech? I focus on these companies because they are a useful window through which to examine network agency issues: these organizations were early to adopt digital technologies and are, famously, a context where network connections are critical for achieving high performance. These firms provide an "early window" into digital relationships, and prefigured most of the technology adoption trends by established complex organizations in traditional sectors where some network agency issues are emerging. Indeed, several multinational corporations find themselves in competition with big-tech firms and adopt similar digital technologies in order to survive. An organization like Multibank is an obvious example, as they explicitly became "like a tech company" and adopted several collaboration and productivity tools for the first time. That is, even though the theory presented here was induced from research on technology companies, I expect it to apply to modern, complex organizations of many types, especially as they adopt digital technologies.

If it is true that digital technologies play such an important role in sustaining network pathologies, then understanding the impact they have on networking behavior may be the key to resolving the central puzzle stated previously: How are networks both the key to individual achievement and the cause of organizational problems? To resolve this puzzle, it is necessary to reframe it. Simply identifying network agency problems is not sufficient. It is necessary to play out the implications of divergent motivations for internal network dynamics and performance in the presence of digital technologies. Rather than consider networking, performance, and technology in isolation, it is necessary to consider their interplay over time.

AN AGENCY THEORY OF SOCIAL NETWORKS

In organizational contexts where conflicts of interest arise, a principal-agent framework has been used to understand the sources and impact of misalignment. In the principal-agent model, the principal is in a position of authority and is an organizational representative either as an equity owner, executive, or administrator with control over the organizational incentives affecting agents.[16] Agency theories have been productively applied to a variety of principal-agent pairs ranging from equity owners and top managers to owners and boards to managers and subordinate employees. The key in this analysis is to identify the source of interest conflict—typically organizational circumstances that lead to incentive misalignment—and then quantify the negative impact absorbed by the organization, often called the "agency cost." In some cases, agency costs can be measured in terms of lost profit potential due to misaligned agency behavior or in terms of the extra governance effort that must be expended to mitigate these behaviors. Interventions can be judged on their capacity to realign interests and change behavior to minimize agency costs.

The idea that social networks may become the subject of agency theory is premised on the notion that individuals may take action regarding their relationships in a manner that serves their own interests.[17] Nonetheless, networks are necessary to achieve virtually all critical organizational objectives, from collaboration to innovation to change, which not all networking serves. In this way, the economic and sociological senses of the term *agency* overlap, as socially embedded action may determine whether collective objectives are realized.[18] The costs of individual and organizational misalignment around networks may be a considerable driver of overall organizational performance.

Network agency costs bear some resemblance to agency costs in other contexts. The most apparent network agency cost is related to the effort, attention, and energy of managers in monitoring and assessing the agent's networking performance and managing the consequences. However, since monitoring and assessment are imperfect, the organization may suffer what is often called "residual loss" in terms of activities and opportunities that are foregone as agents pursue networking that obviates them.[19]

Although there are some similarities, the source of network agency costs may be fundamentally different from the source of agency costs underlying traditional governance problems that have been studied before, such as the separation of ownership and control, a distant board, or imperfect resource dependence.[20] Network agency problems are fundamentally social because they emanate from the network of relationships itself. Unlike other resources, individual networks are directly controlled by organizational members and are more difficult to monitor. Furthermore, network mechanisms are well known to produce nonlinear effects as social effects propagate and are amplified through network diffusion. In fact, many of the nonlinear effects studied by social scientists stem from networks, ranging from the S-curves of practice adoption and organizational change to the increasing returns of market demand due to network externalities.

Network agency problems may exhibit additional complexities due to the various roles that are possible in network and organizational structure. Considering the vertical relationships in an organizational hierarchy, it can be seen that middle managers and lower-level executives occupy the most complicated position as they may alternate between the roles of principal and agent. They are principals with respect to their direct reports and other subordinates, and they are agents with respect to executives. Part of their responsibility is to translate organizational goals into directives for these employees and then find ways to enable and motivate them to carry out these directives.

However, similar to other employees, these managers also act as agents when they attempt to enact the orders of their superiors. Not all of their superior's intentions may be perfectly delineated as orders, in which case the manager must interpret the preferred course of action. This is complicated by the potential for interest misalignments between the superior and the organization, a misalignment that is prone to differences in interpretation as well. Superiors hold real power over managers' fate, but the broader organizational system may demand compliance as well. In this simple vertical setup, managers must discern the interests of three parties—the organization, their superior, and themselves—and translate that into action.

This story is complicated considerably by horizontal relationships. Sometimes horizontal connections hold formal authority—for example, in matrix structures where managers report to other managers of equal position in specific projects or on taskforces where one manager holds sway. Yet even in cases where this influence is informal, one can imagine that the likelihood of incentive conflict about which relationships to invest in can expand substantially in a large network of mutual influence. Managers may think twice about the new ties they form if only to create alignment with their current friends and colleagues. Networks are endogenously evolving systems where individuals have heterogeneous interests with respect to networking that shape the evolution of those networks. New network ties can forge new interests that require new ties, and so on.

These simple issues illustrate the complexity of network agency problems—organizations are a networked multiagent and multiprincipal context with role switching, leading to complexities that may not be easily understood by deduction from first principles. Such complexity may be the reason why an elaborate network agency theory has yet to be developed. It implies that a network agency theory can only progress by abandoning unrealistic microeconomic assumptions around full rationality, perfect information, and homogeneous agents and taking up the more fully socialized assumptions that may stem from organizational behavior, sociology, and psychology disciplines where agents are assumed to be heterogeneous, socially constrained, and sometimes irrational, with multiple motivations and outcomes that are path-dependent. Understanding the governance implications and performance impact of social relationships is different from other agency-theoretic phenomena where social and psychological factors may be assumed away. In fact, it may be impossible to develop predictive models of network agency without an understanding of how social context, behavioral microfoundations, and motivational orientation impact network agency cost.

The divergent performance impact of network agency costs can be depicted in a simple graphical model. Figure 1 shows three ideal types and their impact of networking activity on organizational performance. Each assumes that organizations depend on the individual social capital of their members. The first, arguably unrealistic, ideal type is that of an organization with no significant network ties—that is, a group of strangers. Since these individuals lack a prior history of interaction or knowledge of each

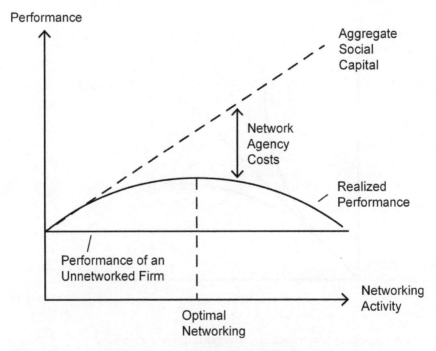

Figure 1: Decoupling social capital from organizational performance

other, they may be able to work together only in a very ineffective fashion that involves misunderstanding and mistrust. Much like individuals interacting in a market, these atomized individuals only interact effectively in transactions where a simplifying mechanism, such as pricing, enables them to resolve differences in underlying interests. We should expect such an organization to generate very low performance if the environment demands complex coordination and cooperation to achieve goals.

A second ideal type is an organization with positive social capital in which members engage in networking activities of various types, including activating their current relationships and forming new ties. In this case, the aggregate social capital of individuals acts as an upper bound on organizational performance. A third ideal type is a more realistic organization in which individuals seek to activate and increase their social capital through networking; however, network conflicts of interest emerge. As networking increases, we might expect cases of misalignment to increase, which will increase network agency costs and performance losses of the organization away from its highest potential. It is the third more realistic model, in which

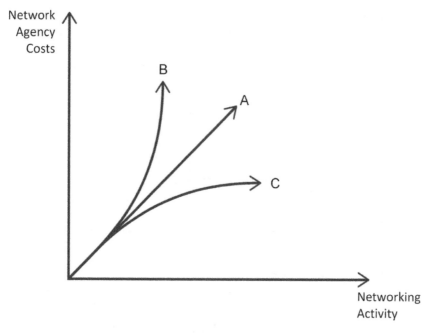

Figure 2: Agency cost trajectories in organizational networking

network agency costs have a real impact on aggregate performance, that is the main concern of this book.

The actual magnitude of network agency costs can vary depending on multiple factors. Some positive dependency on the amount of networking activity must be expected, since members' capacity to act on misaligned interests is dependent on networking. New ties enable employees to achieve additional misaligned goals.

Underlying the performance impact are the dependency of network agency costs on networking activity and their evolution over time. Figure 2 indicates some basic cost trajectories. Although a linear model, such as the one depicted in curve A might be presupposed, we should consider that network agency costs can be nonlinear in networking activity as well. The most pernicious networking agency costs may be increasing in activity, as depicted in curve B—we might expect exploding agency costs if unaligned behavior diffuses to other employees or if the productivity impact of agency problems on work increases with incentive problems. Another possibility is that network agency costs increase with networking activity but with a decreasing rate, as seen in curve C.

If the agency costs are linear (A) or concave (C), they may be managed effectively by principals. Interventions can be designed to cultivate an organizational culture of sufficient employee engagement with networking issues, or perhaps an organizational design can be implemented in which legitimate hierarchies are reinforced and inappropriate networks are disrupted. Convex agency costs that balloon over time (B) are more problematic as they presumably outweigh any benefits the organization derives from its business activities. In all these cases, the agency-theoretic framework points to the issue of incentive alignment and whether it can produce a long-run change in the underlying interests of the principals and agents.

NETWORK AGENCY THEORIES OF ORGANIZATIONAL BEHAVIOR AND OUTCOMES

An agency-theoretic view of organizational networking differs from social capital consensus in ways that might be seen as advantageous by organization scholars. Network agency theory relaxes the assumption that individual social capital aggregates in a simple and monotonic way to produce positive organizational outcomes. Instead, it problematizes network alignment, asking how conflicts of interest around relationships shape networking behavior and outcomes in an organizational system. Of course, such a mandate creates a large white space for possible network agencies theories to emerge. A single research program cannot offer the final word on network agency, yet it is straightforward to note a few common features that any network agency theory is likely to possess.

First, a network agency theory is inherently multilevel, as it considers microfoundational individual interests of employee agents, macroorganizational interests of managers and other stakeholders who act as principals, and the mesodynamics of the network itself, which mediate whether individual and organizational interests come into and out of alignment.

Second, such a theory is both positive and normative, since it is concerned with strategic action in real-world contexts and so must necessarily have implications for both predicted and preferred organizational outcomes. The positive and normative are related because the interventions that managers should enact to enhance organizational performance depend both on the current equilibrium and on how individuals will respond to the intervention.

Finally, network agency theories are fundamentally behavioral, as they must embed some assumptions about how agents and principals are likely to act in light of current network conditions. These assumptions can be more or less accurate, generating the theory's better and worse explanatory and predictive power. Accurate behavioral microfoundations regarding social relationships are likely to produce better predictions about organizational networks.

In this book, I build on these foundations to explore the central puzzle in network agency: How does misalignment of individual and organizational interests generate network pathologies that diverge consistently from the potential of organizational networks, and what is the role of digital technologies in accelerating these effects? The qualitative evidence I provide here serves as a basis for further theory development around network agency problems. In fact, it is possible to build a variety of analytical and computational models to explore network agency dynamics over time.

The simplest model examines divergences between ideal networking for the organization (optimality) and what the organization actually achieves in the long run (equilibrium) using tools from a branch of mathematics known as nonlinear dynamics.[21] Based on a few key assumptions grounded in qualitative evidence—namely, that individuals engage in networking when costs exceed benefits, and that digital technologies reduce the costs of networking and make it more attractive—it can be shown that networks inevitably grow more than what is optimal for the organization because of misaligned incentives for individuals to form more ties in order to manage their own risks and aspirations. As organizations adopt digital technologies, the value derived from an optimal number of ties increases, but the real organizational equilibrium of the number of ties that organizations actually achieve diverges even further from this optimum.

These findings are consistent with the recent experiences of many large organizations. While the digital revolution promises great rewards for large enterprises such as Multibank, their increasing adoption rarely lives up to its promise and can even diminish performance. This occurs against a backdrop of dramatically higher potential performance that a few star organizations may achieve, often only temporarily. Models like this explain this paradox. Suboptimal performance emerges as a natural consequence of digital relationships that are created when digital technologies simultaneously improve potential performance and induce more networking than is useful.

Although this basic model makes a variety of simplifying assumptions (homogeneous agents forming only one type of tie and a uniform organizational objective), a number of more elaborate models can be constructed with similar results. In this class of model, principal-agent problems between individuals and organizations are a foundational assumption, but it is the interaction between networking behaviors and network-enabled performance in the presence of cost-shifting digital technologies that generates overzealous networking.

Network agency theory enables an organizational analyst to focus on several strategic issues that are not as easily considered in traditional social capital research. The first is a consideration of issues related to network ownership and control. Who owns the network? Who controls the ties formed and what they are used for? As organizational relationships are both personal and public, this issue is difficult to resolve on a first attempt. Like other intangible resources, network ties "walk out the door" when employees leave, but they can be reconstituted. Managers cannot control networks by fiat, but they do have tools to shape incentives for tie formation and use. Network agency has an important perspective on this question. If conditions in which organizational interests align with individual interest can be identified, then some instances of heavy-handed managerial intervention can be avoided.

Network agency theory might also inform an important debate about how value created in organizations is captured by stakeholders—namely, principals and agents. A tension emerges because, although personal relationships are not fungible, some relationships confer more benefits on the organization than others. The notion of firm specificity of relationships is critical, as potential conflicts can easily emerge about tie formation choices that favor individual versus organizational benefits. General tendencies can emerge in different contexts, such as an organization favoring internal over external relationships, individuals favoring homophily over task interdependence, or structural patterns where individual and external benefits diverge.

Finally, network agency subsumes a variety of considerations about the broader distribution of benefits in networks. This is related to discussions of inequality in benefits, which is an organizational concern manifested in research about CEO pay, job hopping, and superstar employees. In this book, I reframe these issues as related to the distribution of social capital in organizations. It is possible to construct specific network agency theories of both positive and negative externalities of networking behaviors and note the distributional effects on rewards. Emerging research on patterns of structural externalities is pointing the way toward causal theories, but the root causes are the networking behaviors that are induced by organizational incentives and the divergence of interests this implies.

PERSISTENCE: THE FAILURE OF ORGANIZATIONAL DESIGN AND MANAGERIAL INTERVENTIONS

It is natural to wonder whether managerial interventions or changes in organizational design might have some mitigating effect on pathological dynamics. Chapter 6 explores various managerial interventions using evidence from case research and participant observation. I find substantial variability in the effectiveness of these interventions, with the largest impact deriving from those that target specific positions, ties, and roles that amplify network pathologies or deriving from large-scale design changes such as those in corporate restructurings.

I also investigate technology-enabled interventions that leverage advanced social communication software that managers can monitor, and people analytics systems that can be used to shift job assignment and thereby shape networks. I find some evidence of a temporary performance improvement when these activities limit network growth. While seemingly counterintuitive, pruning brokers and creating silos around effective network groupings may generate the greatest positive effects.

However, the results of this investigation are ultimately pessimistic. After nearly every design change or managerial intervention, I found substantial evidence of "snapback," which I define as an eventual return to network agency problems that interventions were intended to solve. Severing weak ties, strengthening a few relationships, or eliminating brokers and hubs produced temporary improvements as an organization approached the optimum. Eventually, however, the same ties were reconstituted, others came to fill the maladaptive role, or similar pathologies appeared in other parts of the network where there was space for the pathology to spread.

I also explore the deeper roots of persistence. That is, why do typical designs and interventions that organizations produce rarely generate a lasting change in system dynamics? Relying again on qualitative evidence and elaborative modeling, I identify three interrelated reasons—design resistance, network ignorance, and managerial misattribution—and document their effects.

Some persistence is an implication of the dynamics described earlier, but snapback suggests that organizational design or management interventions are unable to change underlying system dynamics sufficiently to have a lasting impact. In view of this, it is hard for an organizational theorist not to think of the "iron cage" of technical, competitive, and resource factors that puts pressure on organizations to become increasingly similar in their structure. Despite substantial heterogeneity in leadership, many organizations adopt similar practices and designs because of environmental constraints. Yet if these broad environmental constraints are the iron cage imprisoning organizations, it is hard not to view digital relationships as the leg irons that keep them chained to the wall and unable to mount a prison break.

THE AGENTIC FUNCTION OF THE EXECUTIVE IN DIGITAL ENVIRONMENTS

Chapter 7 examines the role of executives and higher-level administrators in this new digital environment, providing emerging views of how digital technologies are accelerating network agency problems during the pandemic as we engage in a massive, global, and technology-enabled work-from-home experiment. The pandemic has provided an opportunity to examine technology's role—both positive and negative—in managing people. A focus of this chapter is the leverage related to broader organizational activities that executives engage in organizational culture and talent development and performance management that are sometimes classified as "strategic human capital" or "strategic human resources." I reinterpret these activities through the lens of network agency theory, suggesting that the most successful structures and processes shape the deep structure of networking interests in order to change networking behaviors for the better.

Evidence from interviews with managers and employees who have newly adopted technologies such as Zoom, Teams, Slack, and WhatsApp suggests that these technologies have accelerated and amplified network agency problems. They filled a gap during the pandemic, as working from home without face-to-face interactions could lead to isolation. However, most individuals are reporting more interaction and connectivity than ever before, partly because organizations are mandating these technologies but also because they lower the costs of communication and connectivity to such an extent that they create incentives to increase these activities.[22]

On the flip side, however, reports of Zoom fatigue and overinteraction via Slack and WhatsApp are mounting. In my interviews, I learned that overload is particularly prominent when employees make new connections, since new connections require some obligation of future interaction to solidify. As the theory predicts, employees report having digital relationships— that is, more ties of weaker quality and lower productivity. There is also some evidence that brokers use technologies to solidify their bridges and roles and that network inequality in the presence of hubs may be increasing.

As explained in previous chapters, many one-time managerial interventions generate good outcomes by resolving network agency problems, but they often lack persistence as networks "snap back" and reconstitute offending ties. Hence, if the solutions do not lie primarily in technological or managerial interventions, they may be in the deeper structures and processes that affect people in organizations. This includes how talent is developed and managed in organizations—sometimes called strategic human resource management—and how the expertise of members is applied to organizational problems or strategic human capital management. I explore institutionalized practices—related to what I call strategic social capital management—that shape how employee networking during the hiring, socialization, and performance management processes—and their impact on long-run performance from organizational networks.

Such an agentic role in institutionalizing networking practices and intervening in networks may be uncomfortable for many executives, suggesting that negative consumption value, cognitive dissonance, and stress should be offset by additional organizational rewards. However, there may be no choice for managers but to attempt to influence internal social structure. Perhaps the most pernicious implication of prior social capital theories is that those in management or executive positions should adopt a laissez-faire approach to employee networks and focus instead on expanding their own egocentric networks in order to keep *their own* options open. Such behavior can only serve as an exemplar of disloyal and dysfunctional networking that cascades down the hierarchy. In this way, formal structures like hierarchy amplify network pathology.

By contrast, the theory I develop implies that the proper function of the executive is primarily allocentric as it concerns networking. Effective organizations have managers who dedicate outsized effort to supporting subordinates and colleagues in building a few strong ties and, in some cases, pruning time-consuming weak ties, severing ossified bridges, and ensuring that network scale is not too unequal. Without such efforts, the most pernicious network pathologies may persist.

MANIFESTATION IN DIVERSE ORGANIZATIONAL AND STRATEGIC MANAGEMENT PHENOMENA

Investigating the implications of divergent networking motivations for digital relationships may have broader theoretical implications for macro-level organizational phenomena. Chapter 8 explores the implications for organization design and the "theory of the firm," a stream of research at the intersection of economics, strategic management, and organizational theory that attempts to explain the existence, boundaries, and behavior of firms in different environmental conditions. Why do firms emerge in a market that mediates transactions? What explains the boundaries between firm and market, and heterogeneity in organizational boundaries? Agency theory's focus on maladaptive employee motivations that increase transaction costs is an important microfoundation of most prior explanations. Network agency problems offer a different mesofoundation that emerges from system-level (dys)functions. Table 2 summarizes the organizational and strategic management implications of network agency theory.

Organization theorists are interested in issues surrounding organizational boundaries, including organizational communities with porous boundaries that go beyond the typical corporate form in which the boundaries of membership are more selective. One of the most important phenomena in need of exploration is the emergence of "open"-innovation communities as found in open-source software, social movements, or social media ecosystems that do little to screen, filter, or select members.[23] Open communities are notable for their rampant diversity and unchecked growth, producing substantial innovation in some cases. Open communities can also be conceived of as a network. In Chapter 9, I explore the question of how a network of individuals in an open community differs from that in a "closed" organization, where network agency problems are easy to observe. I also explore how network agency costs may change predictably over the life cycle as organizations change from entrepreneurial to established. Which network agency costs are most relevant in new versus old organizations? Can network evolution predict organizational life cycles? Are open communities superior to closed organizations, and if so why are there so few successful innovation communities compared with the massive ecology of closed organizations?

Digital relationships theory may shed light on these questions. Closed organizations differ from open communities in their design, evolution, and administration of networks. For instance, as closed organizational boundaries are less permeable than those of open communities, they generate natural constraints on network diversity and growth. As discussed earlier, institutionalized organizational socialization and roles might limit the most extreme forms of dysfunctional networking as organizations age. And internal inducements, such as promotions and an appropriate bonus structure, can compensate for a less personally valuable network.

The broader theme of this book is the persistent and significant effect of network pathologies that emerge in digital environments, the new agentic role of managers, and the broader impact of that role on prominent organizational and strategic phenomena. As the predictions here may be contrary to some conventional wisdom about networks and digitization, it is essential to test their underlying theories in a larger sample of data. This book provides a sketch of various theories with testable implications, and I encourage eventual falsification efforts. Yet in my view, we are in greatest need of a deeper understanding of network pathologies that depends on further inductive research in different contexts and data modalities.

In the concluding chapter, Chapter 10, I outline an inductive research agenda that focuses on further case comparison and future ethnographic research, new organizational experimentation studies using randomized control trials to uncover relevant dynamics, and further elaborative modeling to capture essential dynamics and observe the implications of assumptions and stylized facts from the field.

We continue to rely on organizations to address many of the thorniest societal problems and create a better life for all, so it is essential that we improve their functioning. It is my hope that this book will inspire both inductive and deductive research on the network agency–based causes of organizational problems so that we might someday find solutions.

Too Many Ties

DIVERGENT INTERESTS WITH THE FALLING
COSTS OF DIGITAL NETWORKING

This chapter describes how and why organizational and individual networking interests become unaligned during the formation of relationships, the density of the resulting networks that are formed, and the impact of too many ties on organizational outcomes. The falling cost of networking with the increased use of digital technologies is a key factor underlying the proliferation of these network agency problems as it shifts incentives for individuals and enables them to form too many ties.

NETWORKING IN ORGANIZATIONS: INVESTIGATING
SOCIAL CAPITAL IN CONTEXT

Among the most robust findings in social science is the importance of interpersonal relationships. These relationships are often thought of as linkages in a broader network of ties. Scholars sometimes refer to the social capital in an individual's network ties—that is, their productive utility in everyday life. Social capital complements the financial, human, and political capital of individuals, with the idea that social relationships have a unique value that, while sometimes dormant, can be unlocked when needed.[1] Whether the network contains free agents in society or members of organizations (or both), the literature suggests that individuals with more ties have several advantages in accessing, acquiring, and using resources. Social relationships provide a useful foundation for those interactions and exchanges. Individuals with more ties, it has been shown, have more and better ideas, have more financial capital, learn faster, are trusted more, receive more emotional support, achieve better health, live longer, and are happier. In organizations, those with more ties are more likely to hold the best jobs, receive better pay, get promoted faster, have more influence over work, and have colleagues who report greater job satisfaction working with them.[2]

These positive individual outcomes appear to work through similar social capital mechanisms. Achieving goals often requires resources. A relationship increases the likelihood that resources will be given, if only because the source is better able to communicate, understand, negotiate, and trust an exchange partner with whom they have established a prior relationship. Most relationships are renewable in the sense that access to, acquisition of, or use of new and additional resources can flow in the future after some have already been forthcoming. Individuals may maintain relationships even if they are exhausted of resources if only because human connectivity brings joy and satisfaction. Later, serendipity may reactivate the relationship with a different pattern of exchange, since relationships may have some fungibility, as they are useful in different contexts. When multiplied across all ties in an egocentric network, the value of greater connectivity may be additive or even multiplicative if the ties offer some complementary value. Taken together, the truism of social capital theory becomes clear: simply put, individuals with more ties do better.

Social capital is so important for individual achievement that managers have often sought to develop organization-wide capabilities in networking in order to support social capital development and improve company performance.[3] The idea is to improve individual skills in forming and maintaining ties so that employees can enhance their own social capital, based on the theory that individuals with greater social capital will be more effective in mobilizing resources to achieve organizational goals. This involves empowerment though various means. By training employees in interpersonal communication, organizing informal social events, rotating employees through jobs, providing incentives for connecting, and even designing physical spaces effectively, the raw number of good interactions can be magnified. If some of these interactions catalyze into long-standing interpersonal relationships, the effectiveness of the company network can be increased.

Yet there is an emerging view that this dynamic only tells part of the story. Its logic appears to underreport a common experience faced by many individuals who describe negative experiences from overcommunication, frequent and intense interaction, and overcommitment stemming from social relationships. They suggest that too many interactions may result in divided attention that leads to mistakes and distracts from "deep work" that requires concentration or, indeed, any work that extends beyond routine practices.[4]

Most of these popular accounts suggest that overcommunication and very frequent interactions may be a company-wide phenomenon that is embedded in organizational culture, managerial practice, and the shifting nature of work. There are also hints that this growing problem may have a network component, as the evidence suggests that, despite the emergence of more extensive collaboration, the quality of relationships appears to be deteriorating.[5] In this chapter, I report research findings linking networking practices and connectivity to organizational outcomes, before discussing theoretical implications of these findings.

EXPLORING SUBOPTIMALITY IN NETWORK DEGREE: ORGANIZATIONAL IMPACT OF TOO MANY TIES

I conducted field research at a variety of companies to explore the relationship between networking, the individual experience and motivation behind forming new ties, and the organizational performance. I found that in many companies employees are often preoccupied with an endless stream of introductions, interactions, and communications that arise from the network of relationships they maintain. Employees are forming more ties than ever before and while some of these relationships are productive, the net effect has been negative in many cases. Sometimes these efforts are supported by managers and corporate resources, but in many cases tie formation efforts are self-initiated by employees. The examples below illustrate a common impact on social overcommitment and divided attention that decreases productivity and work effectiveness.

NetCo is a computer network systems company I studied in depth. Two decades ago, it was the undisputed industry leader with respect to technological innovation in the network equipment industry. In fact, it provided telecommunication infrastructure that underpinned many corporate intranets. At the turn of the millennium, however, it found itself trailing multiple nimbler competitors in terms of new features and was fast losing market share. To compensate, NetCo developed deep expertise in corporate activity around mergers and acquisitions (M&As). The idea was to use M&As to infuse the organization with fresh talent and intellectual property in the most important technical domains of the dynamically evolving network equipment industry.

However, NetCo's leaders soon found that acquisitions alone were insufficient in maintaining technical leadership in a highly complex industry, especially for infrastructure innovations that spanned industry boundaries. They shifted their approach to developing strategic alliances, especially with other powerful players in the computer industry. To develop these new capabilities, NetCo's managers were aided by many new leadership development initiatives, including an executive education program with a famous professor who taught the importance of networking and developing a matrix structure that ensured collaboration across internal silos and with external players. NetCo's executives encouraged these interactions. Their investments created a platform for NetCo to transform into a "human network company," not just a computer network company.

The initial results were mixed. Company surveys indicated that average interpersonal connectivity increased as a result of a greater number of interactions across the hierarchy, including those between executives, managers, and their direct reports. Examples were new interpersonal relationships across silos and greater interactions with leaders of recently acquired startup companies. Also, new connections to members of established companies in the industry were developed. NetCo funded many expensive trips to conferences, site visits, and off-sites, which facilitated external linkages. Employees would often jokingly compare their Outlook calendars, noting a dramatically higher number of meetings than in the previous year. However, the impact was mostly negative, with an obviously overworked contingent of managers, too many cross-cutting alliances languishing in the initial stages, and other products and initiatives falling behind schedule.

These actions had prominent effects across all levels of the organization. For example, NetCo's hard-driving CEO found he could not convene his typical yearly meeting of executives. Due to scheduling conflicts, his team

could not find a date within a six-month period when a majority of executives could attend. A big factor was his employees' attendance at multiple industry conferences—a growing trend over the past few years. In response, the CEO sent an email to the executive team to "stop going to so
many damn conferences," instructing them to "come back home." Many
responded swiftly by canceling their conference travel. The CEO was forced
to backtrack and clarify that his intentions were to simply "conduct these
ecosystem activities more efficiently" so that the employees would choose
their conferences wisely. The CEO's office took to scheduling yearly meetings a year and a half in advance in order to preempt the yearly conference
circuit schedule.

The broader impact of rampant tie formation at NetCo was the creation
of a culture that saw employees overwhelmingly occupied with personal
meetings, conferences, and events that stemmed from the broader connectivity they were embracing. Nearly all of their interactions could be justified
in work terms: employees argued that boundary-spanning ties would surface
new business prospects and opportunities for learning. New ties were forming both inside and outside the organization, and these resulted in many
more obligations to interact. "The demands on my time are intense," said
one manager. "I attend so many meetings because of the people I know." It
was clear that the organization was engaging in more communication than
ever before. Another manager joked, "It's great to know so many people. But
it would be great to communicate less so we could get back to work."

Some also reported that the organization seemed more political. Fault
lines were emerging around pockets of intensive communication occurring
because more relationships were being formed. "Once I got more connected,
I realized where my bread is buttered, and what people really compete for
the same resources. You start to learn unsavory things about them that get
repeated in your conversations." In other words, although extensive communication did have the positive effect of clarifying interests, it occasionally
resulted in knowledge being shared that was less than positive. Such knowledge can generate misunderstandings and even acrimony.

Employees at NetCo and at other field sites I studied, reported being
overwhelmed with networking activities, including communication and
work obligations and the amplified politics that seemed to be involved. Individuals were in need of practical ways to manage their personal networks
more efficiently. At the organizational level, one might expect managers to

employ all the tools at their disposal to facilitate the right types of networks. In modern contexts, this includes new digital tools to facilitate collaboration and communication. Can the judicious use of digital technologies improve networking?

THE APPLICATION OF DIGITAL TOOLS IN NETWORKING

Many organizations attempt to improve the efficiency of collaboration using digital software tools. For example, both consumer and enterprise social networking tools hold the promise of managing communications more efficiently by bringing them online. There are many perspectives on digital tools and social media, including their impact on education, health and well-being, and civil society. In this treatment, I focus on their impact on networking in organizations.

From the networking perspective, digital technologies improve the ability to form and maintain relationships efficiently, as many face-to-face and telephone interactions can be avoided and dashboards, likes, and chats make it easier to interact quickly.[6] Moreover, casual updates can occur on a broadcast basis as opposed to a series of one-on-one meetings. This holds a particular significance given the COVID-19 pandemic, a subject I will explore in a later chapter.

Despite the potential of these digital networking technologies, accounts of their supposed harmful impacts on work productivity are now commonplace. Social media platforms such as Facebook and Twitter have come under particular criticism, and are often branded as "addictive technologies" or "time sucks" that distract and lead to poor work output.[7] Although enterprise tools such as Trello and Slack have a smaller footprint, there are reports that they have a similar impact in the workplace.[8] Such criticisms are undercut by their widespread adoption and commercial success, however, with many employees actively lobbying for their IT departments to adopt them on an enterprise-wide scale. Understanding their impact on networking in organizations is necessary to unravel their effects.

An illustration is from NetCo. As the company embraced the human networking initiative at the CEO's behest, a group of younger executives sensed an opportunity to piggyback on this transformation project with one of their own. Enamored with new digital tools such as Slack, Trello, and Zoom being widely used in Silicon Valley startups, they lobbied for the wide adoption of these technologies across NetCo in order to enhance connectivity, collaboration, and communication in the organization. They argued that these digital tools were a necessary support to human networking.

However, adoption was difficult as NetCo already had its own internal messaging, project management, and video conferencing projects in development, and many were reluctant to use an external product. The young executives succeeded in convincing the CEO to greenlight an enterprise-wide adoption of Slack and partial adoption of Trello in their R&D centers, but lost the battle with Zoom, as video was considered too important to NetCo and organizational politics around its own product was high.

The effect of Slack was particularly dramatic. Its adoption was rapid, and employees soon found themselves engrossed in various groups and conversations on the platform. In most instances, Slack usage was passive, meaning that employees would simply read what was happening in various conversations. But in other instances, employees found themselves commenting much more on public Slack conversations than in email threads, in which they tended to be more careful about spamming colleagues with too many "reply-all" messages.

In some ways, Slack communication was more efficient than email, especially for informal comments about project plans. However, the ease of sending messages soon led to negative consequences, as managers found themselves answering many queries each day. The new channel of conversations generated some obligation to interact. As one manager said, "When I see the '@myname' tag in Slack I know I have to reply." Typically, employees left Slack notifications on because of the obligation that was created to reply in a quick and timely manner.

Over time, it became obvious that the organization was spending an extraordinary amount of time on the platform. The CEO threatened to "throw out Slack" but knew he would face great internal resistance from such a diktat. One vice president joked, "I wish our own product was that effective at wasting people's time!" Top executives tended to disagree with middle managers about the net benefits of Slack, but all agreed it had created a more connected organizational network that appeared to generate more opportunities and obligations for interaction. Over time, the organization seemed more engaged in communication than ever before, leading to more of the negative consequences they had experienced previously.

To summarize, although digital technologies hold much promise in making our networking activities more efficient, they can actually exacerbate the networking difficulties that organizations face. Communication and collaboration affect networking behavior in two ways. On the one hand, they have the potential to improve relational efficiency—forming, maintaining, and communicating in relationships become easier and quicker. On the other hand, they can lead to productivity losses from overcommitment and divided attention that results from networking.[9] This occurs as individuals face increasing temptation and responsibility to engage in rampant interactions.

In fact, these two effects are intimately related. As networking efficiency increases, networks become increasingly connected. This connectivity entails its own duties, which in turn mean that individuals spend a greater share of their time and attention on networking. In other words, digital technologies that improve networking induce greater networking, leading to networks with many more connections. This is depicted in Figure 3.[10] Digital technologies lower the costs of forming and maintaining ties, leading individuals to overdo it and construct large networks whose macrolevel impact is actually less than that of the smaller networks used before technology adoption.

As these examples indicate, individuals are led to develop many interactions, even though they obviously do not result in more valuable interactions, as predicted by social capital theory. This may occur in society at large, but appears to be a particular feature of organizational life. It is natural to wonder about the organizational outcomes of such a process.

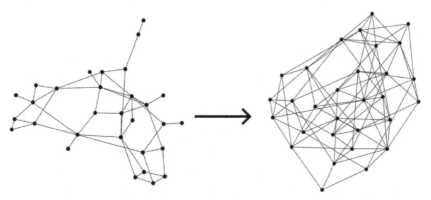

Figure 3: Network growth after adoption of digital technologies

REVISITING SOCIAL EMBEDDEDNESS: SOCIAL
CAPITAL AS ORGANIZATIONAL LIABILITY

Although the emphasis of social capital research is on the downsides of insufficient social relations, some network scholars have noted that individuals may form too few or too many ties. The theory of social embeddedness suggests that, for different reasons, both states are suboptimal. Individuals with too few ties have "underembedded" networks that lack enough connectivity to access resources and gain support. Individuals with too many ties have "overembedded" networks that place too many constraints on their time, attention, and resources to fully exploit the value of any one or a few connections. Too many ties make it difficult to explore new opportunities and are a particularly damaging driver of individual overcommitment to failing causes. Studies have mainly focused on individual networks or those in small firms where the organizational network is synonymous with the network of the founder. These studies have indicated that organization-wide networks can sometimes be overembedded, so it may be the case that the examples are indicative of these individual differences.[11]

But something different may be occurring when larger organizations persist in suboptimal overembedded states for a long time. We might expect a few employees in a large organization to possess underperforming overembedded networks for a time but then regress to the mean after intraorganizational selection pressures take effect. This means that employees with too many ties may fail momentarily but then correct their behavior or are let go. In the employee population, we might expect that different individuals to have either underembedded or overembedded networks but that these different types balance each other so that the organizational average generates a sufficiently high level of performance.

However, organizational networks with too many ties are a puzzle, especially if they persist, not least because underperforming organizations should face their own selection pressures when in competition with other organizations. Yet, almost all large organizations I have studied have too many ties and suffer the predictable consequences of overcommitment, divided attention, and languishing projects. Technology, as stated earlier, might be part of the answer, but it cannot explain these dynamics, which were occurring even before rampant technology adoption. What is most puzzling is how such a state can be created and maintained in light of the apparent downsides. Why would employees and managers not address this problem? Why do some organizations persist in possessing too many ties?

MOTIVATIONAL MODELS UNDERLYING NETWORKING IN ORGANIZATIONS

To better understand how organizational networks move into suboptimal states, it is necessary to explore the motivations that drive individuals to form relationships and particularly how the organizational context affects those motivations. Individuals have a wide variety of reasons for their behavior, and various models have been used to explain and predict action. But specific organizational contexts have a tendency to make some motivations more likely than others. What motivational model explains organizational networking in light of digital technologies?

An important starting point is that relationships in organizations are formed for many reasons, sometimes but not always related to the work roles that individuals play. Individuals may form ties for personal reasons or interests. In what follows, I focus on strategic interests that shape networking. This is not to say that relationships do not sometimes form due to serendipity. However, the focus here on interests offers a pragmatic way to proceed with analysis based on some semistable motivational patterns and differences. In particular, individuals and the organizations they belong to may actually have different interests with respect to networking. So it is useful to consider them separately to see if any stable patterns emerge.

What are the organization's typical interests regarding individual employees' networking? When do they differ from the typical interests of individual employees?

If organizational interests are to be explored, then we must have some common assumptions, such as the notion of organizations pursuing a common purpose with sets of identifiable goals. In reality, organizational goals can be multivaried and a point of great contention. Nonetheless, some common networking interests are often observed.

Managerial and employee roles in network change. Literature on organizational networks has often focused on general topographical features of networks such as density and constraints that shape broader outcomes. Yet while features that can be expressed in network statistics (centrality, density, constraint, and the like) are at the forefront of academic interest, they are often in the background of the experience of organizational members. Individuals often encounter conflict about what ties to form, with many different perspectives and interests underlying the sometimes acrimonious interactions that result. Moreover, a broad topographical view often neglects an important distinction between networking roles, most importantly between employees who are participants in particular relationships and managers who take responsibility for the outcomes of these relationships.

Managers are typically concerned with producing specific changes to network configurations, as new objectives require certain combinations of people to work together on specific organizational goals. As most collaborations benefit from rich, trusting, and collegial relationships, it may become a manager's key task to facilitate network configurations in order to achieve project objectives.

To the extent that an organization is not at risk of imminent demise, its existing networks are often taken for granted as functional and assumed to be a positive contributor to organizational survival. As a consequence, the salience of networking activities may only emerge during times of crisis or organizational change —that is, when the organization faces new work demands requiring fresh collaborative efforts best supported by new ties. This means that organizationally inspired changes to networks may be punctuated by times of relative stability.

By contrast, employees may be more likely to choose changes in ties at any time that are only occasionally aligned with organizational intentions. Sometimes employees may change relationships of their own accord to align with new work objectives. In other cases, managers are tasked with translating new organizational objectives into broader network changes by facilitating changes in employees' ties. A third possibility is of great interest here: individuals may change ties in order to pursue private goals that do not align with organizational objectives. This is a possibility we will explore later in great depth.

Changes in network configuration can be of different forms. Sometimes, the need is simple: two people who have not worked together before must do so now. Managerial attention can then focus on making introductions and facilitating the formation of new relationships that will enable effective collaboration. Creating a single partnership is a prototypical case of managerial involvement in networking. Sometimes, too, complex configurations must be achieved. If projects require multiple individuals from different groups to work together in novel ways, a manager must facilitate multiple complex and interdependent relationships simultaneously. This is complicated by a heterogeneous history of positive, negative, or no prior interactions between the target individuals. Therefore, managers must carefully discern where to apply their facilitative efforts.

If intraorganizational complexity is not enough, prior relationships outside the intended configuration can have an impact on network facilitation too, as they either support or undermine the new network design. In some cases, managers must actively direct workflow away from prior ties to new ties, or even prune prior ties if they sow conflict. The savviest managers find it useful to know the network portfolios of each employee, as prior relationships may affect the probability of new configurations being achieved.

General differences in individual and organizational networking interests. The previous point provides some color about how network changes emerge in organizations, particularly the broad difference between roles. But what motivates these changes? What are the individual interests in networking? How do they differ from organizational interests? Of course, sometimes employees form ties because their manager directs them to do so. This is rare, however; most interpersonal relationships in organizations are not facilitated by managers. In fact, the network benefits described by social capital literature can be a guide to individual networking interests. For instance, employees may seek to broaden their networks in order to obtain valuable information about opportunities, learn and increase their skills through collaboration, or increase their political support in anticipation of promotions or raises. That is, they may pursue personal goals that differ from the networking directives given by managers.

Less instrumental motivations may include connecting in order to help others, express an identity, or support a social cause. Additionally, because organizations are infused with values, employees may seek to form ties in order to support social initiatives and be good citizens. Finally, individuals may be thinking beyond membership in their current organization, especially when turnover is high or when they are members of multiple organizations. In such cases, tie formation outside organizational boundaries may be an imperative. When taken together, these motivations make it clear that individuals may have a range of motivations well beyond the mandate of their current employer.

Compared with individual interests, organizational interests tend to be more tightly constrained because they are based on larger investments in assets and capabilities that limit what is possible. Individual relationships may have great multiplexity, which is defined as different types of interaction and content that flow between the two contacts. Yet only some of these dimensions have organizational uses. Indeed, the different dimensions of multiplex relationships may be both instrumental and noninstrumental.[12] Although noninstrumental dimensions may promote general collegiality in the organization, they may not advance specific organizational goals. And even the instrumental dimensions may not be in alignment with current organizational goals. That is, individuals may participate in more complex relationships whose dimensionality may have the potential to be valuable in the future outside of current organizational contexts.

Differing interests may also explain why macrotopological network statistics of social capital theory—such as centrality, constraint, and average path length—often appear more relevant to analysis of individual social capital than organizational outcomes. By contrast, improvised configurations may be more relevant to organizations than individuals. For individuals with a limited capacity to invest in relationships, short-term connections with a single use seem myopic given the greater value that may emerge serendipitously in long-term relationships. Therefore, a successful strategy is often to preserve most relationships if possible, whereas an organization may prefer to reshuffle relationships. Although organizations also benefit from long-term relationships, they may have a greater capacity to tolerate a set of transient linkages that get the job done during times of innovation, crisis, or change.

It is important to remember that managers are often tasked with reconciling differences since they have the responsibility of translating organizational interests into action. The challenge is that individual employees ultimately enact their own ties. As individuals seek to create a private network portfolio of great future utility, managers may call upon them to leverage their networks for the public (organizational) good, often placing them in network configurations with other privately held ties. We might imagine that managers usually act as network "price takers" and simply accept the relationships that employees have formed and attempt to leverage them. Yet sometimes they may try to facilitate new ties for specific ends. In either case, managers must contend with different organizational and individual interests that stem from differences in objectives, risks, costs, and the time span of activities. Although they differ, it is possible that these interests become misaligned in predictable ways that affect aggregate organizational outcomes.

DIVERGENT NETWORKING INTERESTS IN
THE ORGANIZATIONAL CONTEXT

The previous section outlined basic theoretical rationales for differences in individual and organizational interests in networking. However, it is perhaps easiest to examine misalignment in the case of specific organizational situations that generate individual network changes. The key idea is that individuals adapt their networking behavior based on organizational context, on the likelihood that their current set of ties is sufficient for the current demands of the environment. The goal is to assess differences in magnitude or outright conflicts of interest between individuals and organizations regarding the content and structure of network ties. As I argue below, the different resource endowments, timescales, risk orientations, and exploration preferences of individuals and organizations underlie differences in networking interests. Consider four common organizational contexts in which differing networking interests emerge, with illustrative quotes drawn from various employees I have interviewed.

Organizational turbulence and crisis. Nearly all organizations go through crisis at some point in their lifespan. This is true of technology companies, for example, that consistently face disruption by competitors and copycats. Organizations can also face financial challenges that threaten their health and survival. At a time of turbulence and crisis—such as the one caused by the ongoing pandemic—organizations must draw on their most effective teams to solve problems and respond to challenges.[13] What this often entails is a stable set of interpersonal relationships to accomplish critical tasks in collaboration. Existing ties are often more useful than newer ties during crises because of the trust that long-standing relationships provide.

However, individual interests may differ from organizational interests in the networking domain. Certainly, individuals may benefit from longstanding ties and work hard to preserve them. However, the bigger risk that an individual faces during difficult times is that of job and role displacement. The risk of financial problems is not borne equally by all organizational members. When employees are demoted, salaries reduced, roles eliminated, or jobs cut, it may only impact a subset of employees. The organization as a whole may adapt precisely because a small subset of its employees bears these costs. In fact, this capacity to redistribute costs is a major reason for the robustness of many large organizations. Yet faced with risks to their livelihood, it is not surprising that employees may act to mitigate these risks. To do so, they may form new ties to seek new job opportunities or secure their current job. These ties may be external or internal, with the result being stronger social capital with which to manage the crisis.

Bad bosses. Almost every individual who has worked in organizational settings long enough eventually encounters a bad boss. Bad bosses have a number of traits, including inattentiveness, indifference, narcissism, and even malevolence.[14] However these traits are combined, their impact on employees is to create stress and reduce the productivity and commitment to the organization. They also have other negative organizational impacts such as creating acrimony, reducing collaboration, and damaging the effectiveness of routines. As a result, worthy executives must reform or remove bad bosses who are temperamentally unsuited to management, and enact policies to do so on a routine basis.

The key organizational responses to ineffective management, though, lie in fair processes that adjudicate the issue and take action only when it is appropriate. Procedural justice is required because individuals on either side of the relationship have differing views of appropriate conduct, and organizational representatives must gather facts to judge the case on the basis of company policies. For example, a demanding boss may be perceived as a bad boss even though he or she does not violate organizational policy or norms. Without procedural justice, the removal of managers can become subject to opinion, whim, and bias. Of course, such bosses often survive by virtue of strong ties to other parts of the organization and are difficult to remove. As a result, employees are often frustrated that processes are either delayed or never result in removal.

Organizational conservatism often frustrates employees, although it has its utility in the broader context of management and employee relations. Nonetheless, the impact on individual employees may lead them to take action. Those suffering under a bad boss often cannot wait. Leaving the organization is one option. Short of that, employees may go in search of a new boss in their current organization. Allowing internal job change can be an organizational strength. For the employee, the process usually begins by striking up new relationships to find opportunities to work in different configurations with a different boss.

Promotion and leadership aspirations. The examples above stem from negative aspects of organizational contexts in which employees are forced to respond in some way to protect their role, job, or standing. Other examples derive from individual and organizational characteristics that are usually viewed as positive. For instance, organizations must engage in talent development around leadership and operations in order to fill managerial positions, which many individuals aspire to. Promotions provide greater status and remuneration, so it is not surprising that some employees pursue them.[15]

Promotion and leadership opportunities are inherently competitive because there are often more aspirants than positions available. To make themselves suitable and to be noticed for these roles, employees can do several things to stand out. Leadership development involves taking initiative, working in teams, and taking on risky high-potential projects. Often, the best way to be promoted is to accomplish highly visible goals in collaboration with others.[16] Each of these activities may be suitably supported by forming new connections. Taking initiative involves building support, forming teams that may involve new connections to new teammates, and taking on high-aspiration projects that necessitate new connections to mitigate risks and access resources to ensure project success.

Corporate entrepreneurship and spinoffs. Related to promotions and leadership aspirations, it perhaps goes without saying that in most organizations there are some individuals who are disproportionately responsible for new ideas and projects that improve operations and build new lines of business. This activity—often called corporate entrepreneurship—may be responsible for much of the value created by established organizations. It is a fact, however, that very few good ideas that corporate entrepreneurs advocate are implemented by the organization. There are many reasons for this, including organizational inertia in responding to and executing them. Organizations also face capacity constraints that stem from limited financial resources, management time and attention, and human capital—they can only pursue a limited number of good ideas at a time.

When taken together, these organizational constraints can leave corporate entrepreneurs feeling extremely frustrated. Faced with limited resources and corporate political resistance, employees with an entrepreneurial disposition may wonder if the opportunity to engage in innovation and business building is better outside their company. If so, they have two main alternatives. First, employees may jump ship to another established company. Yet savvy innovators may wonder if the new company will have many of the same constraints as their current company. The second is to engage in startup entrepreneurship after leaving the established company. Startups are riskier, but they do alleviate many of the constraints on innovation. In fact, there is some evidence that frustrated employees are responsible for many successful spin-offs from large companies. They include storied Silicon Valley companies like Intel, Applied Materials, and AMD, that were founded by the former employees of an older company, Fairchild Semiconductor.

When employees are frustrated, it is natural for them to reach out to others and form new ties. Although their current company may prefer them to spend time working through problems and finding a way to conform to constraints, forming ties to stakeholders who may be useful in new ventures is a common activity of frustrated would-be entrepreneurs. In fact, many of the companies just mentioned have a networking story. The founders of Intel, Applied Materials, and AMD all began their ventures by forming new ties with other frustrated employees of Fairchild or with those in other companies, or academia, who would end up becoming part of early top management teams. Without spending the time to form strong relationships, one imagines that it would be difficult to work effectively in risky new ventures.[17]

Organizational politics and resistance coalitions. Another fact of organizational life is that organizations are social spaces where political action is common. Organizational politics occur because the interests of different stakeholders are never perfectly aligned and resources are limited. Diverse groups of employees, managers, and owners may form coalitions that support common causes to mobilize resources in ways that conflict with those of other coalitions. In many cases, employee coalitions are meant to exert pressure on the current managerial regime, which represents strategies for achieving the owner's goals.[18] Yet this may not be the case—coalitions can be split between groups of executives with similar power or even include external stakeholders like customers, suppliers, and citizens who have interest in an organization's functioning.

Organizational politics can sometimes be useful. On occasion, current management requires a powerful coalition to push it to engage in value-creating activities such as adopting new technologies, enacting reforms that ensure fairness, or reacting to a crisis. Seemingly more often, though, surges in organizational politics can be destructive if they waste time, lead to little real change, and create conflict that is long-lasting. In organizations with high political intensity, individuals who initiate coalitions typically develop new ties in order to establish coalitions, and when faultlines emerge, those on the sidelines are often pressured to join and form ties themselves. One imagines that an increasingly connected political organization may spend increasingly more time on organizing activity than on productive work.

Generalizing commonalities across contexts: an asymmetry in networking interests. What is interesting about the examples just given is the asymmetry of networking in each organizational context. In these and many other examples, individual motivations mostly lead employees to make network changes that facilitate network growth—forming new relationships and increasing the density of egocentric networks. Indeed, studies find that most individual efforts in network change are oriented toward tie formation as opposed to tie dissolution. Apart from a few toxic relationships (with a bad boss, for example), active dissolution is rare; dissolution cases are mostly examples of passive "tie decay" in the literature.[19] Organizational interests, by contrast, cause managers to prefer new configurations, including some that may actively separate individual colleagues and promote the dissolution of ties. Many of these preferred configurations are built around existing ties that provide a solid foundation for new projects. An asymmetry emerges because organizations may prefer to leverage existing ties whereas individuals prefer to build new ties.

The key is in recognizing that individuals and organizations may have persistently different networking interests. Incentives often lead individual organizational members to prefer more ties than the organization needs to pursue its specific objectives. Whether these incentives stem from risk avoidance or aspiration, individuals use tie formation to mitigate risk and achieve goals that include at least some private interests that the organization does not completely share. Digital technologies appear to amplify this asymmetry by lowering the costs of forming and maintaining ties and thereby increasing individual incentives to pursue tie formation.

Here, the manner in which both positive and negative organizational conditions motivate an individual's tie formation over dissolution is essential. Viewing individual interests from a network portfolio perspective is useful. In the first two examples, organizational crises and bad bosses, individuals seek to mitigate negative risk through new tie formation. These additional ties are functional if they operate as social insurance in the case of a negative scenario. Yet the organization's interests may not be aligned, as the risk of individual turnover or a few bad bosses can easily be absorbed by the organization. If the additional ties crowd out functional activities, they are often organizationally suboptimal.

In the second two examples, promotion and corporate entrepreneurship, individuals are risk seeking and form ties to explore opportunities. While the value of such ties may be captured by the organization in terms of filled leadership roles or new corporate ventures, there are only enough positions and resources for a few and excessive networking may destroy value. Moreover, much entrepreneurial value may not be captured by an organization if employees leave to form their own venture or join another organization. From a portfolio risk viewpoint, individuals often find themselves short of the productive frontier in terms of preferred number of ties. But the individual motivations they produce may be misaligned with organizational interests to achieve a more optimal tie configuration.

Finally, although political action may not have a positive or negative valence—since differing objectives may be positive or negative—excessive politics usually destroy value even when competing coalitions are advocating for similarly positive but conflicting goals. Moreover, forming coalitions and political action can make things worse by installing a less effective management team. Much of the rampant tie formation and interaction that is a part of political action and coalitions is wasted if the coalition loses its bid for power. And lower-level coalitions can be used to shirk responsibilities without fundamentally changing the power structure. The networking interests underlying excessive politics and conflicting organizational goals are a topic we will explore in later chapters.

ANTECEDENT CAUSES OF NETWORK AGENCY PROBLEMS: WHY TOO MANY TIES?

The network agency problem described in this chapter—too many ties—is the first described in this book, so it is natural now to ask why these problems emerge. Generally, they emerge because of misaligned incentives and social capital inducements that lead to unaligned networking by agents. The evidence in this chapter points to specific organizational contexts—turbulence and crisis, bad bosses, promotion and leadership aspirations, corporate entrepreneurship and spinoffs, and political resistance and coalitions—where they are more likely to be observed.

From these empirical cases, it is possible to generalize a few common causal antecedents of too many ties. First, some individuals seem to form new ties as a form of social insurance. New ties can substitute for older ties or resources should those be disrupted even by individuals who are committed to organizational objectives. In some cases, new ties are formed to pursue new opportunities, often outside the organization or in pursuit of a different objective. Finally, in what may be a middle ground, some individuals seek to simply preserve optionality with new ties.

What of digital technology adoption itself? Is it rightly thought of as an antecedent cause of network agency problems, specifically too many ties? I presented evidence of enhanced network growth after the adoption of digital technologies. In fact, many organizations do not even recognize that too many ties have been formed until long after digital technologies are adopted. Is it the case that what precedes network growth is its cause? Or is this an example of the *post hoc ergo propter hoc* fallacy?

Yet although these associations are strong, I argue that digital technologies should more rightly be thought of as an organizational contingency or a moderating factor of the basic causal relationship between motivational factors (misaligned incentives and social capital inducements) and network agency problems. That is, the motivation to develop new ties may exist independently of any technological enablers. One can imagine network agency problems in pretechnology organizations, even if they are less frequent. Instead, digital technologies appear to facilitate and enhance motivational inclinations that already exist. The fact that network agency problems may become more prominent after digital technology adoption is a marker of the technology's strong moderating force, which shapes incentives and activities that affect employee motivation. In this view, digital technologies are a strong but not necessary moderating factor in the production of too many ties.

AGENCY PROBLEMS IN NETWORKING: INCENTIVE CONFLICT UNDERLYING TOO MANY TIES

The branch of strategic management, economics, and organization theory that most directly considers individual and organizational conflicts of interest is agency theory. Although there is little written about network agency problems, it is possible to draw on agency theory terminology to structure the managerial dilemma around networks. Differences in interests can be framed as a principal-agent problem in which managerial principals and employee agents have different networking interests. The goal is to identify incentives that the organization can use to bring agents more into alignment with the organization.

Some agency theorists view individual characteristics as the prime cause of misalignment, especially as some individuals may possess maladaptive personalities or may be insufficiently prosocial, leading them to shirk responsibilities or pursue opportunistic behavior despite accepting the formal employee contract. However, in the case of networking, this is a difficult argument to sustain because building relationships is an inherently social activity. In fact, antisocial behavior is not required to account for differing individual and organizational networking interests, as previous examples illustrate. It is fair to say that the individual pursuit of network objectives that differ from organizational interests relies on social skill. In each case, differing networking interests result from differences in risk-seeking, aspirational, and exploration orientation of individuals and organizations, suggesting that the organizational context of individual collectives working together on heterogeneous objectives is a cause.

To better understand the differences between dispositional and contextual accounts, it is useful to examine the aggregate impact of divergent networking interests on organizational outcomes. The emerging case evidence suggests a strong association between too many ties and a variety of negative impacts, but a deeper examination highlights the mechanisms linking the two and their persistence. Such an investigation has the added benefit of addressing the relevance of network agency problems and whether managers should concern themselves with misalignment.

For example, NetCo's executives clearly imagined that increasing connectivity and the greater use of digital technologies would improve their employees' capacity to collaborate effectively. In fact, individuals supported these digital tools, and network growth subsequently accelerated as the tools were widely adopted. Yet managerial perspectives soured when outcomes became unsatisfactory. The same executives who advocated for digital technologies—most prominently the CEO—sought to restrain their use, even though the true cause of the failed initiative was never clearly stated.

Sometimes executives mandate moderately connected networks when individual employees appear to be engaging in excessive networking. For example, in ComputeSystems—a computer hardware company I studied— employees shrugged off human resources (HR) leaders' attempts to get them to "avoid overload," "eliminate meetings," and "reduce unnecessary communication." Employees admitted that they were hiding their networking activities, particularly those outside the organization. LinkedIn and follow-on coffee meetings were the main way to facilitate new relationships. In a few cases, meetings were purely concerned with private gains such as job seeking and social insurance, but in most cases individuals explained their activities with reference to the common good of the organization, even if private benefits were ever present in the background.

One director told me, "You can't deny that future jobs can come out of these chats. But you focus the conversations on what good you can do for ComputeSystems . . . or their company. You're trying to understand if there are opportunities for partnerships, alliances, vendor relationships . . . or maybe we can hire them! I found a few. They all materialized from these quick meet-ups and connection building. It's hard to predict which ones will work . . . but that's how the Valley works. And LinkedIn—and Starbucks—have made it so easy to do. I'm connecting so much more now. But it's legitimate. I'm telling you, I'm just trying to do my job. Of course, I want to succeed here."

In many interviews like this, I learned that the private and public benefits of forming relationships were often difficult to disentangle. There was, however, a strong sense that many organizations had too much networking and the time and attention dedicated to it were crowding out essential useful work. Another observation was that digital tools had shaped both the ease and desirability of networking, although multiple informants cautioned me that such a dynamic had existed long before the current slate of digital tools. They pointed out that social communication apps such as Facebook and Slack did not deserve all the blame even if they seemed to accelerate these trends.

To conclude, it appears that managers mostly attempt to facilitate tie formation. In fact, even after recognizing some challenges in overcommitment, they may mandate additional connections. In rare cases, managers may attempt to curtail tie formation or even facilitate dissolution. I describe many of these interventions and their impact in Chapter 6.

A SIMPLE MODEL OF NETWORK AGENCY PROBLEMS

It is possible to build a variety of analytical and computational models of network agency problems. One of the simplest models examines divergences between networking that is best for the organization (optimality) and what the organization actually achieves (equilibrium) using tools from a branch of mathematics called nonlinear dynamics. This is the "blue-sky" model and it is detailed in the Appendix.

The blue-sky model relies on three key ideas that find support in the case data. The first is that, by reducing the costs of using ties, digital technologies can enhance organizational collaboration and thus performance. This means that the potential productivity improvement is foundational, even if the unintended consequences may be surprising. This idea is supported by countless observations, and in fact it underlies the motivation for adoption of digital tools at many of the organizations I studied.

The second idea is that, by reducing the costs of maintaining and forming ties, digital technologies may induce individuals to form and maintain more ties because it is easier to do so. Such an assumption is an implication of employee initiative and is a desired organizational behavior. Forming additional ties no doubt brings both private and public benefits that are hard to disentangle.

The third idea incorporates organizational context into networking. Individuals are more likely to form or maintain ties that increase the likelihood of individual achievement, which itself is dependent on whether the organization is near its networking optimum. This means that individuals modulate their networking based on expected impact, which is related to whether there is a need for additional connectivity.

The blue-sky model explains prior observations and generates new predictions. The relationship between networks and performance, the actual critical points, and the networking trajectories that surround them are illustrated in Figure 4. Organizational performance typically has an inverted-U relationship with the number of ties in the network, with the position of the optimum determined by the costs of networking, c. This means that organizations face the usual consequences of under- and over-embeddedness. Additional insight comes through stability analysis, an analytical method used to identify critical points in a system which define

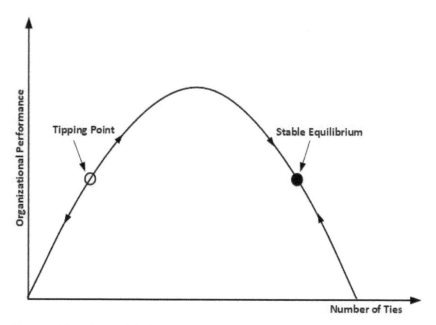

Figure 4. Blue-sky model of organizational networking dynamics

the trajectories that individuals actually follow in forming ties, either more or fewer.

Examining network dynamics on either side of the optimum is useful. Organizations with few ties face an unstable critical point below the optimum (Figure 4, *left*), sometimes called a "tipping point" for the unique differences in behavior below and above it. Below the tipping point, individuals reduce ties and organizational networks decay, while above it tie formation increases and organizations climb the curve toward the optimum. Thus, the lower critical point operates as a threshold of critical scale below which networks may degenerate due to insufficient internal connectivity.

By contrast, the critical point above the organizational optimum (Figure 4, *right*) is a stable equilibrium. Individual interests on either side of it drive organizations with more ties back to this suboptimal value. The organization possesses more ties than can be maintained sufficiently to generate peak performance outcomes. This occurs even if the system started at the optimum, suggesting that moments of peak performance may be transitory. Because the critical point is stable, organizations maintain this inertial state indefinitely without performance declining.

The impact of adopting digital technologies that reduce the costs of networking, c is examined in Figure 5. Comparing an organization with high networking costs (*top*) with one with moderate costs (*center*) reveals that unaligned interests emerge only when networking costs fall. In the top graph, organizations with too many ties seek to reduce them as they approach the optimum, although that is difficult to maintain if the ties diminish too quickly and fall below the optimum. By contrast, the center graph indicates that with a lower c an organization can achieve higher potential performance with more ties. As c declines, one critical point splits into two while descending along the inverted-U curve. That is, two critical appoints emerge from one in the relatively empty 'blue sky' of the curve.

The bottom graph indicates an extreme state with the lowest c, perhaps due to the rampant adoption of digital technologies related to collaboration and communication. The critical points have fallen even further down the curve.

The blue-sky model sheds light on a lacuna in the study of entrepreneurial and established organizations, if we interpret organizational age and size through the lens of network density. Digital technologies appear to have a more positive impact on entrepreneurial than established organizations, and not only for the usual competitive reasons (such as disruption); but also because of how they shape internal collaboration.

Startups usually suffer from a liability of newness in which they have few ties and need to develop more or they will perish. As c falls because of digital technologies, this threshold falls and it becomes easier to develop sufficient ties for organizational viability. In contrast, established organizations already possess sufficient ties and are pulled toward a stable, inertial point. As c falls, this critical point becomes more suboptimal and performance falls as well.

The equilibrium created has paradoxical implications for performance. Figure 6 superimposes curves with moderate (solid lines) and low (dashed lines) networking costs in order to compare potential optimal performance and actual performance critical points as c falls. A general result is that as c falls, the critical point moves farther away from the optimum so that potential performance and actual performance diverge. Under some conditions, the performance of the lower c critical point is actually below the performance of the higher c critical point, suggesting the paradox. Cost-lowering

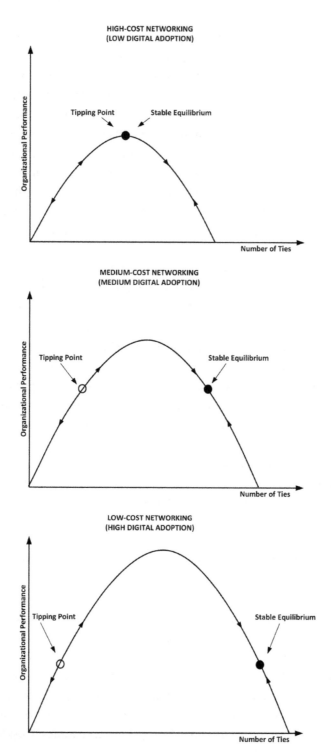

Figure 5. Emergence of critical points in the blue-sky model

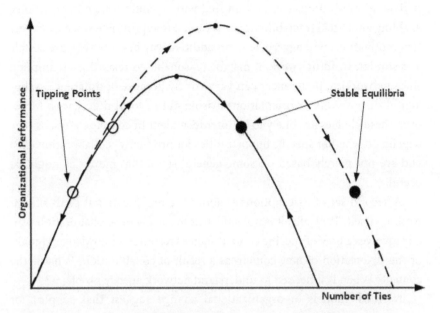

Figure 6. Comparison of potential and actual performance in the blue sky model

digital technologies may simultaneously *increase* the potential performance of organizations, as Figure 6 illustrates, which means that the position of the optimum *increases*, while the performance that these organizations actually achieve in their critical equilibrium *decreases*.

These findings are consistent with the recent experience of many large organizations: the digital revolution promises great rewards for large enterprises such as NetCo, but increasing adoption of digital technologies rarely lives up to that promise and can even diminish performance. This occurs against a backdrop of dramatically higher potential performance that a few organizations may achieve, even if only temporarily. Models like blue-sky explain this paradox as the emergence of suboptimal performance is a natural consequence of digital relationships created when digital technologies simultaneously improve performance and induce more networking than is useful. Principal-agent problems between individuals and organizations are a foundational assumption, but it is fundamentally the interaction between networking behaviors and network-enabled performance in the presence of cost-shifting digital technologies that generates overzealous networking.

Of course, this model makes multiple assumptions; some are for convenience, and others are more fundamental. A first assumption is that individual motivations can be captured with a single system of equations, enabling analytical tractability. In this case, it is appropriate since we expect that motivations will aggregate in an additive way because they are simple and similar. In future work, it may be reasonable to relax this assumption since networking preferences can vary widely because of different psychological dispositions or orientations arising out of local differences. Moreover, these choices are likely to be interdependent in complex ways, as they depend on whether specific opportunities for productive collaboration exist and are not merely based on some general sense that more ties might be useful.

A second set of assumptions is about the organizational goals of networking itself. Typically, it is not sufficient to form a tie. Collaboration usually involves a flow of specific content such as resources, knowledge, signals, or the co-creation of new content as a result of collaboration. What is the content? When is it needed to understand network agency problems?

Network models of organizational change suggest that support for new initiatives flows across network ties. Information about a new practice or initiative diffuses across ties, with mass adoption the usual goal. But network models of technical work suggest that expertise is rare and only needed locally. The local application of knowledge in a specific time and space is all that is necessary to "get the job done." Mass diffusion results in costly redundancy. Whether the right knowledge flows across ties is a critical contingency.

Finally, innovation is the hardest case as it typically involves the recombination of existing knowledge into new and useful forms, often during collaboration. Therefore, the right knowledge elements must be available to the collaborating partners so that a new combination can be formed and deemed useful. Taken together, these can be seen as three prototypical use cases for organizational networks that actually imply different outcome measures by which managers can judge the effectiveness of relationships. Although common agency problems may underlie tie formation in all cases, the form of the impact might differ depending on the outcome. In each case, simply forming a tie is not sufficient; what flows across and is created in network relationships, and its organizational utility, is paramount.

A third assumption is for convenience. In the blue-sky model, it is assumed that the relationships themselves are homogeneous, which is to say that all are equally effective for collaboration or to allow resources to flow or be created. Of course, relationships vary in a number of ways, the most apparent being their relational strength. Some ties are stronger than others, where strength is commonly defined as the frequency of interaction, the extent of emotional intimacy, and the degree of mutual confiding. Of course, these simplifying assumptions make it possible to gain traction on a difficult problem, but they also point the way for future applications. I relax these assumptions in developing new ideas about other network agency problems in later chapters.

This chapter examined individual networking in organizations, focusing on the simplest network characteristic: the number of ties. It noted many organizational contexts in which the networking interest of individuals and organizations—in the number of ties formed and maintained—can become misaligned. Wide differences in aspirations and risk preferences tend to lead individuals to prefer more ties than are in the best interest of the organization. When this interest misalignment is acted upon, it often pits managers against employees. The formation of too many ties by organizational members can lead to overcommitment and divided attention, which make it more difficult to achieve work objectives and result in organizational political conflict that often entails pursuing private individual goals that conflict with public organizational objectives.

The adoption of digital technologies by either organizational mandate or individual choice can lead to more networking interest misalignment, acceleration of actual tie formation, and denser networks. Although based on overly simple assumptions, the blue-sky model reveals the network agency difficulties that underlie the decoupling of an organizationally optimal number of ties and the equilibrium of ties that organizations actually achieve; digital technologies only widen this suboptimality. In fact, adopting digital technologies may increase the potential value of the optimum, consistent with the promise of these digital tools, while making that value more difficult to achieve.

By investigating network density, this chapter took some first steps in exploring network agency problems, culminating in a simple model of optimality and equilibrium. Yet the impact of social capital on organizational outcomes extends far beyond degree, with the quality of ties, the network position of individuals, and the distribution of ties in the broader network being known to have distinct effects on individual social capital. Thus, it is reasonable to expect that such network attributes may have an impact on organizational outcomes if individual and network agency problems emerge. Models of these features will likely need to relax assumptions about homogeneous motivations, uniform tie strength, and stereotypical tie content to make headway in predicting and explaining networking dynamics around these issues.

Ties Too Weak

INSUFFICIENT FIRM-SPECIFIC SOCIAL INVESTMENTS TO MOBILIZE DIVERSITY

This chapter focuses on network agency problems related to the quality of relationships that individuals form, noting that individuals often have incentives to create weaker ties than are necessary to accomplish organizational goals. Digital technologies that enable employees to maintain vast networks of weak ties amplify this effect. Employee motivation to form weak ties is related to the firm-specificity of strong ties in organizations. Although weak ties are often associated with heterogeneous resource access in markets, stronger ties may be necessary to mobilize diverse knowledge and resources necessary to achieve heterogeneous objectives in organizational contexts.

ACCOUNTING FOR RELATIONAL QUALITY AND TIE STRENGTH IN ORGANIZATIONS

Chapter 2 dealt with a challenge of degree—organizations tend to move toward an equilibrium of too many ties. The time and attention required to maintain these ties diminishes organizational performance. Yet this theory does not capture the quality of the ties and their capacity to achieve specific organizational goals. There is, however, an implication of this finding that is relevant here: organizations that have too many ties tend to have weak ties.

The strength of ties is defined as in social capital literature: strong ties are relationships characterized by emotional intimacy, frequency of interaction, and trust. Weak ties lack these features. Usually strong ties are thought to be necessary to engage in complex joint activities involving uncertainty and risk, including innovation and organization change.[1]

If we assume that individuals have limited time and attention for networking, then as the number of ties increases, it becomes untenable to maintain them all at the highest levels of intimacy, interaction, and trust. Some become weaker as a consequence of the limited time and attention available for relational investments. That is, too many ties and ties that are too weak go hand in hand. As described in Chapter 2, the divided attention and overcommitment of innumerable ties hinders the accomplishment of important organizational goals and impacts the quality of relationships. Yet there may be other behavioral motivations for relational quality that impact organizations in different ways, if only because tie strength impacts the quality of joint activities beyond simple attention and commitment mechanisms.

This chapter focuses on the broader implications of weak ties. What are individual and organizational interests with regard to relational quality? Do employees develop too many weak ties? If weak ties are detrimental, why would employees not invest more in these social relationships to improve them?

It is useful to recall the organizational example from Chapter 2 in light of the strength of ties. In NetCo, employees formed many ties. But several ties were new, so they started weaker by definition—individuals began by knowing very little about each other as they launched new collaborations.

Unfortunately, most of these new ties never strengthened substantially because employees were too focused on maintaining vast portfolios of ties or forming ever more new ones. Moreover, some important older ties weakened or became dormant as individuals shifted their attention to new partners. Digital technology played a role, with many individuals using email or social media to maintain larger networks of weaker ties without regard for their organizational usefulness. In some cases, employees used technologies like social media and job recruiting sites to form ties because these technologies enabled them to hide ties from managers.

Some employees were remarkably frank about how they managed their vast networks of weak ties. "For me," said one, "it's all about LinkedIn. Every day, I spend time sending InMails to my LinkedIn contacts, just to maintain those connections at a minimal level. I also try to make some new contacts. You never know when you'll need them. . . . How many? Some days it's more LinkedIn messages than NetCo emails. It's definitely under a hundred, though."

Others pointed to messaging apps like WhatsApp, where group chats are popular. According to one employee, "The great thing about WhatsApp groups [is] that you can interact and broadcast so widely. Everybody's on WhatsApp, and you can add them to groups without their permission. I find the key is to send at least one message a day so everyone remembers who you are. Of course, many are doing the same thing! So I'm getting hundreds of messages a day . . . but it helps me remember who these people are."

Recall that employee motivations in developing ties are often self-interested. Employees wish to learn about new job opportunities and stay connected with those who have the power to help professionally. Consistent with prior literature, weak ties may be sufficient to keep these options open for learning and support. There is an additional motivation regarding weak ties that has important implications in organizational contexts. Many employees feel caught between competing political coalitions, whether inside or outside current organizational boundaries. They reason that weak ties to multiple coalitions allow them to credibly claim nonpartiality. "The important thing is to not take any sides. Just listen and stay connected to everyone," a NetCo employee said. WhatsApp, LinkedIn, and email are the technologies that enable this impartiality.

However, even weaker ties require some degree of investment to maintain. Sending updates, replying to requests, and scanning long threads are daily obligations. Digital technologies have made networking with weak ties more efficient, but a larger impact has been the increasing capacity to manage larger portfolios of weak ties, which individuals in my interviews often emphasized. The focus of this chapter is on individual choices in relational quality investment, including the preference for weaker ties, and its impact on the broader organization.

THE CONSENSUS LINKING NETWORK DIVERSITY AND KNOWLEDGE DIVERSITY

To better understand the relationship between tie strength and organizational outcomes, it is helpful to outline existing theory and evidence about tie strength and knowledge in networks from prior literature, even though they have been primarily focused on individual tie portfolios and outcomes. This research is organized around a theoretical consensus that emphasizes diversity, both in the knowledge that flows through networks and the diversity of networks themselves. The main idea is that there are many different types of resources that may be needed so employees must seek different contexts where they can access them. In many cases, it is necessary to bring together different types of specialized information, skills, and expertise to get important work done. The key, therefore, is to access diverse sets of resources in whatever way the social situation allows.[2] What role do network ties play in this process?

One of the most prominent theories that address this question is "the strength of weak ties" theory developed by Mark Granovetter. One might imagine that strong ties are always optimal. Weak-ties theory was revolutionary because it identified a context in which strong ties may not be the best option for achieving individual goals. In a study of job searches in Boston, Granovetter (1995) found that people were more likely to find a job through their weak ties (for example, mere association, general contact, or schoolmates) than through their strong ties (such as family members or longtime work colleagues).[3]

Strong ties maintain their value, since individuals in those relationships are often highly supportive and willing to refer their contacts. Yet those contacts often lack connectivity to new job opportunities for the seeker because they are connected to contacts similar to the seeker. That is, their friends and even "friends of friends" tend to be the same. Instead, weak ties are more likely to give access to a new job opportunity because information about new jobs usually comes from contacts who are not known well by the job searcher. In this way, weaker ties may provide better access to a wider variety of opportunities by virtue of the wider variety of contacts they link to.

Without weak ties, a form of market failure may emerge in which it is too costly to search for opportunities. A network of only strong ties may be less extensive than one with weak ties—strong-tie networks often have few or sometimes no paths between large network components. Because weak ties take less effort to maintain, networks of weak ties tend to have more connections between parts of the network than strong ties alone. That means a network of weak ties is likely to have access to diverse sources of information in its more socially distant parts that can unearth a job opportunity—more so than strong ties, which tend to have similar, often redundant, information.

Of course, weak-tie theory is an individual social capital framework. However, it has proven useful for organizational theorists as it builds logic often used in group-, team-, and organization-level studies. Job searching shares some similarities with innovation in companies, as individuals may be seeking a single good idea in a sparse network which can be applied to a number of problematic organizational goals.

Such "low-hanging fruit" may require not coordination but simply judicious application of a good idea in the right context. Just like individuals, organizations need to ensure that they do not converge on homogenous solutions, information, and expertise. Groupthink and conformity are of strong interest to organizational behavior researchers as a leading cause of innovation failure. Both constructs have been linked to closed networks where people share strong ties, suggesting that weak-tie theory may have application in organizational contexts as well.

Weak-tie theory relies on an important assumption that real constraints on time and attention create a sparse network with heterogeneity in tie strengths so that not all ties are strong. Weak-tie theory may be less applicable to isolated tribes, for instance, where a large proportion of people may all have strong ties. Yet most networks in the modern world are sparse, with only a few strong or weak ties but mostly disconnection, suggesting that limits on time, attention, and resources constrain how many strong ties are possible, and the effectiveness of search.[4]

In sparse networks, weak ties may be more likely to access distant parts of the social space or span holes in the network when compared to strong ties that are more localized. Those with strong ties tend to think similarly and of the same things because of their more frequent interactions and likelihood of demographic similarity. In other words, weak-tie theory relies on an assumption about the equilibrium state of sparse networks, in which knowledge tends to be more similar among strong ties and less so among weak ties.

In fact, this finding about weak ties may be an instance of a broader theory in which diversity in the structure of networks is linked to more diverse knowledge and resources that can be accessed by network members.[5] Weak ties are one form of network diversity in that they link to more widely different parts of the network than strong ties. Yet there are other forms of network diversity such as the type of tie (family, friend, work colleague, etc.) and type of content in interactions (gossip, education, collaboration), sometimes called multiplexity. Each of these produce a different form of network diversity that may sustain knowledge diversity because actors with different ties are likely to have different kinds of information and interactions. Moreover, broader structure features such as different groups, long bridges that link different groups, and substantial holes in structure may also create local social conditions in which actors have different viewpoints and knowledge[6]. Taken together, these sources of network diversity may enable better mobilization of different ideas if their participants have multiple avenues to view ideas in different lights. The broader theory is one of network diversity in all its forms and its capacity to contain, access, and mobilize diversity in resources.

NETWORK DIVERSITY CONFRONTS ORGANIZATIONAL REALITY

As satisfactory and generalizable as this emerging theoretical consensus may appear, there are reasons to believe that organizational contexts may be different enough to call this consensus into question. Organizations may have multiple objectives and goals, and so need to leverage specific idiosyncratic resources like ideas, knowledge, and expertise possessed by different people, not just some generic diversity. So, while individuals may need only one job or idea to apply to a problem, organizations must assemble a specific configuration of activities and work to achieve meaningful objectives.

In economic language, individuals may be "price takers," who may accept a wide variety of new resources resulting from ties as long as doing so satisfies and gives sufficient value beyond some threshold. In fact, many individual needs can be satisfied in this manner, even creative work that appears idiosyncratic. Artists and inventors are famous for bricolage, in which they recombine resources that are close at hand. In fact, some research indicates that individuals may need to participate in only one creative project if its success is sufficient to provide value and occupy time.

However, organizations do not have that luxury. The complex and dynamic market environments in which organizations operate generate specific opportunities that top managers translate into resource requirements.

The scope of useful resources is limited. Typically, organizations must assemble complex configurations of specific resources, some of which may be idiosyncratic, to achieve objectives. Product innovation is a classic example: often, the catching on of a new technological trend requires that specific new components, algorithms, or processes be utilized. Multiple projects are the norm, and a sizable portfolio of experimental activities requiring idiosyncratic resources may be optimal.

Organizations can take on new projects with serendipity, but there are some essential projects that are required to "keep the lights on." Completing such projects may require that both strong and weak ties be accessed at different times. The difficulty of this process is magnified if knowledge is easily locked up in organizational silos or by individuals with tacit knowledge, which is often easier to access when participants have some strong ties. Managerial networking must bring together resource combinations across group boundaries, which is often very difficult even with ideal network conditions.

I explored how individuals choose to invest in relational quality in organizations and what the impacts of such investments might be. As described in Chapter 2, organizational members tend to be overwhelmed with ties, and technology can amplify that process. In further exploration, I found that these extensive tie portfolios were often too weak to achieve complex, risky, and challenging goals that require extensive coordination and trust. Individuals reported being spread too thin—with attention diverted into many relationships—to accomplish a few tasks at the highest level of effectiveness. Other important issues emerged related to relational quality: motivational issues also emerged, with many reporting that they lacked trust in or commitment to their colleagues. Miscommunication and confusion was frequent as well, as these shorter-lived relationships lacked enough foundation for mutual understanding. When viewed through the lens of relational quality, these impacts can be seen as instances of insufficient tie strength, which develops when individuals form too many ties.

It is useful to recount an example in a large software company I call Digital Forest. One manager there confessed he spent a lot of time maintaining connections with school ties—those with whom he attended college and graduate school years earlier. While these ties seemed innocent, the manager admitted that his primary motivation was not friendship but finding angel investment opportunities, since many of his schoolmates were involved in early-stage technology startups: "I am learning a tremendous amount about different industries where software is useful. But I invest rarely since only a few of these ideas are really great." Fortunately for him, weak-tie theory seemed to have worked by enabling him to find a few high-value opportunities, with three of his angel investments resulting in large paydays.

The trouble appeared when the manager's own division at Digital Forest faced technology disruption in web-enabled video. "I actually knew a lot about this space from my angel investing, so I spoke up often at our all-hands meeting. In fact, I even had connections at one of the main upstarts in this space, which some were thinking would be an ideal partner or acquisition target for us."

His being vocal at the meeting seemed to create an expectation that he could help solve the problem, and so he was assigned to the team tasked with addressing the disruption. Yet over time the manager came to realize that his knowledge of web-enabled video was not deep enough to address the specific integration and security problems that Digital Forest faced in the video space. Although he knew many things about video, he did not know how it could fit into his company's own complex set of constraints.

Nonetheless, he mined his external connections for further information, including trying to find a contact at the startup. "I couldn't find the right contact there. In fact, those folks wouldn't return my calls, even though they were asking for my money nine months before! I felt like I let my team down." In fact, Digital Forest only made contact with the startup two months later when its founder reached out to the CEO. Unfortunately, the startup was in the process of being acquired by one of Digital Forest's biggest competitors by then.

I found many examples like this in many contexts, including R&D, investment, and hiring, in which a potentially useful tie existed but lacked sufficient strength to provide access to useful resources. A commonality was that the weak ties that employees formed primarily for their own benefit were unable to be repurposed for organizational ends.

In some cases, individuals do mobilize their relationships for the organization's sake, but the inherent downsides of these weak ties come to the fore. For example, another manager at Digital Forest was known to have connections with entrepreneurs in a different country who were working on an innovative video conferencing product. This manager knew the founder from industry conferences and thought him a potential alliance partner or possible acquisition target: "My company really needed something good in video so I felt pressured to make the connection. I called many meetings with my executive team and [the founder's] team, and later it moved to technology sharing to see if we could integrate our investments. Wow, did that blow up in our face! After a month of knowledge sharing, they cut off communication, and we later learned that they were copying the features of our product and reaching out to steal our biggest customers! Unfortunately, his company was in a different country, so we couldn't sue. I should have never trusted him. I felt horrible, but luckily my managers didn't blame me since they put the initial pressure on me to interact with him."

As these examples illustrate, weak ties do not always translate into useful knowledge that organizations can put to use. Although the knowledge may match organizational needs, the relationships may be difficult to mobilize; when they are activated they may be characterized by well-known trust and commitment problems inherent in weak ties. Although weak ties may benefit individuals in their private objectives, these benefits may not accrue to the organization and may even distract or harm it.

In many cases, weak ties may be more than a distraction or a cause of insufficient relational quality for mobilization. Networks with weak ties may also be a strong precursor to destructive organizational conflict. An organization with weak ties makes it difficult for legitimate authority to defend itself from the emergence of political coalitions that seek to enact some sort of regime change in management.

For example, a top executive at NetCo was leading an effort to open up the company's platform to enable third-party companies to interact with it, potentially generating millions in additional revenue. In fact, he had the authority to make these changes as the head of platform strategy, and many of his executive colleagues had given their consent to the idea. Unfortunately, most of the linkages between executives were weak. A group of midlevel managers and directors started organizing against the idea when they realized that this immense third-party revenue might cannibalize their own product line or, at the least, make NetCo's achievements pale by comparison. Although the dissenters only had weak ties themselves, they organized effectively over WhatsApp to create a common language before they petitioned their executives' bosses.

When the executives simultaneously heard from these managers, they were struck by the weight of the onslaught, as so many were against an open platform. The original executive tried to organize against dissenters and re-state his case, but to no avail. As he put it, "It was horrible . . . they basically just put it to a vote . . . among people with conflicting interests! I think we failed to use our executive judgment, and NetCo lost a big opportunity as a result. I guess my colleagues weren't willing to stick up for me."

When these examples are taken together, it becomes clear that weak-tie theory and other social capital theories of network diversity reach some boundary conditions in organizations. Social capital theories are designed to explain individual outcomes, so if the objective is to explain how employ-ees can access resources that are different from what they had before, ideas like weak ties may work in organizational contexts. Gaining access to new roles, new opportunities, or new roles may indeed be related to weak ties. But when we shift the focus to achieving organizational objectives, these often require resources that, while diverse, are idiosyncratic and specific to the task at hand. Accessing and combining these resources is an act of in-tensive collaboration requiring trust, suggesting a need for strong ties even if they are rare in many organizational networks. Network agency theory explains the reason for this mismatch: individual interests lie more in the realm of weak ties, and organizations find it difficult to provide incentives for producing enough strong ties in light of these misaligned interests.

THE ROLE OF TECHNOLOGY IN MAINTAINING WEAK-TIE PORTFOLIOS

It is interesting to ask whether digital technologies can be used to miti-gate the downsides of weak ties in organizations. Arguably, their capac-ity to enhance efficient management of weak ties should free up attention and resources to be dedicated to organizational objectives. They may even make it easier to maintain strong ties. However, Chapter 2 showed that individuals actually use technologies to develop many more ties, most of which I found to be of a weaker character. In the process of rampant tie formation, many older, stronger ties may weaken. The resulting portfolios of mostly weak ties are less readily mobilized by managers to meet orga-nizational objectives.

How does this occur? Digital tools do enable employees to lower the costs of maintaining and forming ties. This has led to more ties being formed which, as illustrated subsequently, are particularly useful for maintaining a vast portfolio of weak ties at low—but not zero—cost. One challenge, however, is that the sum of these costs can be significant across such a portfolio.

Another possibility is that some digital technologies can be used by management to monitor and discourage vast weak-tie portfolios. Perhaps, as some claim, enterprise software solutions lower the costs of network governance as well. However, I find this claim to be exaggerated. The impact of cost reductions on employee networking greatly outweighs the impact of reduced costs of network governance.

Social media platforms like LinkedIn, Twitter, and Facebook are prominent examples. Digital Forest encouraged its employees to be active on social media and engage in thought leadership. In fact, Twitter was encouraged even during work time. Company executives felt that, although external reputational benefits might be minimal—since only a few employees were verified influencers—at least their social media presence would enable them to source new ideas.

The executives analyzed their employees' social media presence to see its impact. What they found was shocking. The majority of social media activity fell into two categories: politics and entertainment. Employees were either politically tweeting, with both progressive and conservative camps being represented, or they were tweeting about movies and comic books. Very few engaged in technical or business conversations, although there were some discussions about Digital Forest's products.

When executives learned of this nonwork focus of social media activity, they asked employees to redirect their posts away from politics in particular, because it appeared to be increasing divisiveness in the company culture. They also celebrated technical tweeting when it occurred, particularly if it was used to address customers' problems with Digital Forest's products. However, further analysis of employees' tweets revealed that there was no real shift in focus. Indeed, company pronouncements had given further prominence to political conversations.

Later, ahead of the US presidential election, Digital Forest took the drastic action of banning social media on company time altogether. There is some indication that this reduced social media presence, but unfortunately both technical and business engagement on Twitter dwindled too.

LINKING ORGANIZATIONAL RESOURCE MOBILIZATION PROBLEMS TO DIGITAL RELATIONSHIPS

While employees may be engaged in forming and maintaining many weak ties for their own needs, managers must call upon them to mobilize some of these ties for organizational goals. The key difference lies in the purpose of mobilization whether for individuals or the organization. Employees may form many weak ties to find opportunities and keep their options open, not necessarily to collaborate deeply with them. Weak ties may actually be ideally suited to meet these goals in an individual's tie portfolio, which is a key motivation for maintaining weak ties.

At Digital Forest, employees' new weak ties did not go unnoticed. In many cases, managers heard about them and followed up by asking that they be put to work to achieve organizational goals. Employees were called upon to start new projects with either weaker new ties or dormant older ones. Yet predictable problems relating to miscommunication, misunderstanding, and mistrust emerged when the weaker ties were applied to complex, ambiguous, and risky collaborative work.

Much of the negative organizational impact of relational quality at Digital Forest can be traced to this mobilization problem: weak ties were being created and acted upon as though they were strong. In fact, participants seemed to sense this was true. As one manager pointed out, "We all sensed we lacked the trust to engage in these difficult tasks. We really don't know each other well. But we had no choice but to dive in—it was a real leap of faith."

In fact, they may have had very little choice. There was very little variation in tie strength in the company network because nearly all ties seemed to be of a weak character. As a result, managers and employees ignored relational quality as an important variable and proceeded to work with any ties that seemed to exist beyond a very minimal threshold in strength. This was even reflected in their language. I found that many individuals had taken to calling weak-tie contacts "good friend" or "partner" or "mentor," even though they may have met this person only once or twice.

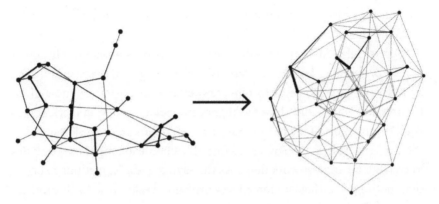

Figure 7: Diminishing relational quality after adoption of digital technologies

I call these vast portfolios of weak ties "digital relationships" because they resemble the 1s and 0s of digital technologies. As organizational members increasingly adopt digital technologies, they use them to increase connectivity, albeit of a necessarily lower relational quality. In fact, at Digital Forest digital technologies were often the key to maintaining such digital relationships at even the lowest level, but they did very little to encourage the strengthening of relationships. Figure 7 depicts a network undergoing a transformation after the organization-wide adoption of digital technologies, transforming from a moderately dense network with both strong and weak ties to a larger network of mostly weak ties.

The real problem in organizations emerges when managers and employees attempt to act on weak relationships to achieve organizational objectives, since even a large portfolio of weak ties is insufficient to get organizational work done. The digital-relationships dynamic appears to underlie many popular accounts of overwork, overcommitment, and organizational automation that have emerged over the past decade. Testaments to "shallow work" or "overcommitted organizing" suggest that digital technologies may be a factor. My research is consistent with this, but suggests an important mediating mechanism: the biggest negative impacts come when digital technologies encourage rampant formation of digital relationships—that is, weak ties supported by them. The irony is that even though these weak ties are usually unsuited to organizational activities, each still requires a minimal level of investment to maintain; the sum of many digital relationships can overwhelm the time and attention of the individuals who maintain them.

Digital relationships can ultimately be viewed as a scaling phenomenon in preferences for social relationships. Scaling in this sense is driven by technological change, with most ties tending to cluster around a given tie strength, which shifts lower as digital technology adoption increases. In equilibrium, most of the ties in individual portfolios are at the lower end of the strength scale so employees are forced to choose among those weak ties to collaborate and get work done. As the saying goes, "something is better than nothing," so they are forced to work with weaker ties. In short, there are few alternatives given that sufficiently strong ties to optimally match organizational goals are not present. The key irony of digital relationships is that they may be the only connections available for mobilization even though they are the most difficult to mobilize for organizational ends.

There is a broader perspective on why organizations may support digital relationships. Max Weber found that one of the main trajectories of bureaucratization is the depersonalization of organization structures so that a wide variety of people can occupy the necessary roles and relationships. The value of this bureaucratization includes clarity in roles, better alignment to objectives, and robustness to turnover and new occupants in positions. To the extent that roles and relationships are idiosyncratic to a specific charismatic person, it may be hard to replicate their activities and knowledge when they leave the organization. Thus, if roles and relationships can become specialized and limited to their essential functions, organizational structures can remain robust to turnover and personnel change.

While bureaucracy theory does not explicitly consider the number or strength of relationships, Weber speculated that hybrids of charismatic and bureaucratic control may actually be the norm. For example, the kind of administration we observe in craft guilds often combines particularistic networks of artisans supported by staff with more characteristic roles. Yet in this world only a few strong ties between artists may be necessary—the others may be replaceable. Such hybrid structures are perhaps becoming more prominent with the advent of leaner, digitally enabled organizations. Of course, the fully autonomous organization has yet to emerge, and even modern software organizations rely on small armies of coders who are often interchangeable. In other words, digital relationships may be a continuation of bureaucratic impulses as much as a consequence of digital technologies.

NETWORK AGENCY THEORIES OF RELATIONAL QUALITY

Underlying many resource mobilization difficulties is the fact that organizations face a variety of governance problems. If different individuals are to contribute resources and work together in specific configurations, a set of appropriate incentives should be in place to support them. To achieve this, governance must mitigate the asymmetric risks discussed in Chapter 2—for example, that developing a few stronger ties in a few high-aspiration teams may leave the individual at great risk of failure. At a basic level, individuals must trust that their collaborative efforts will be rewarded if they go well or punished if they go awry.

But because managers are rarely present to direct every interaction, employees are usually called upon to translate organizational, group, or team objectives into their own choices about who they collaborate with. This additional risk of collaborative failure is borne by employees. It is therefore not surprising that they would use prior interactions and the strength of relationships as a proxy for the risk in each choice to collaborate. Such risk is even implicit in weak-tie theory, in which a minimal strength threshold is presumed to be necessary for any interaction. The risks are, presumably, higher for weak ties than for strong ties.

The threshold of acceptable tie strength to accomplish goals may be higher for the organization than for individuals accessing opportunities in markets. The risks of collaboration may be higher when it depends on multiple actors who are interdependent or when interactions must unfold across organizational silos. Moreover, organizational goals often involve the combining of actors with complementary expertise, although these actors may be less likely to be conversant or know each other well, particularly in dynamic, global organizations with high turnover.

In organizational cases where collaborative risk is higher than when working alone, we might expect individuals to deliberately avoid collaboration. Some employees may even shirk the idea of collaboration. Given this possibility, it is natural to ask whether individuals will collaborate with the right people or invest in relationships that make sense for the organization. Will it happen automatically? When do local individual interests conflict with global organizational interests? What role does tie strength play in mobilizing the diverse knowledge necessary to achieve organizational objectives? And when does a firm have more claim on ties or more likelihood of influencing them?

MOBILIZING FIRM-SPECIFIC SOCIAL RELATIONSHIPS: MANAGERIAL INFLUENCE OVER TIES

An important issue in organizations is the extent to which managers can mobilize their employees' ties towards organizational ends. There are reasons to believe that this is not an easy task. As discussed earlier, different objectives may require different roles and relationships, each with its own motivational foundation. Ultimately, ties are owned by people and not by the organization. So the key question is what influence managers and organizations have over them. Of course, managers can define the general incentive structure for willingness to mobilize ties. In specific cases, they call upon employees to use their ties in service to the organization.[7] These general managerial capacities will be the subject of later chapters. What is essential here is to find general patterns in relational embeddedness that make managerial interventions more or less difficult.

When does the firm have more or less control over individual ties? Some general patterns can be inferred from the features of organizational networks. Many individual networks that organizations take advantage of actually span boundaries, meaning that individuals have contacts both within and outside their current organization. In some cases, the organization relies upon individual relationships that are completely outside its boundaries—for example, the relationship between contractor and subcontractor. For the issue of network boundaries, it is easy to infer some basic mobilization patterns. It should be the case that fully internal individual relationships (between two members of the focal organization) are more readily mobilized than boundary spanning relationships (between a member and a nonmember). The latter, in turn, is more readily mobilized than a fully external relationship (between two nonmembers).[8] The formal incentives and authority of the organization and the informal influence it affords managers in this common organizational space should increase their capacity to compel or induce members to use their ties toward organizational ends.

There are perhaps less obvious but equally important patterns of relational quality for ties within organizations. The most important pattern is a difference in tie strength. The key insight from my fieldwork is that managers are better able to influence, mobilize, and control strong ties than they are weak ties in their organizations. As tie strength increases, it is more likely that these trusting relationships will be long-lived and specialized to the needs of this particular organization. While strong ties may be of great use to those who possess them, the social capital that individuals possess may be less useful for outside endeavors, which decreases their bargaining power in interactions with managers.

Strong ties are also likely to be more complex in that they take on many dimensions (work colleague, friend, mentor, etc.), which enhances their robustness and applicability to different managerial tasks. And they are likely to be more visible to others, as they are more likely to be within an organization's transactive memory. This enhances their capacity to be mobilized by managers. Taken together, these factors suggest that strong ties may be more subject to managerial suggestions, requests, and diktats.

The inverse dynamic illustrates the logic as well: individuals with many weak ties have diversified their risk across a greater number of contacts. While they may be less effective at accomplishing any single difficult and complex project, they actually have greater bargaining power since they have little resource dependence on a few ties. In some cases, such individuals can ignore administrative requests because of their broad base of social support. This is true in dynamic industries with high turnover, in which internal weak ties even increase the likelihood of workers sourcing job offers from former colleagues now at other companies. Weak ties are also less trusting and less complex, making them less likely to be mobilized effectively to meet organizational goals.

Moreover, weak ties are more likely to be hidden from view than strong ties, especially if interactions take place either on digital platforms that managers cannot access or on public platforms that are less likely to be monitored. The result is that these digital relationships are not well suited to organizational objectives and less likely to be mobilized effectively for them.

Indeed, there is strong evidence that firm specificity of knowledge, expertise, and other elements of human capital shapes individual motivation and behavior. It is not too big a stretch to imagine that the firm specificity of social capital may be a motivator of organizational behavior as well.[9]

An example from NetCo illustrates the firm specificity of strong ties. Two engineering vice presidents, one focusing on network security and the other on wireless connectivity, had a long-standing and strong relationship, having worked together for almost ten years at NetCo on different projects and in various roles. They had risen through the ranks together and become friends. Even their families knew each other, and they often vacationed together. "We weren't natural friends at first. Honestly, we began by rankling each other. But we were both around for a long time so we got to know each other and became close." Over time, they often worked as a "dynamic duo," such that executives would run new product ideas or technical initiatives by both of them at once.

Although friends, the engineers' work relationship could be viewed as somewhat conflictual, since the domains of network security and wireless connectivity sometimes had conflicting objectives. Over time they learned to critique and supplement each other effectively. "It's true we argue a lot, but what newcomers may not see is that we trust each other implicitly. Our arguments are about ideas and perspectives only. I know he's in it for the long-term, so I trust there is always goodwill there. In fact, behind the scenes we are often protecting each other in a system that can be a little cruel. It isn't always perfect, but we have thrived together."

There were times when the relationship appeared detrimental to them both. Executives and others in the organization treated them as a unit, and this may have held back their career prospects at various times, since promotion of one before the other threatened to break the pairing. Both also recognized that their unique value to NetCo was that they were co-specialized. "Yeah, I joked that I can never jump ship unless he comes with me! I guess the CEO already knows this. [laughs]. Anyhow, I get pulled into so many NetCo things, partly because of him, that I don't have time to look elsewhere. I guess it's a choice . . . although I don't see many others making this choice. Most people here are free agents . . . or lone wolves."

The broader idea in this chapter is to apply the idea of firm specificity to strong ties. Firm specificity as a concept in strategy literature is characteristic of resources that are tightly held by the firm and therefore not easily appropriated by others, whether competitors or employees who may threaten to use them for private benefit.

Firm specificity applies to physical assets, but has most often been applied to knowledge-based resources that have little value outside an interdependent system of resources.[10] Often, resources become firm-specific when they have high value only when used in conjunction with other resources that the firm owns or controls. That is, combinations of resources are often firm-specific, which is why the topic is intimately related to resource diversity.

Individuals may have firm-specific expertise if the value of what they know cannot be captured by a competitor that might hire them. In such cases, individuals of great value to the firm may have very little bargaining power vis-à-vis the firm because they have fewer high-value options outside. A prime example is an engineer working on valuable technologies that are not interoperable with those of competitors. By contrast, individuals who occupy high-value but interchangeable positions and whose population is limited may have low firm specificity and relatively higher bargaining power. Examples include lawyers and accountants who can find work in many companies against competition which is limited by the many years of education and professional licensing necessary to enter the profession.

The ideas just presented concern the firm specificity of social relationships. Any intraorganizational social relationship has some degree of firm specificity just by virtue of the physical location and social foci of the organization in which it was created, so individuals are more likely to continue enacting relationships there than in other places. I argue further that strong ties are more likely to be firm-specific than weak ties because the longer, more intensive, and multidimensional social investments that two members make in a strong relationship are more likely to be specialized in roles that benefit the firm than they would be in a weak relationship. In fact, there is some indication that individuals' preference for weak ties is at least partially motivated by a desire to avoid firm specificity so as to maintain their bargaining power.

A key dynamic underlying the prevalence of weak ties may be the incentives for making the social investments that organizations engender. Individuals may sense that investments in strong ties are more firm-specific and that organizations capture more of the benefits as compared with weaker ties in which individuals capture nearly all of the benefits. That is, this dynamic is endogenous and reinforces individual inducements that are already in place. Firm specificity of strong ties can lead individuals to avoid making long-standing social investments that are useful to the organization.

As before, it may be tempting to view digital technologies as a causal antecedent of this network agency problem because vast weak-tie portfolios are mostly observed there. Yet although this is possible, I argue that digital technologies are mostly playing a contingent or moderating causal role in the production of ties that are too weak. Indeed, failing organizations with weaker relational quality were observed long before the dramatic increase in digital technology adoption of our era. Instead, the more fundamental antecedent cause of ties that are too weak appears to be motivational, as a product of either misaligned incentives or social capital inducements. Sometimes employees form ties that are too weak as a logical consequence of incentives and inducements that lead to too many ties, as described in Chapter 2. But this chapter presents additional evidence that employees specifically avoid investing relational energy in strong ties because they tend to be more firm-specific and therefore less robust to network disruptions and organizational changes that do not favor them.

MANAGERIAL INTERVENTIONS IN NETWORKS WITH CHRONICALLY WEAK TIES

It is useful to understand management's perspective on employees' social capital, particularly tie strength. There is evidence that some managers are aware of the firm specificity of strong ties and attempt to enhance it with interventions in network structure.

One manager told me, "I always try to assign critical tasks to pairs of people who have known each other for a long time. In fact, I may rely on the same pairs too much. Work relationships are tricky and I know these few work partners will trust each other, work out their differences, and find a way to divide the work to achieve the goals. . . . Frankly, it's a big problem that most people who work together don't know each other very well. I understand it from their perspective; who wants to spend outside time with work colleagues? But that's what it takes to become real friends. People want to work with many others. They demand to be rotated to learn more. I get it. But it means we're always working through basic trust and communication problems. It's frustrating."

Another executive told me of his attempt to intervene in an organization that seemed to have too few strong ties. "I noticed that despite being an established organization, people didn't seem to know each other. So I began by organizing social events, but these were like cocktail parties where people bounced around a lot. A lot of people stood in the corner. So that didn't work. Then I had an idea that the best way to cultivate was to assign people to common projects, and have them work together. Perhaps multiple times. Then they really developed esprit de corps."

Over a year, this executive implemented a policy of partner assignment for one of the business units in his charge. The results were mixed. He recalls, "I think everyone developed deeper relationships as a result, but the real test was whether they would choose to hang out with each other socially or work together on their own once my little experiment stopped. Honestly, maybe only a few people continued, since I think the rest preferred to go back to the other way of working. But at least I can be proud of the few connections I catalyzed. They've become really important contributors." Although most of the pairs did not sustain or maintain strong ties after one year, a few success cases were noted and continued.

It is possible to generalize these findings on types of intervention. Of great importance is whether managers have an inkling that strong ties are preferable from the perspective of organizational goals. If so, there are two types of intervention that improve a network with too many weak ties. Managers can support the development of strong ties through enhanced rewards, formal reassignment, or other means. Yet this may be insufficient if the social environment creates incentives for weak ties. Such a dynamic competes for relational investment in strong ties. The other type of intervention focuses on discouraging weak ties themselves. Managers can focus on discouraging large numbers of weak relationships in particular.

The two types of intervention work together if discouraging weak ties frees time and attention to invest in strong ties. While it does appear to be possible, I must admit that I found very little evidence that managers would discourage ties or even intervene to forbid them simply on the basis of their weakness.

The findings here add nuance to the theory. As individuals invest in social relationships at work, whether the benefits are captured depends on social control and ownership of social capital. Organizations require sufficient control over social resources to accomplish goals, and individuals may exchange mobilization of their social capital for compensation, monetary or nonmonetary. In an ideal world, these negotiations meet an equilibrium that is perceived as fair.

The agency problem arises because management has difficulty governing these relationships. Individuals may "own" ties, but who controls them in each encounter? It is natural to imagine that intraorganizational relationships are somewhat immovable and not fungible, so they should naturally be under the organization's control. But because relationships have a performative element and are difficult to monitor, individuals have local choices that can shift the equilibrium away from what may have been agreed upon when taking the job. The preference for weak ties and the agency cost of guarding against them result in an organizationally suboptimal equilibrium that is only exacerbated by digital technologies. Digital technologies lower the cost of tie formation and maintenance, enabling individuals to more effectively pursue private objectives. In this view, relational quality is always the subject of a potential agency problem where misaligned incentives are possible and organizational outcomes become decoupled from private achievement.

DECOUPLING NETWORK AND KNOWLEDGE DIVERSITY: MODELING MOBILIZATION FAILURES WITH WEAK TIES

What has been described above—that resource mobilization problems arise as individuals choose to underinvest in relational quality—is not captured in the theoretical model presented in Chapter 2, which focused narrowly on the structural issue of whether there are too few or too many ties.

An optimal number of ties may shift and diverge from actual behavior, but does not account for the tension that organizations experience around mobilizing a portfolio of ties with varying strength. Although the examples given indicate that many organizations make do with ties that are too weak, it cannot be assumed that fewer ties of sufficient strength are always the best option. As described before, the equilibrium may diverge from the organizational optimum.

It is useful to understand the optimal distribution of tie strength to achieve organizational objectives. Providing occasions for tie strengthening or inducements for forming more weak ties may be among the most practical policy levers that managers have at their disposal. It might be particularly useful to understand the relational optimum when organizational innovation is the goal, where the underlying model is one of recombination distributed across individuals with different social capital endowments, in which both strong and weak ties are likely to be relevant. Accessing diverse resources, such as knowledge, is an important first step in the recombination process that underlies innovation. Weak ties have been shown to be involved in various innovation efforts in which key inputs to recombination come from acquaintances. This idea is consistent with the network and resource diversity theory described earlier.

The model in Chapter 2 emphasized an optimal number of ties, but it did not touch upon any trade-offs in the strength of ties that might shape the decision to invest in longer-lived and strong relationships. One reason that that mathematical model cannot address this issue sufficiently is that it has no way to capture the heterogeneous preferences of individuals that drive different investments in relationships. The long-run preferences of individuals may be shaped both by the capabilities and social skills that are innate dispositions of individuals and by the network context itself.

In short, networking preferences can differ substantially across a population of employees, with some individuals acting as "gadflies" who connect early and often and others focusing more strategically on ties that will pay off in the long term. Individual investments in relationships are local—they depend on opportunities to form and maintain ties and the individual preferences that confront them.

Of course, it is possible to build such a model, as I explain next. The essential features are agents with diverse preferences who seek to form or maintain ties with others based on their prior experience of collaborative success, whether in work, the gain of new knowledge, or innovative knowledge production itself. That is, network ties and knowledge-based collaboration co-evolve in an endogenous fashion based on what individuals learn about each other, meaning that decisions about whether to explore collaborative opportunities with new individuals in new ties or to exploit ties with current partners becomes critical. Elaborating such a model may have substantial payoffs if it can provide insight into equilibria and optima related to tie strength and knowledge diffusion, production, and innovation in endogenously evolving networks.

A BANDIT MODEL OF COLLABORATION
AND RELATIONAL QUALITY

To address issues discussed in previous sections, I developed a computational model of heterogeneous knowledge, collaborative preferences, and tie strength. This model endows employees with choices about whom to collaborate with based on tie strength and prior knowledge of the likelihood of success with each employee. Collaborative success depends on tie strength and the implicit quality of partners. Tie strength evolves endogenously as employees allocate their limited time and attention to choices of old partners or new ones. Experiments explore how tie strength increases the aggregate performance of employees engaged in collaboration.

A key aspect of the model is whether employees should choose current partnerships for additional collaboration or explore new partnerships. As this is a process of learning by doing—involving exploration and exploitation— it is based on a standard bandit model, which allows the experimenter to vary the degree of exploration in a parameter, τ. In bandit models, τ shapes whether actors lean toward exploiting current options or toward exploring new ones, much like the choice of a gambler who can choose to play the current slot machine or switch to a new one in every time period. Since the choices in this model are multivaried among possible network ties and

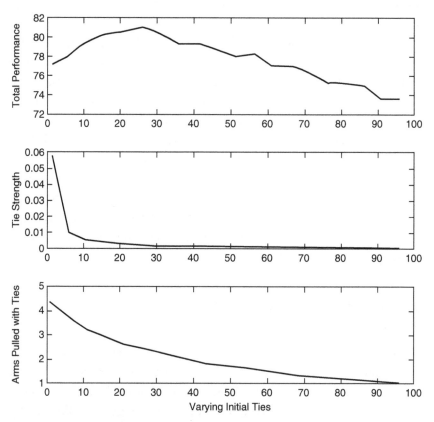

Figure 8: Tie strength and performance in a multiarmed network bandit model

potential collaborators, and the preferences for τ are heterogeneous, I call this the multiarmed network bandit (MANB) model. Such a model has the potential to provide a better understanding of relational quality and organizational outcomes.

A key finding of the MANB model is that, as the number of initial ties in the network increases, the heterogeneous knowledge accessed by each individual decreases. This is depicted in Figure 8. Although seemingly counterintuitive, this occurs because the average tie strength in a network with more ties is less than that in a network with more ties. As networks with more ties evolve, the likelihood that individuals rely on network connections to make collaboration choices decreases—the number of arms pulled in the bandit model of those with ties decreases. Individuals increasingly collaborate with suboptimal partners who have a lower likelihood of successfully providing access to new knowledge. In other words, in this endogenous model, where individuals can choose to explore new ties or exploit existing ones, the capacity to effectively build on effective relationships is diminished with more ties precisely because of the declining relational quality.

The model confirms an intuition about digital relationships illustrated by qualitative evidence: in the presence of more ties of lesser quality, individuals will satisfice to act on any relationship at their disposal. Digital relationships imply two interesting features in networks that evolve endogenously—that is, where tie strength, outcomes, and choices about tie strength dynamics depend on each other freely. A main effect is that large networks with any ties are treated as a minimally viable linkage for organizational work, with predictably lower performance outcomes as a result. Another effect is the diminishing importance of tie strength as a decision criterion. If tie strength is no longer a reliable predictor of expected performance, individuals will come to rely on apparent network quality even less when making collaboration choices, with relationships playing less of a valuable role in improving organizational outcomes.

Entrenched Brokers and Ossified Bridges

MONOPOLIES OF INFORMATION AND CONTROL

This chapter details network agency problems related to prominent network positions, using brokerage relationships that span structural holes as a primary example. Misaligned networking interests emanating from entrenched brokerage positions and ossified bridges are explored. Brokers as a cartel are considered, with the notion of brokerage monopoly developed to explain anticompetitive networking behavior at the group level. Contrary to some expectations, digital technologies can be used to solidify brokerage monopolies and sustain their rents.

SOCIAL POSITIONS IN ORGANIZATIONAL NETWORKS

A prominent strand of network literature focuses on the benefits of various positions in the network structure. Since a network of ties is not uniform, individuals may hold vastly different sets of relationships, some of which may be more valuable than others if they enable better access to resources.[1] Much of the literature focuses on the social capital of brokers, who are defined as linking individuals (sometimes called "alters") who are otherwise disconnected (Burt 1992). Brokers play a unique role in networks because they act as bridges that span structural holes between alters.[2] Since alters must rely on brokers to access information or resources from other alters, brokers can benefit from this relationship by gaining greater prestige, respect, attention, favors, or even direct payments in exchange.

Substantial evidence indicates that brokers who span structural holes enjoy several benefits by virtue of their position. They are likely to be paid more, be promoted more, be respected more, and even be happier than nonbrokers. Yet not all brokerage positions are created equal: some brokers derive more benefits from their structural holes than others. An emerging literature on the differential "returns to brokerage" seeks to understand why some brokerage positions are more beneficial than others. The key idea that shapes the magnitude of brokerage returns is the "threat of disintermediation"—that is, how likely it is that alters can "cut out the middleman," the broker, and interact directly. If the threat of disintermediation is significant, alters can leverage it during negotiations with the broker to diminish the value the broker captures from exchanges.[3] In these negotiations, the cost of direct interaction between alters determines the continuity of the brokerage. If the cost for alters to interact directly is low enough compared with the benefits of direct exchange, then alters may avoid interacting through the broker altogether and close their structural holes.

Put another way, one can ask why structural holes continue to exist if closing them provides benefits to alters. There are several reasons. Direct interaction between alters may be challenging because of different thinking styles, culture, or language, or simply because they have few ways to communicate with ease. The broker may be useful in facilitating interactions and saving the alters these costs. Of course, a broker may help without payment simply by being altruistic. However, this may not be possible for most brokers over a long period. If we examine brokerage relationships over a significant duration, we should expect the broker to derive some value from the alters for facilitating their interactions. Thus, an implicit exchange logic may take hold in which brokers perform a useful function that alters compensate. In markets, brokers' compensation is usually monetary. However, in social networks it is frequently respect, deference, favors, or support for the broker's preferred causes and interests in the social system.

BROKERAGE UTILITY IN ORGANIZATIONS

Though much of the literature has documented the benefits of the brokerage position for individuals, considerably fewer studies have focused on the utility of brokerage for organizations.[4] One can imagine that the impact of bridging might be positive for organizations since many of the organizational objectives that are important in the modern age require individuals or groups to work together when they lack rich connections. Brokers can fill that gap. For instance, functional or divisional silos—groups of individuals who are densely connected in clusters but possess diminished connectivity outside the group—are prominent in many organizations and seem to be responsible for failures to coordinate. Brokers who span boundaries are often the key to mitigating the negative effects of silos since brokers act as the necessary connective tissue that enables information and resources to pass between these otherwise separated groups. That individual brokers benefit in terms of greater returns may be counted as adequate compensation for their organizational functionality.

In fact, the idea that brokers are beneficial for organizations is an assumption that permeates the literature on managers' facilitation of networking. Managers are often advised to leverage brokers or become brokers themselves in order to facilitate interactions between their direct reports or to bridge horizontally in the organizational hierarchy. Is this accurate? Should organizations encourage more brokers? Individual social capital logic seems to suggest that this is the case: brokers enjoy benefits because they perform useful functions that benefit others. Does this logic hold in organizations? How does individual brokerage in an organization differ from brokerage that might be found in a market of free agents?

What is interesting about typical social capital theories of brokerage is that their treatment of brokers undersocializes them in various ways. Generally, individuals only play stereotypical roles as brokers or alters. Some research has added notions of individual differences and cultural context, but what is particularly relevant here are typical features of organizational life that affect brokerage.[5] It has been suggested that the heterogeneous patterns of behavior that brokers exhibit range from spanning holes to maintaining the separation between alters.[6] It has also been noted that informal social positions such as brokers can often translate into formal roles and ranks. Brokers may become managers themselves.[7] In fact, many brokerage positions in organizations may arise because of team, function, or division boundaries across which individuals need to interact. Brokers may productively translate knowledge or exchange resources between these groups.

A dimension that is often neglected is that of time. Social relationships in structural holes can unfold over long periods of time, and some emerging brokerage literature has recently started exploring the dynamics of these relationships in organizations and other socially bound contexts. The effect of time may be experienced differently across social contexts if network dynamics unfold across different timescales. Brokerage research suggests that brokers can develop relatively stable strategic orientations—facilitating interactions or maintaining disconnection—based on their experience with alters. Some brokers may strategically toggle between these orientations at selected times when either facilitation or separation is more useful. For instance, recent research has revealed how structures change over time and has uncovered mechanisms of creation and sustenance of brokerage.[8]

In organizations, time is a particularly important variable of interest because organizational activities, routines, and cognition can quickly become inertial. Organizational inertia implies that activities and routines become repeated and thinking becomes stale in fixed frames. These effects can make it difficult to respond to change because members either do not see the need for change or do not have the tools to create it with enough urgency. Brokerage relationships may be thought to mitigate inertia if they connect parts of the network that enable the organization to pursue new opportunities. As brokers are often considered to have a vision advantage and to be a source of good ideas because of their position, they may be on the front lines of effective change efforts.

However, it is also possible that time may affect brokers themselves if the connectivity they provide does not match the purpose of accessing good ideas, enabling recombination, and diffusing best practices. Bridges may become problematic if the specific interactions they facilitate are no longer a good fit for the environmental demands of the organization—that is, whether they are suited to upcoming projects or current business. In order to understand how brokers can simultaneously help and harm organizations, it is necessary to consider time since organizational networks can exhibit substantial stability over multiple timescales even though they sometimes become less useful. Specifically, it is important to examine how individual interests emerge and change over time even while some relationships may remain the same.

INVESTIGATING BROKERS IN THE ORGANIZATIONAL CONTEXT

Prior research on individual brokerage and structural holes may lead us astray in organizational applications. As brokerage research highlights the importance of bridging ties, its natural implication is that the longevity of a broker's relationships should enhance organizational returns, if only because the broker becomes more efficient in exchange and enhances her or his reputation as a broker. One might even assume that individual relationships become specialized to better fit the tasks at hand or adapt to changes. A longer relationship may also mitigate the sense of risk inherent in undertaking uncertain innovation projects. Considered together, the literature suggests that brokers are useful for organizations and that the more experienced or long-established they are in their particular brokerage role, the more value they create for their organization.

Although this conventional wisdom is appealing, my research on organizationally embedded brokerage across multiple settings yields conclusions that are in stark contrast. I find that brokers are often surprising linked to lower innovation outcomes in organizations, with less diffusion, connectivity, or adaptation. Long-established brokers are most likely to be associated with negative outcomes. As brokers become entrenched in their position, they are less involved in innovation or change and the bridges they form between alters become ossified. These entrenched brokers tend to conduct self-similar types of exchange and information flow that are ill-suited to the pressing needs of the organization. How exactly does this occur? What mechanisms lead older bridges to become ineffective? Examining specific brokers in context may shed light on these issues.

The first example comes from Digital Forest and a marketing director named John. Although John was employed in a customer-facing marketing role, he had a background in product development, where he forged many connections with engineering specialists. The marketing division was tasked with sourcing customer needs and feeding them to the product teams and understanding the product features deeply and, with the assistance of sales managers, communicating them to customers.

John described how he became a broker: "Well, I like to say I'm a translator or problem solver, not just an information conduit. In the early days, I noticed that the way engineers and customers interacted was missing some big opportunities. First, the corporate office was becoming more complex, and there was no way for our engineers to think about new product features without knowing what the important trends were. And customers couldn't see how our new technologies could solve their problems. I was responsible for launching our new customer segmentation and bundles about ten years ago. That was highly innovative, and really increased our growth. Well, it was an important component of our broader strategy. Ever since then, I've been involved in virtually every interaction between the engineers and customers."

A few engineering managers spoke of this role as well, although they questioned its value. "Every time we source customer requirements, John has to be on the call. And sometimes, he'll take calls for us. He's very protective of his bundles. They are long-standing here at Digital Forest, so every engineering change has to be interpreted through that framework. As a result, he has to be involved. But honestly, that schema is pretty old—a decade, right? I'm not sure why he must be involved. We understand the customer well enough to chat them up and that might honestly lead to a reimagining of the space. But it's not the way things are done. I'll admit it might be a pain in our necks to do it ourselves, so we continue this way with John involved."

Over time John's brokerage role focused less on true innovation with alters and more on information packaging, translation, and transmission that maintained his position. Given his experience, he could have been involved in creating new pitches that targeted customer's needs, but there is little evidence that he did more than advocate for the old way of doing things. John revealed his logic: "Well once I had proven my value, I focused on reinforcing it. The bundles work. No one really questions it. So I just make sure that customers and engineers are both happy enough with my transition work."

Another example comes from interfirm alliances. Alliances are a particularly good setting to study brokerage and its impact on organizations because bridging ties that span boundaries are highly prominent and seemingly necessary for the success of an alliance. Moreover, brokerage processes across boundaries are usually more discernable and so can be more easily analyzed. In a technology-based alliance that I studied, the collaborative work relied on one manager, Ross, to form connections between companies. An executive in the partner organization described Ross as "a great guy. . . . He used to work here . . . so I think that in itself broke down a lot of barriers. He understood the culture, what the goal was. He was there when we were rolling out [I-tech] and so to have a guy like that inside [the other company] really removed a lot of barriers for us."

Despite the executive's requests that Ross help other employees "get connected," "find the right partners," and "work closely" with each other, he actually made no attempts to do so. Instead, he preferred to sustain the disconnection between alters because it served his purposes. Indeed, he tried to limit interactions between others and canceled progress reviews of the alliance or joint work activities. The impact of these sustained disconnections was increasing technical hurdles and an inability to translate technologies into commercial products. After months without any positive outcomes, the executives dissolved the intercompany alliance.

The broker in this example represents what is often called *Tertius Gaudens* (TG), defined as a cluster of behaviors in which brokers actively work to maintain the separation between alters. This is contrasted with the *Tertius Iungens* (TI), in which brokers facilitate connections between others (Obstfeld 2005). Most of the literature generally presents these as stable strategic orientations that brokers pursue—a mix of personality traits, preferences, and orientations. Newer literature suggests that brokers can strategically alternate between TG and TI behaviors based on the task at hand and goals.[9] My research joins this latter tradition in seeing TG and TI behaviors as a choice, but it adds the idea that a stable pattern in decision making may emerge under specific social-organizational contexts: I found that as bridges age, brokers tend to engage in more TG behaviors that sustain disconnections between alters and solidify their positions. The key difference with prior literature is to consider the difference between individuals and organizational interests in brokerage: employees who are long-standing brokers may resist TI even though their managers request it to achieve organizational objectives.

Indeed, there are many examples of mismatch in which managers requested that brokers facilitate interactions between alters and expected them to do so, only for very few interactions to actually occur. This suggests a certain puzzle: brokers are needed to facilitate exchanges between the disconnected in various organizational activities, but they do not. Why do brokers choose not to broker?

BROKERAGE MONOPOLIES: CREATING AND SUSTAINING ADVANTAGES THROUGH SOCIAL POSITION

The key to resolving the puzzle is a better understanding of brokerage behavior in organizational contexts and its typical impact on organization-level outcomes. The literature on individual social capital has found that individuals benefit from occupying brokerage positions. Yet those very same benefits, which constitute the social capital of brokers, create incentives for brokers to lose alignment with organizational interests, which depend on managers to facilitate interactions between employees, many of whom are alters in a structural hole. This sustains existing brokerage relationships and leads them to become inertial and maladaptive. Put simply, brokers may decline to facilitate interactions if they feel that doing so threatens the value they derive from brokerage.

Threats of disintermediation. A key idea that animates the literature on returns to brokerage is the threat of disintermediation. A threat of disintermediation affects the value that brokers derive from structural holes, if only because it describes the costs that alters incur should they want to eliminate one alternative to brokerage: direct intermediation ("cutting out the middleman"). However, many other alternatives to current brokerage arrangements are used in negotiations to diminish the returns to brokerage. For example, alters can permanently acquire needed skills or resource so that interaction with another alter is not necessary. They may also find a way to diminish the value of the broker's capabilities. For instance, a change in organizational policies may sanction the exchange of informal favors or make it difficult to defer to informal positions like brokerage. Perhaps the most useful remedy is to find alternative brokers to exchange with or, at the least, use these possibilties in negotiations to diminish the current broker's value. These options may be readily available in organizations, which act as social foci for alternative relationships: in organizations alters may be more likely to find alternative brokers with whom to exchange. Over time they are likely to make use of these mechanisms to decrease their disadvantage vis-à-vis the broker.

To better understand the broader dynamics of brokerage in organizations, it is particularly useful to apply the idea of monopoly to network positions. A brokerage monopoly is defined here as a state in which an individual broker dominates information flow and control rights in a local social structure to such an extent that the broker extracts nearly all of the benefits of exchange in that structure. Brokers do not always have monopolies. In fact, the brokerage position can be transient and only weakly rewarded, as I discuss subsequently. However, it is useful to analyze brokerage advantages from this perspective and the monopolistic ideal type.

How are brokerage monopolies created and sustained? As I will explain, brokerage monopolies can be sustained for "natural" reasons related to the broker's skill or the organizational context in which they are valued. However, of greater interest are brokerage monopolies resulting from some intentional anticompetitive action on the part of would-be monopolists who sustain their brokerage position and advantages.

It is useful to recall corporate monopolies because they share features with individual brokerage monopolies in social networks. In industry, company monopolies are thought to exist in an equilibrium that is sustained indefinitely unless it is broken up at a very high cost to those involved or by some external third party who sets policy, such as the government. This occurs because companies can use excess profits to cement their advantages if they remain unchallenged.[10]

Similarly, the costs to disrupt brokerage monopolies are high because once brokerage positions are established, a broker can use the information and control advantages of the position to resist changes that threaten returns. In fact, in a brokerage monopoly the broker may control the distribution of rewards. Typically, brokers parcel out sufficient rewards to alters and other partners to ensure that the brokerage structure is retained while maintaining a significantly higher surplus for themselves. In a perfect brokerage monopoly, the broker's returns are maximized while the organizational benefits are minimized in such a way as to sustain the brokerage. The actual magnitude of the organizational benefit may vary, as I discuss.

Entry barriers to brokerage. It is essential to realize that brokerage monopolies need not depend on formal structures at all. Brokers often do not occupy the highest positions in an organization. Instead, brokerage emanates from informal social relationships and may not serve organizational ends. This genesis can magnify misalignment because the broker's true source of advantages does not depend on organizational compliance. Strictly speaking, brokers are a particular case of double-sided monopoly (since both alters may be completely dependent). To use the specialized language of industrial organization, the brokerage can be a monopoly and a monopsony simultaneously since both the source and the recipient of any information or resource exchange depend on the broker.[11] This dual dependency makes brokerage monopoly a powerful structure.

The brokerage monopoly idea is useful because it offers insights into how misaligned brokerage arises and is maintained. The key idea is the notion of entry barriers, defined as the costs that alters or others have to bear in order to establish a new brokerage position that at least partially substitutes for the position that a current broker occupies. These are the costs of establishing a new structural hole that serves the same purpose as the existing one, or some new purpose for which alters are willing to supplant existing brokerage relationships. For example, if the current broker acquires ideas and certifies that they are valid before passing them along, then the entry barriers are precisely the costs of finding another individual with similar expertise and certifying power to do the same. Alternatively, alters may arrange a new structural hole in which the broker is the key stakeholder, which eliminates the need for certification altogether.

COMBINING DISINTERMEDIATION AND ENTRY BARRIERS INTO BROKERAGE

Entry barriers to brokerage differ from the threat of disintermediation often discussed in brokerage literature, since the latter is confined to the costs of alters closing an existing structural hole. Entry barriers raise costs for new brokerage in general. Both factors affect brokerage in existing triads. Disintermediation is primarily concerned with the alters in a given structural hole, whereas entry barriers are concerned with potential brokers outside the hole. However, the two may be related in a dynamic equilibrium. For instance, if alters find a potential alternative broker, they increase their negotiating power with the current broker, thereby diminishing the current broker's advantages.

However, the implication is broader than the existing local structure in the triad and its current alters. One can imagine a new structural hole triad emerging, with three entirely new individuals, competing in function with the prior triad. This alternative arrangement competes with the current structural hole by reducing the returns for all individuals in that triad with the offer of a substitute. Thus, potential triads may have two effects on existing triads, by diminishing the value that both the existing broker and existing alters derive from the previous arrangement. The determining factor is whether the existing alters can credibly join new triads with new brokers. If so, the negative impact is borne primarily by the existing broker.

These dynamics are particularly relevant to organizations where there is often a relatively stable supply of individuals with somewhat redundant skills who are competing to become brokers and alters in alternative structural holes. Unlike in markets, where brokerage may be temporary or transient, brokerage in organizations may run longer in many cases because these same individuals participate for the length of their employment and the network of relationships is more transparent. Considered in its entirety, the brokerage monopoly frame may offer a clearer picture of brokerage dynamics that are well suited to organizations. Both entry barriers and the threat of disintermediation determine the utility of being a brokerage position since they determine whether such a monopoly—however partial or temporary—can take hold, be sustained, and generate substantial returns.

A few examples are useful to illustrate the key difference between threats of disintermediation and entry barriers to brokerage. For instance, in the example discussed previously, John faced a threat of disintermediation by his colleagues, who were considering whether to speak directly to customers. This threat was not particularly serious, though, because John, as a broker, offered some translation value at relatively low cost to his alters. A higher potential value in customer-centric innovation was possible, but his colleagues were busy and risk-averse.

This suggests a useful thought experiment. First, if John leaves the organization, what will his colleagues do? They almost certainly will pursue innovation since it provides much greater value than mere "translation" work and the learning curve may not be too much steeper than the learning curve to perform that translation function exactly as John did over many years. Yet they do not disintermediate John when he is present. Such a thought experiment indicates how brokerage relationships can be caught in a suboptimal local equilibrium when the broker is present for long periods of time.

I found many examples of potential brokerage substitution related to barriers to entry in brokerage. These were of three main types. First, I encountered many brokerage triads where there were potential alternative brokers "waiting in the wings" who could act as substitutes for current brokers. The major barriers included the lack of strong enough ties to both alters and the inability to provide whatever added value constituted the broker's relationship.

In a second category of barriers to entry, I observed some cases in which a potential alternative broker offered to serve some new brokerage function for which alters were willing to forego the original broker's function. This was often a new way of interacting that the alters had not considered, such as a new way of organizing projects, co-investing, or social events that made the original broker unnecessary. In this case, prior relationships were often the only credible barrier to new brokerage.

The third category I explored was a potential broker who intermediated new alters in such a way that the value of the entire prior triad was diminished. Typically, this was a broader combination in which, for instance, the new triad outcompeted the old triad or made it redundant. I observed these redundancy-making triads in many organizational functions ranging from new ways to organize the product portfolio or the sales approach to new ways to reorganize the accounting function. The barriers to this new brokerage were particularly hard to raise by the old brokers, as old relationships between older alters were not necessary. Typically, the only barriers were "on the merits"—did the old triad offer more value than the new triad?

SUSTAINING BROKERAGE MONOPOLIES: INCUMBENCY ADVANTAGES AND STRATEGIC ACTION

Under what conditions do brokerage monopolies emerge and endure? There are some general patterns. First, the costs for an alter to disintermediate, connect through an alternative broker, or become a broker are often much higher than those of maintaining the current connection. This is especially true in the long run since the broker becomes more experienced in dealing with alters and in making exchanges more efficient for all involved. Each of these alternatives to existing structural holes requires an upfront investment in connections that did not exist before. It requires forming and maintaining connections that are at high risk of lower performance simply because they are new relationships.

In fact, brokers often do make improvements to exchange relationships, and they can do so with substantially lower marginal costs than would-be brokers can because they build on an already functional relationship. Since existing brokers have a stronger influence over the current distribution of rewards, they have greater latitude to adjust should alters require additional compensation to put down competing offers.

A major benefit of incumbency is that improvements to already strong brokerage relationships are easier to formulate. Unlike in existing relationships, in incumbencies convincing others to enact a new structural hole may require strong ties that are lacking. Sufficient tie strength to take on such a risky project may not exist in modern organizations with weak digital relationships, as was discussed in Chapter 3.

There is a final factor, one that has not been extensively explored in research on brokerage. Brokers are powerful agents in organizations, capable of taking decisive and often effective action to protect their interests. Often, action is directed at raising the costs of entry into brokerage. Therefore, it is reasonable to believe that existing brokers might block potential brokers by excluding them from interaction or attacking them or their reputation in some other way. Controlling their own alters is easy because of the dependent relationship that already exists. As for potential brokerage rivals, they must mobilize their power externally to their relationships. In either case, we should expect a baseline impact as they leverage their information and control advantages to thwart challenges to their brokerage position and returns.

In fact, I witnessed multiple examples of misaligned strategic behavior by brokers. These went beyond mere defensive maneuvers meant to preserve relationships in the current triad. They often focused on preventing both disintermediation and brokerage entry, even if closure or new brokers might be organizationally useful. The former was perhaps to be expected: there were many cases of brokers maintaining active separation between their alters by engineering separate meetings and events so that the alters would not encounter each other. In an attempt to sabotage a budding relationship, brokers sometimes intervened when alters interacted. They may have sown mistrust between the parties or selectively revealed negative information not balanced against positive information. In fact, disrupting budding relationships between alters was usually easy for brokers since, by definition, alters trust the broker more than they trust each other.

Other forms of strategic behavior emerge when brokers attempt to actively block efforts by would-be brokers that may substitute for the original broker's activity. Thus, while the actions described previously are concerned with eliminating threats of disintermediation, these behaviors focus on raising barriers to entry. In such cases, brokers tend to lean on their generalized power and skills as opposed to any specific relational, informational, or control advantages they may have in the triad. For example, I observed some managers using their sway over resource allocation or their presence on promotion committees to persuade would-be brokers to give up their attempts.

ANTICOMPETITIVE BROKERAGE BEHAVIOR: COLLUSION AND CARTELS

Barriers to entry in brokerage mirror those in industrial organizations, where there is an important distinction between natural and anticompetitive barriers. Industries with natural entry barriers are those where incumbent companies have economies of scale and scope by virtue of their prior investments and product market choices. These factors raise the costs of entry of potential rivals who hope to compete against incumbents.[12] Similarly, a broker's reputation for effective intermediation or social skill in effecting such exchanges raises the cost for potential brokerage competitors. That is, sometimes brokers are functional, performing tasks of helpful translation, exchange, and coordination. If these skills are rare and costly to develop in others, one might expect outsized rewards for brokers without their harmful interventions.

It is more novel to consider the anticompetitive barriers to entry into brokerage across industries. Incumbent companies may act to limit competition, including but not limited to consolidatory acquisition, preemptive alliances, tacit collusion, mutual forbearance, predatory pricing, and various nonmarket strategies targeting preferential government regulation. All these actions have the net effect of lowering incentives for rivals to enter the market and compete with the incumbent. That some actions are illegal is a testament to their destructive power over society and customers.

As discussed above, noncompetitive strategies that brokers employ are mostly oriented toward direct prevention of tie formation by potential brokers and alters that would weaken the broker's advantage. However, one can imagine social versions of other noncompetitive strategies as well. For example, a broker's preemptive tie formation with other potential brokers can be used to decrease the likelihood of the latter creating competing structural holes. Brokers can also engage in a version of predatory pricing: they can minimize their value extraction and sustain temporarily high rewards for alters in order to force potential brokers to give up or leave the organization, after which the rewards are reduced. Versions of collusion may also exist if incumbent brokers collaborate to exclude newcomers. For example, they may engage in mutual forbearance, where they agree to recognize each other as the key intermediary in their respective domains and refrain from actions that would upset each other's uncontested disintermediation.

One idea that is particularly useful here is that of a brokerage cartel. In industrial analysis, cartels are defined as groups of firms that use both explicit and tacit collusion to improve their profits and dominate the market. Similarly, brokerage cartels are groups of brokers who cooperate to improve the value they extract from their positions. They attempt to maximize their rewards by reducing the impact of the two mechanisms described earlier: threats of disintermediation and barriers to entry into the brokerage class.

The key to understanding brokerage cartels is identifying a set of brokers who might collude. Typically, brokers occupy organizational positions in distinct, noncompetitive domains, and then agree to identify each other and offer assistance to (or at least tacit acceptance of) each other's activities. For instance, brokers who intermediate R&D and marketing functions are common. However, in multinational organizations, there might be multiple such brokers across the regions in which the company operates. The R&D-marketing broker in one region may coordinate with R&D-marketing brokers in other regions to ensure the stability of this brokerage role, since its legitimacy may depend on organization-wide acceptance.

Yet brokerage cartels need not be between role equivalents, as just described. Often, brokerage cartels comprise individuals in complementary brokerage roles that have negotiated definitive spheres of influence. These spheres of influence may be organized around content areas or around sets of alters. In each case, the content and/or the people are divided among brokers. This is related to ideas of mutual forbearance, in which colluding multibusiness firms agree not to compete with each other in their spheres of influence. It is notoriously difficult for outside regulators to prove that mutual forbearance has occurred, specifically because internal deliberations and negotiations are not visible and competitive choices could have been made for other reasons. Similarly, brokerage cartels may engage in mutual forbearance that reduces competition in a way that cannot be monitored by principals.

The *sine qua non* of cartel behavior is agentic action to maintain the preferred behaviors and boundaries of a cartel so that cartel members can capture value from others. The first challenge in maintaining a cartel is minimizing defections, as the benefits of a cartel can usually only be maintained if members comply with norms that ensure that members capture rents. Usually this is done by sanctioning and punishing members who defect. It is also important to combat threats from the outside by taking unified action against outsiders who attempt to become brokers.

I found multiple examples of sanctions for cartel members, such as members attempting to help outsiders become brokers only to be pushed back by the cartel member whose brokerages advantages would be dissipated thereby. More interestingly, cartel sanctions can be a group phenomenon. In one example, an executive, Mark, tried to help a junior colleague set up a new business that involved brokerage between engineers and customers. However, the new business might have disrupted a business managed by Jia, another broker in the cartel. Interestingly, yet another cartel member felt obliged to speak up for Jia's interests: "I went straight to Mark and told him what he was doing would hurt Jia's portfolio, including her new product launch. I made it abundantly clear I would speak up very vocally about this at our committee meeting. It was actually no skin off my back, but I was thinking about the future: if we don't protect each other, then someday it could be me. Jia's relationships with the engineers and customers were already established. There is no reason to disrupt them."

Mark's story is illustrative of brokerage cartel behavior: existing brokers may act informally to protect each other's interests in maintaining ossified brokerage relationships. Sanctions for members or outsiders who challenge the cartel may come from any member, since responsibility for cartel norms may be broadly shared. Most important is that the abnormally high returns for the broader class of brokers are maintained by individual behaviors that support the group, much like corporate cartels in industries.

There are other strategic actions that resemble industrial organization. For instance, nonmarket strategies can be used by analogy. Individual brokers can employ organizational structures to cement their advantages. When companies lobby for preferential regulation, governmental subsidies, or restricted licensing, they are essentially appealing to a governing authority to institutionalize their advantages in policy. Similarly, brokers may appeal to the leaders of the organization for preferential treatment to be institutionalized through policy and design. The clearest example is when brokers shape the promotion process by leveraging their social influence to gain acceptance in more powerful positions in the hierarchy. Brokers may also shape the hiring and firing of others in order to create fiefdoms. While not always brokerage-related, larger teams that report to the individual may stem from the initial advantage that brokerage provides.

ANTECEDENTS OF MALADAPTIVE BROKERAGE BEHAVIOR: BRIDGE LONGEVITY AND BROKER AGE

Underlying the discussion of maladaptive brokers is the idea that a potentially productive social position may often be unproductive in an organizational context. In any given organization or across a range of organizations, one may find organizationally productive as well as unproductive brokers. In the large, established organizations that I studied, I found more clear examples of maladaptive brokers than clearly functional brokers. However, this distribution suggests a puzzle: Why are brokers often maladaptive but sometimes functional with respect to organizational objectives? What explains this difference? Can any key patterns be detected here?

In my research, I found that brokerage age is a key factor. New brokers appear to be more productive and aligned with organizational interests on average than older brokers. To be clear, I am not speaking of an individual's natural age. In fact, in the technology companies I studied, I found that many young brokers were connected to older alters. What appears to be the critical factor is the age of the bridging tie itself in the organization. As bridging ties age, brokers become more effective in using strategic actions to maintain them even as they become increasingly decoupled from organizational usefulness. Why would individual brokers do this? The reason is that brokerage positions maintain their value for individuals brokers, or grow in value, even as they decrease in utility for organizations.

In fact, as I examined the brokers in my research, it became increasingly clear that older brokers were responsible for most of the maladaptive behavior in my sample. Indeed, it was so apparent that sometimes younger brokers within the cartel seemed aware of it, and it distinguished their behavior. One new broker commented, "I'm relatively new to this translation activity between engineers and customers for my product. But Roby has been doing it for years. He doesn't come up with new ideas, but he has incredibly sharp elbows about his turf and he's teaching me to do the same. You know if you don't, some new guy will come along and make you irrelevant! Anyhow, I'm still in the idea phase, but I get his point."

Indeed, I observed that anticompetitive behavior becomes more likely as brokers age in the role (or when bridges are of longer duration). This can perhaps be attributed to brokers discerning greater advantage in behaviors aimed at keeping alters apart and lessening brokerage rivalry. The decreasing utility of the bridging tie may itself be a prompt to defend the tie by anticompetitive action. Some evidence also suggests that brokerage cartels as a group become more solidified as time goes on, since brokers have more time to organize strong collusion and to sanction defectors, in this way establishing destructive collaborative norms. As the brokerage cartel becomes more powerful, its individual members should extract more value from their brokerage roles.

REINFORCING POSITION-BASED ADVANTAGES WITH DIGITAL TECHNOLOGIES

What effects do digital technologies have on the advantages derived from network positions? There is some promise that the adoption of digital technologies will lower the barriers to entry into network positions. The analogy with companies in industries lends some plausibility to this idea since adoption seems to have made it easier for corporate rivals to find the information necessary for business operations, including information about the network of suppliers which can be reverse-engineered to substitute for industrial brokers. This information has the net effect of decreasing the costs of entry and effective competition. Much of a broker's advantages may derive from the lack of transparency in the social structure as, for instance, when alters do not even know they are being brokered. It is reasonable to assume that digital technologies accelerate information transfer and aid transparency within organizations to a degree such that current brokers might be threatened by the increased rivalry.

However, the reality is that brokers can effectively use digital technologies to maintain or even increase barriers to entry. On the one hand, digital communications technologies are particularly useful to the broker's aims, as they can be used to broadcast key features of the social structure. For example, digital technologies can make it abundantly clear who the brokers are, which may enhance the brokers' advantages if their reputation for intermediation is good. On the other hand, digital technologies may disclose the high costs and risks of unintermediated exchange, such as when two alters attempt to exchange without any prior relationship and experience a high-profile failure. In short, digital technologies may simply institutionalize existing exchange relationships and make them appear as unassailable facts of life when the true costs and benefits of functional structural holes are exposed.

There is some indication that digital technologies can help in the creation and maintenance of brokerage cartels. This is depicted in Figure 9, where dark lines indicate older ties (not necessarily stronger ties as in prior figures). It shows that more digital technology adoption may increasingly enable brokers with older ties to act as monopolists, using strategic action inside brokerage cartels to eliminate would-be brokers.

Again, prior research on industrial competition indicates that increased information flow should diminish the capability of incumbents to maintain cartels, since many of these cartels rely on secrecy to minimize threats to this nefarious form of cooperation. In some cases, digital communication technologies have been used to expose illegal collusion that would have previously remained hidden. However, brokerage cartels are of a different character because they rely on individuals and their social relationships, whose reputation and effectiveness can be exposed through digital means. Even though digital technologies expose hidden brokerage relationships, it may become clear to would-be brokers that they cannot compete with current brokers because of the latter's reputation and skill. Finally, unlike corporate cartels, social brokerage cartels are rarely illegal even though they are anticompetitive. In fact, organizational culture may even promote the cartel as opposed to sanctioning it.

Perhaps the biggest difference is that brokers can use digital technologies themselves to form the cartel or expose defections. They also use digital media to communicate strategies or refer exchanges to the appropriate broker. And they may expose would-be brokers and try to diminish their

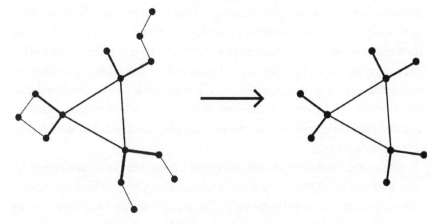

Figure 9: Increasing strategic action in brokerage cartels after adoption of digital technologies

efforts. Finally, they may help brokers lobby for institutionalization through a formal structure, as described earlier.

It also relates to the finding about brokerage age mentioned previously—one may argue that older brokers are less willing to adopt new technologies than newer brokers. Yet it is important to remember that broker age and bridge age are not necessarily demographic but rather features of organization and network structure—the age of the brokerage triad is relative to that of other triads. In fact, many brokers with the most entrenched positions and ossified relationships are not so old that we might guess they would be unwilling to adopt digital technologies. In the technology companies I studied, even the most senior people, from an organization perspective, were often in their fifties and sometimes in their forties or thirties.

In fact, I did not observe any large differences between brokers in their willingness to adopt technology. The key difference seemed to be in the technology's use. As predicted, older brokers were more likely to use these technologies to take strategic action to maintain their own brokerage triads, extract more value from them, or maintain the brokerage cartel. The use of technology is not always straightforward, but the net effect seems to be to increase the broker's advantages. I note some examples next.

First, it should be noted that I observed that the transparency afforded by digital technologies helped alters mitigate their disadvantages vis-à-vis brokers. Sometimes brokers maintained their advantages because alters were unaware that they were being brokered—that there was another alter involved—or they were unaware how much the broker relied on the other alter to create value. Had the alters been aware, the likelihood of disintermediation would have increased. In a few examples, digital technologies revealed the full extent of brokerage relationships, which helped alters negotiate better outcomes or close the structure hole altogether by disintermediating the broker.

In the great majority of other examples, however, the increasing adoption and use of digital technologies seemed to increase brokers' advantages. Brokers can use digital technologies to amplify their information and control advantages in the structural hole in ways that may be much more numerous than the transparency benefits for alters. For example, digital technologies enable them to more closely monitor alters' contributions. They also enable brokers to more broadly amplify their reputations, which only cements their advantages. But the most important effect of digital technologies seems to be anticompetitive: brokers can use digital technology to maintain cartel boundaries, expose and sanction defections, and oppose would-be brokers.

As in prior chapters, I argue that digital technologies play a contingent and moderating role in generating this network agency problem. The true antecedent cause of entrenched brokers and ossified bridges appears to be misaligned incentives and social capital inducements. Brokers seek to preserve and amplify their information and control benefits with the strategic actions described previously. Digital technologies amplify incentives and capacity to do so.

MANAGERIAL INTERVENTIONS IN MALADAPTIVE BROKERAGE

Managers may attempt to intervene in maladaptive brokerage relationships in many ways. Before I describe these interventions, one must ask: How can managers identify maladaptive brokerage in the first place? Of course, managers can, and must, make inferences based on observation of network outcomes, but with brokerage this can be challenging. Because brokerage triads are local structures in which exogenous managers are not involved, managers may not be able to identify the triads, let alone whether their effects are productive or maladaptive. The first step, then, is often to identify entrenched brokerage positions and ossified bridges. This may be a case where technology is managerially useful, as social media, networking, and people analytics software can be combined to find associations between older brokerage relationships and negative outcomes.

I observed many interventions that attempted to mitigate maladaptive brokerage once it was discovered. Yet, as I will note, in most cases such attempts tended to be resisted or were ineffective, or the brokerage snapped back to its original state after managerial pressure dissipated.

There are multiple interventions that managers can try. First, they can encourage disintermediation by asking alters to connect directly, although this is often resisted, first of all, by alters themselves because they have often arranged their work portfolios to rely on broker activity. There is an additional fixed cost and an ongoing variable cost of interacting directly. While it may be worth it in the long run, from both the alters' and the organization's perspective, short-run considerations may create resistance. Of course, brokers themselves may then resist, which increases the costs for both managers and alters.

An alternative intervention is for managers to directly enlist brokers in helping alters connect and eventually replace the brokerage relationship. Initially, the challenge is that brokers will use their information and control advantages to directly resist. This may involve significant political cost to convince them to give up their structural hole. Yet the greater challenge by far is that brokers will comply in name only but resist secretly. Unless directly involved, it is very difficult for the manager to monitor behavior in these relationships. Brokers can uphold "the letter of the law" without its spirit. In fact, I found instances where brokers would introduce alters but hide their brokerage activity or even sabotage direct interactions between alters. The net result was that brokerage activity went on and brokers continued to extract value from this relationship.

The most effective interventions that I found were directly focused on the broker themselves. I studied these interventions in many contexts, but it is perhaps no easier to observe them than it is to observe boundary-spanning brokers and bridges—the structural holes that span boundaries across organizations. These boundary spanners are often brokers who indirectly connect alters in different organizations and often create inter-organizational alliances. Managers in these alliances sometimes employ a useful pruning process to directly remove brokers who have outlived their usefulness or become maladaptive.

Consider an example from ChipVision, a noted semiconductor company. ChipVision's managers, in an alliance focused on security standards, worked with a broker, Bob, who had a history of facilitating productive interactions. Said one manager, "Bob is very responsive to our needs. He is at the right organizational level and has the right expertise. We communicate all the time with each other. . . . Bob and I laugh about it all the time. . . . I feel like I practically work for the other company! We've become really loyal to each other."

But ChipVision's managers began to find Bob's focus on prior content related to technology standards less than useful for the security collaboration. "We can't afford to have gatekeepers," one said. "We need to move faster. We don't want to feel like we're waiting," said another. As a result, they asked Bob to cease communication about standards with his contact in the other organization and focus his efforts on the new innovation project. Bob complied, and consequently this tie played no role in the developing relationship.

ChipVision's managers found out that another broker, Ted, was purposely derailing the collaboration's focus, always shifting meetings to his own agenda, focused on marketing. As a result, they removed him from the project and, along with his ties, from the network. After Ted and his ties disappeared, negotiations refocused on innovation opportunities and a new collaboration network coalesced.

Comparing the two examples just given is instructive. The pruning mechanisms differed—managers asked Bob to sever his relationship with his contact in the other organization (meaning that they cut the tie), but asked Ted to leave the collaboration team altogether (meaning that they removed the node), but the consequence was the same: the ossified bridging ties disappeared from the emerging network.

In these cases, pruning removed entrenched brokers and ossified bridges from the network, having the broader impact of improving project outcomes. Unfortunately, however, in this case and others, I found that brokerage problems persisted as maladaptive brokers resumed their activities or new brokers entered to occupy similar positions and take up similar maladaptive behaviors. That is, once managerial energy was no longer focused on the current alliance or project, a maladaptive brokerage structure returned because the underlying incentives and opportunities to rebuild it did not fundamentally change, suggesting the difficulty of enacting persistently effective interventions in network agency problems.

Scale Too Free

NEGATIVE EXTERNALITIES OF INEQUALITY IN SOCIAL CAPITAL

This chapter examines network agency problems related to the distribution of social capital in organizational networks. It focuses primarily on the degree distribution of ties, noting that networks often converge to hub-and-spoke networks in which social capital is unequally distributed with a few hubs possessing far more ties than the average node. Status dynamics lead to social capital inequality in networks that has an overall negative impact on the amount of high-quality collaboration in organizations. Digital technologies are shown to accelerate these dynamics as hubs disproportionally use these tools to cement their advantages.

EXPLORING INEQUALITY IN SOCIAL NETWORKING

Earlier chapters emphasized that individuals may form too many ties that are too weak while the bridges that span the network may persist for too long. These network agency problems are amplified by the adoption of digital technologies: when aggregated to a higher level, they generate predictable negative effects on organizational outcomes. Mechanisms such as overcommitment, mistrust, and exploitation become barriers to achieving organizational goals. In other words, this theory is microfoundational in that it explains how individual behaviors aggregate to macroorganizational outcomes. Yet like other theories attempting to bridge these levels, network agency theories proceed from the assumption that the average effects of social capital are the main determinates of aggregate outcomes. It is sufficient to argue that when the average individual has too many ties or too many weak ties, or participates in ossified bridges, the negative impact of many such individuals aggregates to the organizational level.

What has been less well explored is the impact of network heterogeneity on organizational outcomes. The key issue is the distribution of social capital in organizations. How are social relationships distributed across people in the organization? Do employees have more or less the same number or quality of ties? The study of distributional effects in social science has a long history, particularly at the macrosocietal scale, such as when economists and sociologists compare income inequality across countries and attempt to link it to various societal outcomes. So far, distributional issues related to social capital have not been studied extensively in organizations, which is somewhat puzzling. If network science has any lesson to impart, it is that not all individual networks are created equal. Networks of all types exhibit significant heterogeneity, with some members having more and different ties than others.

This is true even in seemingly constrained environments such as organizations where we might expect individual members to share some basic network similarities. Nevertheless, even in organizations it is reasonable to expect that some individuals have more ties than others. The fact that we can speak of different network positions, such as occupying structural holes or a more central position, speaks to this heterogeneity. In fact, we can characterize and compare the heterogeneity of different networks and ask whether the distributions we find there might lead to differing organizational outcomes related to group-level innovation, learning, and change. A key issue is inequality. Can organizational networks be said to exhibit different degrees of inequality in network positions and the social capital they create? How can inequality be characterized? Are there predictable differences in social capital across individuals in organizations and, if so, do they shape organizational outcomes? Do digital technologies have an impact on these dynamics? This chapter will address these questions.

DISTRIBUTIONS OF SOCIAL CAPITAL IN NETWORKS: CHARACTERISTIC SCALE IN ORGANIZATIONS

There is little research on the organizational effects of network distribution beyond a few studies focusing on macrotopological structures.[1] Most of this research is by inference—scholars infer various network mechanisms from organizational outcomes. For example, a tradition of research in the Carnegie School of Organizational Research theorized that a well-connected dominant coalition is often useful for producing macroorganizational change; in the language of networks, one can imagine that some highly connected clusters or cliques must underlie this coalition while weak coalitions may not have this connectivity advantage.[2]

Another macrostructural feature that is thought to be useful is short network paths that connect individuals who are members of highly connected subgroups. Prominent here is small-world theory, which argues for the utility of a combination of clusters and short paths connecting them.[3] Such a combination creates "small worlds" in which most individuals can be connected by a few links, as illustrated in the famous finding that most people are connected by "six degrees of separation." It also suggests a distributional difference. Those in the clusters have more ties than those whose ties create the path, even if those bridging ties may provide information and control advantages of brokerage as described in Chapter 4.

The two macrotopographical features—coalitions formed around subgroups and short paths that connect clusters—are suggestive of underlying distributional differences. In fact, in each case it may be that individuals with rare network features—a high degree of betweenness centrality and far from the average—are the ones who drive organizational outcomes. Although suggestive, these research streams do not directly describe the distribution differences that a manager can use to make population-level decisions about networks.

The majority of networks have some real differences in individual networks, but the idea of social capital inequality is to quantify these differences at the population level. Most prior social capital research investigates the existence of stable variations in networks that have predictable consequences for individual outcomes, including how much value is created and the rewards that individuals capture. In some cases, social capital may be more substantial: many managers recount individuals who seem abnormally popular. In these situations, the network somehow "revolves" around such individuals, suggesting that their abnormally high social capital is a network-level phenomenon with implications for behavior in the broader collective . Characterizing the network distribution may be a necessary step in developing a truly organizational theory of social capital.

Scale-free theory. The research that has the most direct bearing on network distribution effects has come from network science scholars with training in mathematics and physics. Although it does not have its roots in social science, this theory directly describes the network distribution of ties in a population and therefore might promote understanding of social capital inequality as well. Here, the most prominent framework is scale-free network theory, in which populations in which individuals have several ties that are roughly similar (or scaling only in linear differences) are said to have a "characteristic scale." For example, all populations in which all members connect only to a few closest family members, or in which most belong to small groups that are almost fully connected, have a characteristic scale. In this research, the degree frequency distribution can be used to quantify the characteristic scale of the network. Networks with a characteristic scale are well described by a normal degree distribution with a mean degree around which most individuals cluster.

However, the key finding of the scale-free theory is that many of the world's networks lack a characteristic scale—in these networks, some members have very few ties, others have a moderate number of ties, and still others have many ties.[4] As a result, the variance is so large that the largest outliers mostly determine the mean. In scale-free networks, a rare few members may have an extremely high number of ties, so that when the network is drawn they resemble hubs that connect most of the other spokes in the network. Many scale-free networks are of this "star" or "hub-and-spoke" type, with one or a few central players surrounded by most of the other players.

When the degree distribution of scale-free networks is plotted, it often conforms to a power law of degree, with individuals with few ties acting as a very long tail and hubs acting as a peak. Barabasi and Albert (1999) found that scale-free network distributions are remarkably easy to produce in growing networks where new members form their first ties based on a principle of preferential attachment—that is, they are more likely to form ties with individuals who have more ties. Over time, hubs emerge and the networks exhibit a power law distribution. A remarkable finding is that networks in many applications conform exactly or approximately to power law criteria; these include ensemble acting, co-authorship, and the internet. Networks without a perfect power law distribution but long tails in a degree are sometimes said to be "approximate" scale-free networks.

Scale-free networks in organizations. Scale-free networks have a few useful properties that may have relevance for organizational science. When compared with regular networks having a characteristic scale, scale-free networks may have the advantages of accelerated transmission, stability, and robustness. Hubs are the key drivers of these advantages, as they are the rare few that can reach many others directly. Modeling shows that scale-free networks are particularly robust to loss of members since a random nodal loss is unlikely to eliminate a hub that indirectly connects others in the network because they are rare. Further, when hubs are lost, the network is unlikely to be disconnected if lesser hubs sufficiently connect members. One can imagine that this is an important feature in organizational networks, where turnover is relatively high compared with that in other social networks that have been studied (such as kin, church, and neighborhood).

In scale-free organizational networks, the few individual hubs are often highly visible due to these relationships; their virility and prominence generate high social status and these individuals are often viewed as stars.[5] In organizations, status can be functional; that is, being called a star may be useful if stardom is aligned with achievement, as it promotes a sense of fairness around meritocracy. Moreover, some markets are naturally winner-take-all and reputation-based, and organizations may need to tap into a few individuals with sufficient status to access the resources in these markets. If social capital is aligned with human capital, it is natural that an organization must have some stars.

Some organizational roles are associated with hub status because of the opportunities they provide to connect with many others. For instance, salespeople are often hubs because they make contacts far beyond organizational boundaries. Top leaders may be more likely to be hubs if their authority enables them to form ties unimpeded. This may not always be the case if the upper echelon is insulated from employee interaction, in which case some key middle managers may act as functional hubs that executives call upon for support. Indeed, corporate gadflies often do not take the top job because they prefer to benefit from their networking and its benefits in the middle ranks. Finally, in scholarly fields and other knowledge communities, editors may act as hubs because of the many authors and reviewers they interact with to evaluate submissions.

In these cases, the process that produces and sustains hubs mixes mechanisms stemming from formal organizational authority and informal social status. By position and authority, an individual occupying an organizational position may have a greater capacity to form ties efficiently and, in some cases, by fiat. For instance, top leaders can dictate interactions with subordinates. While these interactions may not guarantee true friendship—Michael Scott's failed attempts to make friends with his employees on *The Office* come to mind here—what matters is that many of these interactions will rise to the level of a relationship that can be called upon in the future. Seeding networks with somewhat artificially constructed relationships is a time-honored tactic used by new bosses.

Although organizational positions can be used to catalyze networks, the main processes used by hubs to form and maintain their large networks in organizations relate to informal social status. Those with sufficient ties can leverage them to convince others to form ties as well. Social network mechanisms such as transitivity, reciprocity, and cohesion often promote a "rich get richer" dynamic in which others connect to those who already have many ties.[6] The social status theory describes this as "mere affiliation," wherein extensive networks signal a level of desirability that may be unassociated with true quality. Celebrity dynamics may take over in which an individual is so well known because of his many ties that others approach and attempt to affiliate with that individual for the sheer benefits of mere association.[7] Taken together, the combination of these social mechanisms increases the likelihood of those with ties acquiring more ties and becoming high-status hubs in the organizational network upon which many depend.

IMPACT OF SOCIAL CAPITAL INEQUALITY IN ORGANIZATIONS

A critical question is whether hubs and the scale-free networks in which they are embedded are useful for organizations. The organizational effects of individual social status or its distribution have been surprisingly under-studied, but some basic arguments can be constructed in favor of scale-free networks and hubs. For instance, we may expect that organizations benefit from scale-free networks because of their advantages of transmission, stability, and robustness. Robustness to turnover was discussed earlier. However, information flow is more fundamental since it is critical in most organizational activities, such as practice adoption, adapting to the environment, and innovation. The hub-and-spoke structure has been shown to facilitate diffusion if the hubs are capable of broadcasting and disseminating information to their many contacts.[8]

There may be an appropriate application of scale-free networks to a core issue of organizational design: managers may wish to assign individual hubs to critical organizational tasks requiring outsized social capital, especially those that need boundary-spanning outreach, such as sales, recruiting, and ecosystem functions. For example, in the technological arena developing effective new platforms often requires forming a host of new partnerships. Individual hubs with connections in the industry may be essential to new boundary-spanning connections. Launching and selling the first product may also be a context in which scale-free networks are useful, if only because salespeople who are hubs may have more contacts with potential customers.

Much as in the discussion of brokers in Chapter 4, both of the examples just given indicate that hubs can be conceptualized as network positions that organizations mobilize to meet organizational objectives. Managers can assign hubs to key tasks such as platform ecosystem development or new product sales. Scale-free networks provide ample opportunities to mix and match positions with certain tasks. Managers may leverage inequality in social capital for productive organizational ends. Again, network distributions in organizations have not been extensively studied. Yet, as the arguments here demonstrate, it may be reasonable to extrapolate from the mechanisms underlying the scale-free theory and expect that social capital inequality will have positive effects if individuals with extremely advantageous positions can be mobilized to further organizational objectives.

As I illustrate below, it is not always the case that scale-free networks and the hubs that characterize them are useful for organizations. As documented subsequently, scale-free networks create organizational dysfunction because the social inequality they involve generates network agency problems that inhibit effective collaboration and create incentives that may not align with organizational objectives. In organizations with unequal networks, hubs act as bottlenecks that curtail rich interaction and information flow in comparison with networks where more individuals have sufficient ties to interact. These hubs may have misaligned incentives to facilitate interactions between others if their greater social status enables them to capture outsized rewards. It is perhaps more surprising that nonhubs may have diminished incentives to facilitate their ties and become hubs themselves, as they rely on indirect ties from current hubs. That is, nonhubs may find themselves in a suboptimal equilibrium in which they implicitly support the current scale-free regime and its dominant hubs.

In the organizations I studied, managers and other employees became dependent on hubs; they preferred to continue their collaboration with high-status individuals. However, because hubs were themselves limited in time and attention, they could not attend to every collaboration with sufficient energy to maximize its potential. The utility of relationships was diminished although they were not dissolved.

I found some evidence that networks without hubs, where individuals possess ties more equally, outperform hub-based networks. Although this may be a desired state, in hub-and-spoke networks a collective action problem emerges in which no single individual has sufficient incentives to curtail interactions with the hub and form new ties. The result is convergence toward a more static network with unequal social capital that generates fewer effective collaborations than may have occurred otherwise.

Some examples illustrate the negative impact of hubs on other network members and on the organization more broadly. For example, consider ComputeSystems, the hardware company discussed before. In this firm, a director named Alan had clearly become a hub. Having gained notoriety with his outside speeches, blog posts, and involvement in technical standards committees, he was now the "go-to guy" for one important segment of the wireless chip market. Since many ComputeSystems activities involved interfacing with wireless systems during this time of intense interest in mobility, Alan became the man everyone wanted to connect to.

On reflection, however, Alan's technical and market expertise was matched by that of at least ten other people in the organization, but his status made employees feel that they had to reach out to get him involved in ongoing projects. In fact, executives often asked their managers, "Has Alan looked at your proposal?" and would not proceed with resource allocation without his blessing.

Alan's attitude toward this situation was ambiguous: he clearly relished being helpful and making connections, but genuinely did not want to be a bottleneck—the volume of requests seemed to overwhelm him. "I have so many requests to read proposals. I just can't get to them. They tell me I'm slowing them down, but I just can't work 200 hour weeks. In my role, you should read these specs deeply but it's hard with so many. You know there are others who can do the same thing, right?"

One possibility when hubs become bottlenecks is that fewer projects can be pursued. Another possibility is that projects receive less investment than they would otherwise. For example, to meet requests, Alan admitted to reducing his investment in most projects. "Honestly, I just speed-read them now. I feel bad about it. It's kind of like throwing my training out the window. But I realized I was slowing down decisions. What they really want me to do is bless the project so they can move on. So I guess we've become like the Lean startup ideas. . . . We're letting the market decide more than the experts inside."

Unfortunately, the market was making some decidedly negative evaluations: three or four projects that Alan had quickly read encountered setbacks, including technical glitches or customer complaints that might have been caught earlier had Alan read them in depth. The important point is that there were other experts who could have evaluated them. One leader, Susan, an expert in marketing wireless solutions with some technical background, told me, "Honestly, I could have caught some of those mistakes. But I wasn't asked to evaluate them. Alan is the star here and everyone wants to associate with him. I get it. But if I had eyes on that proposal, I would have caught it. Maybe they didn't want me contradicting Alan. I don't know. It's too bad, though. These were costly mistakes."

Alan's story illustrates the more general logic underlying the impact of hubs: by collecting a disproportionate share of network ties and collaborative opportunities, hubs inevitably crowd out other network ties because others prefer them to nonhubs. Hubs may grow their social capital for self-serving reasons. But even those with good intentions eventually reach attention and energy limits, leading to lower work standards. The outcome is a lower equilibrium in which negative performance outcomes outweigh the benefits of associating with a hub who is stretched too thin.

The key mechanism of dysfunction in unequal social structures is over-reliance on hubs and underreliance on nonhubs for collaborative work. Individuals make seemingly rational choices to form and maintain ties with high-status players and have little incentive to engage in collaborations with others, given the risks of new tie formation. These choices, each of which may be reasonable from an individual perspective, magnify the hub's personal network advantages and subsequently diminish the value that others can derive from collaboration. How does this occur?

The reality of scale-free networks is that hubs are often perceived as individuals with substantially higher social status than others in the network. Those others may not see the extent of a hub's entire network, but they consider the hub to have a special aura, which separates them from everyone else—the *sine qua non* of high social status. The literature on status has documented a strong link between network centrality and social status, to the extent that most research actually measures status with centrality measures. With their higher status, hubs can use influence to secure a greater share of relationships than may be warranted. It also gives them greater influence over organizational decision-making and other processes in which resources are allocated. High-status actors can use these resources to further cement their advantages. A major contribution of the literature on status is that it highlights the extent to which status ranking is relatively well-known and agreed upon by members, even if they are contesting it.

The example of Alan indicates that high status enables some hubs to capture an outsized share of rewards, leading to diminished opportunities for nonhubs. It is equally important that high status may come at a cost to the organization as well. In the examples discussed previously, others are drawn to high-status hubs as though they were a star, even if their performance is suboptimal. ComputeSystems employees admitted they were waiting for Alan and that collaborative performance was declining for that reason. Often, they doubted their own judgment, preferring Alan's because he was high-status: "Everyone else is connecting to him, shouldn't I too?" In many cases, a connection with lower-status nonhubs would have been a higher-value choice. Many employees waited for the hub, Alan, bypassing partnership formation opportunities that were more appropriate. Further, interacting with the hub often came at a higher cost in terms of attention, effort, and energy expended on the interaction, if only because the hub's disproportionate power in the relationship could push most of the effort in the collaboration on the weaker party.

Put another way, social capital inequality may lead individuals to form ties that are locally optimal over ties that are known to be globally optimal. More distant connections that take longer to come to fruition may wither; moderately connected individuals may be eschewed for connections to hubs that are quicker to instantiate even if they create less value. It is interesting to recall that social status theory finds its greatest application in contexts with high uncertainty and ambiguity. It is particularly useful in cases where individuals have difficulty judging who the best partners are. Status can be used as a useful proxy to do this. The case here indicates that relying on status can create its own ambiguity and uncertainty, especially in situations where the hubs are prominent and most decisions are driven by status. Even against the evidence of their own experience, partners doubt what the most appropriate collaboration opportunities should be and use status as the determining factor.

DIGITAL TECHNOLOGIES AND THE
DISTRIBUTION OF SOCIAL CAPITAL

In line with other network agency problems described in previous chapters, there is some evidence that digital technologies amplify and accelerate the pernicious dynamics associated with scale-free networks. As detailed earlier, hubs have a general advantage in forming and maintaining ties compared with nonhubs since others prefer to affiliate with a hub over a nonhub, all else being equal. It may be recalled that the main effect of digital technologies is the reduced cost of forming and maintaining ties. One might imagine that this would provide an opportunity for nonhubs to connect to other nonhubs, if only because it is easier, thus democratizing networks with unequal scale.

As I show next, the adoption of new digital technologies favors those who are already hubs by allowing them to form and maintain ties even more easily. Of course, nonhubs can connect with other nonhubs more easily too, but a larger effect is to make it easier for them to reach out to hubs in a more

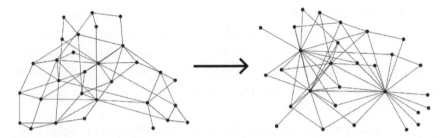

Figure 10: Increasing social network inequality after adoption of digital technologies

efficient manner, enabling them to pursue these locally optimal ties over globally optimal ties to other nonhubs. The overall impact of digital technologies is to increase social network inequality and increase the presence of some highly connected hubs, as depicted in Figure 10.

Many digital technologies also make network ties transparent, and that increases the likelihood that others will correctly perceive that a hub has many ties. The result is ironic: members may rely less on an ambiguous aura of social status when making their choices because they can directly verify who has the most or the best ties and make their affiliation decisions based solely on network connections. Even while hubs may have even more ties, however, they may be less productive. Taking all issues together, the ultimate outcome of digital technologies is to accelerate networks toward pernicious scale-free topologies and increase the advantage of hubs in these networks.

In one internet company I studied, Digital Jungle, the importance of hubs seemed to be amplified by the adoption of corporate IT tools. For example, after the company adopted an internal corporate messaging system, employees became reliant on the information it provided. Users could easily observe who was most prominent in conversations and how many followers each had. Existing hubs had an early advantage because their many real-life contacts followed them onto the platform. As time went on, other employees started using follower counts to decide which projects to support and whom to follow.

One employee described the dynamic: "I needed to find a security protocol expert to support my new API project. The database told me we had many employees who had the right technical training. But when I saw that

Gina had hundreds of followers I reached out to her and she joined the project. In the old days, I would have asked around about a few candidates, but this platform makes it so easy to see who's popular now." Indeed, it appeared that with the adoption of the corporate messaging system, mere popularity had become a more important metric in decisions ranging from staffing to promotions to remuneration.

It is useful here to return to the broader view in light of digital technologies—that is, whether organizational networks can be seen as equal or unequal in social capital in light of new communication technologies. In other domains, such as the study of financial, political, or human capital accumulation, there is an idea that digital technologies are an equalizing force because they democratize information access and flow. However, this idea has been challenged by accumulated evidence, which sometimes demonstrates how elite actors use digital technologies to magnify their advantages. In the Digital Jungle example, social media technology primarily benefited the highly connected individuals who formed so many ties, since the efficiencies of digital network management grew larger with larger network size. Even though digital technologies appear to create opportunities for newcomers to access information and pursue new opportunities, an even stronger effect is sometimes seen as the amplifying of advantaged parties' benefits, especially by allowing top members to pull away from the pack. Thus, far from being a democratizing force, digital technologies promote inequality in social capital. The number of ties may be the most fundamental example of this as high-status individuals use digital technologies to reveal, leverage, and maintain their status through numerous social interactions.

It may be tempting to view digital technologies as the primary cause of social capital inequality. Yet I argue that they are more properly viewed as a contingent moderating factor because high network inequality can occur in some unique premodern networks. Instead, misaligned incentives and social capital inducements, such as seeking disproportionate rewards in networks or allying with those who do, may be the more fundamental antecedents of network inequality. As long as individuals are motivated to capture a disproportionate share of the value created by networks, we should expect that they will do so. Digital technologies amplify these incentives and employees' capacity to act on them.

MANAGERIAL INTERVENTIONS IN PERSISTENT
SOCIAL NETWORK INEQUALITY

A critical question is whether unequal social structures are persistent or disappear quickly due to some internal fragility. In most of the cases I studied, I found that organizational networks with high social inequality persisted for long periods of time, typically around the same hub-and-spoke structure.

Sometimes hub-and-spoke structures form because the hub has access to a critical resource that others want to access. Once they form, though, there is typically a marginal benefit to connecting to the hub compared with some other individual simply because of the greater certainty that the benefit derives from the hub's higher status. As mentioned earlier, the use of digital technologies makes this more likely as it means that individuals can identify who is a hub and who is not.

Once hub-and-spoke structures are in place, they solidify and grow as interaction patterns become routine and institutionalized as normal practices, and sometimes even decoupled from their original function. For example, one manager admitted to me, "Honestly I can't remember why we always get Bob's signoff when we begin a new project. He's not our superior. But it's what everyone does. It might be because he is from [an important region]. He used to be the only one, but now we have lots of people from there! Anyhow, I honestly don't know why everyone consults him first, but everyone does. If you didn't do it, you'd be the strange one now."

Examining interventions is useful to understand the core mechanisms that lead to the sustainability of unequal social structures. One can imagine that if scale-free structures were dysfunctional, managers would seek to change them. For instance, managers might wish to equalize social structures by reducing the connections flowing to single hubs or by creating alternative hubs. Yet intervention in hub-and-spoke networks and other unequal structures is difficult precisely because those with the most social capital are the same individuals who provide the most value to the organization. These are high-status actors who may also have the most power to resist managerial efforts to rein them in.

I studied one enterprise software organization where executives realized that the salesforce had grown in power, with certain senior salespeople capturing a very high percentage of the value. On a closer look, executives realized that the basis of these disproportionate rewards were not only strong ties to large customers but also younger sales staff's insistence on including these senior salespeople in their own sales deals. Many deals did not benefit from a senior salesperson's expertise; the seniors were included because the juniors hoped to benefit from their outsized status or to be included in their future deals. The result was a hub-and-spoke network that spanned boundaries between the sales team and the entire customer base.

Executives implemented policies barring inclusion of more than one senior salesperson per deal. Junior salespeople responded by remunerating seniors in other ways, such as giving them new sales leads or a larger percentage of sales fees in deals. Because executives could not completely bar senior involvement (since their presence did increase the likelihood of some sales), the sales network reached a rough hub-and-spoke equilibrium that seemed unchangeable.

More broadly, I observed that after most attempts to sever ties, make policies, or dictate that nonhubs must link to other nonhubs, employees would often find a way to forge a hidden link with hubs, waiting until management began to pay less attention to the matter and then resuming their prior compensation and connection activity.

Perhaps surprisingly, I saw that the most resistance to managerial interventions came from a hub's partners, who relied on the hub and did not want it eliminated. Interventions to create new, minor hubs to compete with major hubs with a fraction of the ties seemed to be somewhat more effective, as creating networking alternatives was often the only way to combat pernicious network dynamics. But even minor hubs usually connected to major hubs, deferred to them, and so cemented their advantages.

The key problem is that making incremental interventions in unequal networks, as managers usually do, is contrary to the dominant "rich-get-richer" trajectory of these networks. It is easy for both parties to reject managerial interventions to block or dissolve a few of the hub's ties or engender moderate tie formation in the spokes. Prior relationships can be reconstituted by hubs with the same strong incentives that maintained them, and hubs may find that new relationships are less effective or riskier than those they had before. In short, when managers attempt to sever a few old ties or create substitute ties, they are often undone.

The only effective intervention appears to be to remove or substantially diminish the hub's status, typically by severing all or a majority of their ties at once. Unsurprisingly, however, managers often shy away from this highly expensive intervention because it entails a short-term loss of value creation. It is important to recall that hubs have some organizational utility, though suboptimal. Even a partial intervention risks revenge against management, as observed previously, such that permanently disrupting hubs without risk that they will reconstitute their ties and their base of power may only be possible through a dramatic intervention to fully eliminate the unequal structure. As the saying goes, "If you go after the king, you best not miss."

It should be made clear that eliminating the hub structure is typically not sufficient to achieve organizational goals or even result in long-lasting network changes. Managers usually must enact a broader organizational design with an attendant network structure; otherwise, a new suboptimal structure may emerge in the vacuum, normally entailing multiple new ties, roles, and groups to be formed with new ways of interacting sanctioned by management so that employees see the more equal structure as a true alternative to the unequal structure from before. Short of this, the network may not change effectively.

The most dramatic example I observed was when an executive fired two particularly recalcitrant hubs who refused to facilitate others' ties. In the short term, the executive noted some improvement in networking among the former partners. In perhaps the greatest irony, however, when the executive revisited the network a year later, two new hubs had emerged to take the old hubs' place. They had constructed network structures nearly identical to the earlier ones, almost as if they had come to occupy their position in a network vacancy chain. Indeed, it seems that individual routines with connectivity may have produced a remembrance that was easy to reconstitute by new actors.[9]

A key theoretical construct that might be involved is the idea of network memory. Individuals recall a macrotopological structure, including one in which they benefited from specific hubs. Reconstructing a hub-and-spoke structure may appear to be the most salient or even the only option. Although old hubs are gone, those that are left remember the network structure and develop interaction routines and scripts for working in hub-and-spoke styles. If not redesigned, the organizational workflow may support a return to this structure and style. Without a broader option, employees may fall naturally into unequal structures. One can imagine that partial solutions lead to moderately unequal networks with an effective hub removal but a partial new structure in which individuals are at odds with the type of network formed, equal or unequal. Nevertheless, this still relies on some experience, with the past shaping what is possible in the future. More broadly, network memory may come to be perceived as a key factor in why organizational redesign is difficult, because individuals will seek to reconstitute old structures even when they have been dismantled.

Overall, such interventions are instructive. They show that unequal structures are persistent and resist incremental managerial interventions, not only because of network agency problems related to incentives of hubs and spokes but also because network memory reinforces these options and makes unequal structures more salient.

A MODEL OF NETWORK DEGREE DISTRIBUTION INEQUALITY IN ORGANIZATIONS

As indicated by qualitative evidence, the microdynamics of individual choices of collaboration involve mechanisms that generate inequality in social capital at the local level. Although I observed hubs in many organizations, it is important to know if inequality is generated organization-wide as a consistent effect. I observed the immense stability of these seemingly scale-free (or nearly scale-free) networks and noted their persistence and their resistance to intervention. The adoption of digital technologies seemed to accelerate and amplify social capital inequality and the negative consequences of less and ineffective collaboration that the organization absorbed as an agency cost.

What is interesting to know is if these effects of organization-wide social capital inequality can be generated from micromechanisms. As data on a population of organizations is lacking, simulation modeling may be a useful way to build on current insights from the field and extend them to theorization.[10] Fortunately, there is a canonical model that can be adapted to the organizational case—the preferential attachment model used to understand scale-free dynamics (Barabasi and Albert 1999) that was described at the beginning of this chapter. It is an endogenous growth model in which new links are added to the network with a probability of connecting to any other node that is proportionate to the total fraction of links that the node possesses. That is, the probability of connecting to node i is

$$P_i = k_i / \Sigma(k_j)$$

where k_i is the degree of node i and the sum is of all nodes j.

I modify the model to reflect some organizational reality. Each individual can make new collaboration choices according to the preferential attachment rule in every time period. This modification approximates the networking agency of individuals in organizations. Also, to lend greater realism to the individual and organizational costs of network choices and the success or failure of collaboration, the likelihood of collaboration success reflects a number of factors that must be considered. First is the history of interaction between individuals, where the likelihood of success increases with experience in prior interactions. Second is the underlying quality of nodes, q_i, which reflects their human capital, attitude, organizational fit, and many other factors. The key is that not all actors are equally high-quality collaborators, and this underlying distribution may shape collaboration choices, if only indirectly by using network status as a proxy for quality. Finally, the cost of implementing successful collaboration, c, may vary in differing environments, which we interrogate primarily through digital technologies under the assumption that investments in digital communications increase the likelihood of success for any single dyad. Thus, the probability of collaboration success in the next time period, $K_{int} + 1$, is given by this simple equation:

$$K_{int}+1 = q_i * [(1-c) * \Sigma_t(K_{int})/t]$$

Using this preferential attachment model, we can investigate a variety of issues. In this chapter, the application focuses on the interesting issue of social capital inequality. Inequality is often measured by the Gini coefficient, which ranges between 0 (uniformly equal) and 1 (perfectly unequal) for any given capital stock distributed across a set of actors. Fortunately, the Gini coefficient statistic has also been computed for the degree distribution of networks such that low numbers indicate a relatively more equal distribution of ties and higher numbers indicate more inequality, suggesting scale-free structures at higher values.

Because digital technologies are so central to network agency theories of social capital distribution, I ran multiple experiments to investigate the

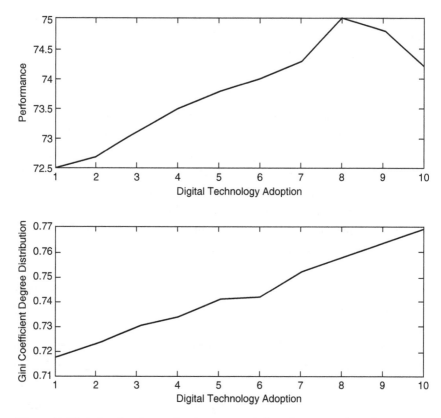

Figure 11: Digital technology adoption, network distribution, and performance

impact of digital technology on the overall performance of individuals in an organizational network. In these experiments, I varied c, the costs of collaboration, as a proxy for digital technology. In Figure 11, I plot digital technology adoption, $1-c$, versus performance and the Gini coefficient of network degree distribution that evolves endogenously as individuals make their own networking choices according to preferential attachment. The figure indicates that as the organization increasingly adopts digital technology, both hubs and social capital inequality increase. This has some positive impact, as hubs possess an increasing number of ties that can be leveraged for successful collaboration. At some key point, however, they possess so many ties that opportunities for nonhubs to collaborate diminish and performance declines.

These equilibrium effects are produced as individuals make choices based on the current distribution of ties. They indicate that social status,

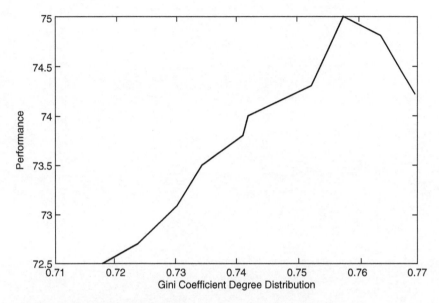

Figure 12: Social capital inequality and organization performance

according to its usual measure based on network centrality, can act as a suit-able proxy for quality up to a certain point, after which increasing network status is a less effective decision criterion, even though individuals continue to use it as such.

The relationship between social capital inequality and organizational outcomes is particularly stark when the relationship between performance and Gini coefficient is clearly plotted as in Figure 12. In the equilibrium steady state, there is an inverted-U relationship between the degree of in-equality and performance, indicating an interior optimum that is driven by digital technology in the model.

PART II
THEORY OF THE FIRM

Network Agency Problems in the
Organizational Context

Persistence

MANAGERIAL INTERVENTION TRANSIENCE AND
THE REEMERGENCE OF AGENCY PROBLEMS

This chapter summarizes key network mechanisms underlying the impact of four network agency problems described in prior chapters, the misaligned incentives and social capital inducements that are their antecedent causes, and the misaligned political content that pathological social capital often supports in organizations. The persistence of problems is related to the inability of interventions directed at specific network structures and networking behaviors to fundamentally change the organizational incentives and opportunities underlying misaligned networking. Digital technologies are shown to often support resistance to intervention aimed at resolving network agency problems more than these interventions themselves.

LONG-RUN EFFECTIVENESS OF MANAGERIAL
INTERVENTIONS IN NETWORK AGENCY PROBLEMS

The preceding chapters described network agency problems that emerge because of misaligned interests in networking between organizations and their individual members. As with other misalignments, it is the responsibility of management to intervene and find ways to gain or regain alignment. Various realignment tactics were described in the prior chapters to address too many ties, ties that are too weak, entrenched brokerage, and unequal network distribution. Some of these tactics were successful and others were not. A key issue underlying the impact of these interventions is managerial agency: Exactly what influence do managers have over networks and the networking behavior of organizational members? The degree of network influence that managers have determines whether the harmful effects of network agency problems can be reversed or avoided altogether.

Of course, whether or not managerial interventions are effective ultimately determines whether managers carry them out, since managers almost always face more problems than can be resolved given their available time and attention. Discerning managers target their limited resources toward network interventions that are likely to be most effective. When are managerial efforts in network intervention justified? In this, both the costs and benefits of interventions must be considered.

As I detail subsequently, it is most useful to see this problem through the lens of time. How long do social capital pathologies persist? If they emerge but quickly dissipate, the downsides may be absorbed by most organizations, making intensive managerial interventions unnecessary. Also, how long do any positive interventions last? Answering such a question shapes whether and when interventions should be made and whether they underlie productive network governance.

One can take an extreme view and argue that social capital pathologies may not last long. If network problems are truly harmful, presumably managers have incentives to intervene and resolve them. Minor pathologies can and will be ignored. Organizations and their members undergo selection pressures. Any networking phenomenon that persists may be assumed not to be highly destructive, as managers only intervene when the benefits exceed the costs. In this view, current network pathologies may represent the best of all possible worlds.

Of course, there is another perspective that can be summarized by the famous quote "The optimist proclaims that we live in the best of all possible worlds; and the pessimist fears this is true." Network pathologies may be crippling, but the alternatives may be worse. Organizational ecologists have famously argued that inertia may be a necessary cost of the reliability, accountability, and legitimacy we desire in most formal organizations. Similarly, network pathologies may be a necessary cost of using social relationships for collaboration, coordination, and learning in organizations.[1]

Both optimistic and pessimistic perspectives share a common view that the network structures we observe reflect a stable equilibrium that accounts for managerial intervention. Yet according to the evidence in preceding chapters, managers may be continually intervening in networks with dynamic and highly varied impacts on network structures and outcomes. Why do network agency problems persist? When fixed, do they stay fixed? These related questions are the missing ingredients in understanding what we are likely to find in organizational equilibrium. They encompass various behavioral issues that have a direct effect on individual agency in networking. Do employees continue with misaligned networking behavior after the managerial intervention? The fact that network agency problems can be observed in cross-sectional organizational analyses where managers routinely intervene may indicate their persistence.

In other words, the effectiveness of managerial intervention is often directly related to the persistence of network problems. Since network agency problems themselves logically precede any interventions to resolve them, it is useful to review the common roots of these problems before considering the impact of managerial agency. I summarize the key behavioral mechanisms underlying network agency problems' impact on performance as well as the key antecedent causes of those problems. These features of network agency theory are summarized in Table 1.

NETWORK AGENCY PROBLEMS: IMPACT OF BEHAVIORAL MECHANISMS AND ANTECEDENT CAUSES

Too many ties and connectivity overload. The formation of ties illustrates how employee motivations can become unaligned from organizational interests and generate negative outcomes. Chapter 2 focused on the density of ties that make up organizational networks, describing a network agency problem in which individuals form more ties than are useful for healthy organizational functioning. The key mechanisms here are divided attention and overcommitment. Individuals with too many ties often split their attention and activities between too many relationships rather than sustain sufficient commitment to a few relationships to produce better collaborative

Table 1: Network agency theory: misaligned incentives, social mechanisms, and organizational impact

Network agency problem	Antecedents: misaligned incentives and social capital Inducements	Social and behavioral mechanisms	Political and relational content	Organizational Impact	Contingent and moderating role of digital technologies
Too many ties	Social insurance; Preserving optionality; Pursuing external opportunities	Overcommitment; Divided attention; Excessive communication	Pursuing new and counter-organizational agendas	Lower-quality projects; More mistakes; More delays; Fewer goal achievements	Primarily messaging tools and social media; Reduced cost of forming and maintaining additional ties
Ties too weak	Firm specificity of stronger ties; Consequence of inducements to form too many ties	Mistrust; Miscommunication; Misunderstanding	Signaling perfunctory organizational commitment; Mere association with causes	Difficulties mobilizing heterogeneous resources; Ineffective resource recombination	Primarily social media and communication tools; Near zero cost maintenance of large weak-tie portfolios
Entrenched brokers and ossified bridges	Preserving and amplifying information and control benefits of brokerage	Disintermediation threat minimization; Raising barriers to brokerage entry	Preserving status quo	Reduced information flow; Fewer new collaborations; Reduced resource recombination likelihood	Primarily internal communication and social media; Brokers' monitoring of disintermediation and entry attempts
Scale too free and social capital inequality	Seeking rewards proportionate to social capital; Allying with prominent actors and endorsement and affiliation benefits	Misallocated and underutilized social capital; Rich-get-richer/Matthew effect	Consolidating power; Coalition formation and affiliation	Unequal distribution of rewards; Fewer productive collaborations; Status/reputation-driven decision making	Primarily broadcast social media; Broadcast search and dissemination; Automated interaction and messaging groups to manage largest tie portfolios

outcomes. Often, they expend their energies switching between relationships and engaging in obligatory communications and interactions.

The effect of divided attention and overcommitment is profound. Employees find themselves overwhelmed with obligations stemming from these ties ranging from unnecessary project participation to payback for prior collaborators to excessive conversations and responses to inquiries. Of course, the obligations of reciprocity and communication can be a generator of value for others in the network, but there is evidence that these behaviors, which stem from large networks, lead to less effective collaboration. Inside organizations, individuals with too many ties have project outcomes that are low-preforming overall, with more delays, more mistakes, and less in line with project goals. Evidence suggests that such mesolevel outcomes result in organizational failures to release new products, respond to disruption, and effect organizational change.

Like all network agency problems, misaligned incentives and social capital inducements are the antecedent causes of too much tie formation. The primary casual mechanisms range from social insurance to preserving optionality to the pursuit of new opportunities. It is important to recognize not only that the large number of ties formed by individuals represents additional, redundant ties whose content is irrelevant, but also that they are often formed with the intention of pursuing private objectives that are not aligned or are in direct conflict with publicly stated organizational objectives. These can include private job offers, secret projects, and plots to take down an opponent. Forming additional ties is often necessary to accomplish these aims. What is ironic is that too many ties of this type can crowd out more aligned ties that could be formed if individual members were not too busy or consumed with private political agendas.

Ties too weak and insufficient relational quality. Network agency problems also underlie the quality of relationships. Chapter 3 focused on the development of too many weak ties, a network agency problem in which an ever larger proportion of the ties in individual portfolios are of a lower relational quality than is useful for accomplishing organizational goals. The key mechanisms are mistrust and miscommunication, which diminish the ability to work together and mobilize resources needed to accomplish tasks. When individuals have ties that are too weak, they encounter trust and communication problems, which make it difficult to meet complex organizational goals requiring intensive interaction and coordination. The point is that, even though strong ties are known to be a better foundation for such goals, individuals mostly have weak ties that they are forced to rely on and so take on considerable relational risk in interactions that do not warrant it.

The organizational impact of ties that are too weak is multidimensional. Poor relational quality results in collaborative efforts that may suddenly explode in acrimony or suspicion on the basis of differing perspectives or misinterpretations that might have been predicted. This often results in canceled projects or blocked career trajectories. A deeper impact is related to innovation. The strength of weak ties is often thought to be their ability to surface new ideas and opportunities, which are difficult to execute in organizations when ties are too weak. Without sufficient relational quality, heterogeneous resources available in the organizational network are not utilized by would-be collaborators and the best innovations do not emerge.

The misaligned incentives and social capital inducements that are often the antecedents of weak ties are related to the private interests that individuals pursue with weak ties. In fact, individuals often form weak ties with the express purpose of discovering new ideas and opportunities such as outside employment or international assignment. Sometimes weak ties act as a personal insurance policy in enabling individuals to mitigate the downside risks of participating in organizational projects that may fail. What is clear is that strong ties are more often oriented toward organizational objectives, perhaps because stronger ties become more firm-specific as they develop over time. This is related to another motivation: individuals seem to sense that investing in stronger relationships will enable the organization to capture more of the relationships' value, so they prefer to invest in weak ties.

Entrenched brokers and reduced collaboration. Network agency problems are often related to network position. Chapter 4 focused on how entrenched brokerage positions can become monopolies as brokers maintain control of ossified bridging relationships over long periods of time. The key mechanism here is a reduction in direct interactions between alters or between alters and alternative brokers that, if not reduced, could lead to more productive collaborations that benefit alters and organizations. With brokerage positions that are sufficiently entrenched, alters can find it difficult to sustain a short-term cost of forming new relationships or finding alternative brokers, even though such a choice may produce better outcomes in the longer run.

The organizational impact of entrenched brokers and ossified bridges is often seen in reduced information flow or fewer collaborations of the type that might threaten the broker's position. Brokers may expend considerable effort in strategic action to decrease disintermediation threats and participate in cartel-like behavior that cements their brokerage advantages. This activity is both destructive and a waste of time from an organizational perspective. Moreover, monopoly brokerage positions enable brokers to capture a large share of the value of alters' efforts even though the arrangement is less value-creating in the long run than direct interaction or an alternative broker. This means that less value is available to compensate others or to invest in higher-value activities.

The misaligned incentives and social capital inducements of entrenched brokers and ossified bridges are most obviously linked to the pursuit of private gain. Typically, actions can be tied directly to the goal of amplifying the information and control benefits of the broker position. To cement their advantages, brokers often defend the status quo in terms of organizational initiatives and relational content. This includes blocking new initiatives or ideas and hiding information that might be useful for others. Many new initiatives require new bridges to be formed or current ones to be disintermediated. However, since both actions threaten the advantages of the current brokerage cartel, brokers often oppose new relational content that is relevant for necessary innovation and organizational changes. Equally important is that alters themselves rarely oppose entrenched brokerage relationships of which they are a part, usually because they cannot overcome the high costs of disintermediation that reflect brokers' strategic actions. Moreover, potential alternative brokers may rarely mount challenges to entrenched brokers if they correctly perceive that the entry barriers have been maintained at a sufficiently highly level to prevent entry into the brokerage cartel.

Social capital inequality and uneven reward distribution. Network agency problems also emerge in organizational network distributions. Chapter 5 focused on an agency problem in which the number of ties becomes unequally distributed across the network, with a few hubs having a very large number of ties but most others having very few ties. These scale-free or near scale-free networks undergo a self-reinforcing "rich-get-richer" dynamic in which most actors prefer to connect to hubs for reasons of affiliation or uncertainty, even though the ties to that hub are less likely to be effective than other ties. The inequality of social capital that is created entails a misallocation of human capital to a few social relationships and an overdependence on a few high-status actors.

The organizational impact of this is often felt in terms of fewer productive collaborations between individuals who may have complementary expertise and therefore might generate more productive outcomes. In fact, individuals may have many ties, but because so much focus rests on connecting to high-status hubs, ties that are a better fit lack sufficient investment. Another impact lies in the distribution of rewards due to unequal social capital, with unequal financial, learning, and reputational benefits often following as a result. Hubs have superior access to the best opportunities, which stem from their many connections with nonhubs. Hubs are rewarded both informally in terms of social benefits and formally in terms of greater job attainment and remuneration. Nonhubs may be rewarded with dramatically lower benefits, some of which may flow from mere affiliation with the hub, leading to the avoidance of risk in severing the very ties that block more rewarding opportunities for collaboration with others.

As with the other network agency problems, the antecedents of social capital inequality are misaligned incentives and social inducements. Of course, individuals may wish to become high-status hubs, and those who are already hubs want to remain so. What is interesting is the motivation of others. The primary motivation of individuals to disproportionately connect to hubs appears to be status affiliation, which enables them to signal quality in the organizational social system, although sometimes they cite critical resources that can only be procured from hubs through direct connections. As hubs gain even more ties, these incentives increase for the marginal next tie to connect to a hub, as status and reputation become more important and competitive in the social system. In a world of growing social inequality, where individuals are increasingly connecting to hubs, the downsides of connecting to a lower-status actor increases, as actors have less experience doing so and less time to dedicate to these interactions.

Network agency problems generate a network of digital relationships. Taken together, network agency problems can have dramatic effects in real organizational networks. Organizations where these problems persist have vast networks of weak relationships with ossified brokerage positions and few hubs. I refer to these networks as comprising "digital relationships"

because of their all-or-nothing (1 or 0) character, which allows them to pro-
liferate and grow. The impact of digital relationship networks resembles
the organizational inertia that has often been attributed to organizational
age. Inertial organizations often fail to capture market opportunities or
changes, make many costly mistakes, miss critical deadlines, and do not
use the capabilities or the best knowledge of their members. They also allow
entrenched elites to act as bottlenecks, blocking key projects, and they dis-
tribute rewards unequally among members. Each of these inertial outcomes
is a result of specific network agency problems. In fact, digital relationships
serve as an alternative explanation of inertia that can operate independently
of organization aging, or at least serve as a proximate cause or social mechanism by which inertia is produced by aging as networks grow.

Individuals pursue digital relationship networks in line with their private interests even though such networks can harm the organization's interests or the public's interest. Often, pursuing private networking interests is a
waste of time, attention, and resources. Yet evidence shows that individuals
often pursue private networking goals that are contrary to stated organizational objectives. That is, an additional motivation underlying network
agency problems is that they may be used to pursue organizational politics that are at odds with organizational mandates. More weak ties, ossified
bridges, and hub-like structures can all be politically mobilized by those
who control these social structures.

NETWORK AGENCY PROBLEMS AND THE
POLITICAL CONTENT OF RELATIONSHIPS

The network agency problems described in the previous section mainly reside in the structural and relational features of networks; these are generalizable features of social capital that can be analyzed across organizational
contexts. In addition, some evidence shows that network agency problems
often entail real differences in the political and work content of relationships
that are contrary to organizational goals or those of other members. That
is, power and politics are another lens through which to examine network
agency problems. There are a few interesting patterns that emerge.

Qualitative evidence suggests that the political content of ties may be
at least as important as structural character in shaping network agency

in organizations. I discovered some interesting associations between network agency problems and political motivations. For instance, I found that forming large numbers of new ties is often a precursor to agendas that are counter to organizational goals. Existing partners are often locked into old ways of thinking, and forming a new tie is necessary for new political action. By contrast, weak ties are more associated with perfunctory organizational decommitment, as they are often used to mitigate organizational risk by insuring against disruption. In some cases, weak ties are used to signal commitment to organizational causes so as to minimize the risk of being exposed as disloyal. Of course, entrenched brokers are better able to achieve nonorganizationally sanctioned goals because of their greater control over resources, which they use to achieve private ends. Finally, unequal social structures as hubs can mobilize coalitions to oppose organizational authority. In fact, forming fast coalitions of intensely motivated individuals around a few hubs is a standard recommendation in the organizational change literature.

Oppositional political action helps to situate network agency problems in traditional agency theory. Classical agency theory accounts of individual motivation concern individuals choosing to shirk, act opportunistically, or pursue private objectives that are intentionally unaligned with those of management.[2] Of course, these negative motivations can be pursued without a specific networking orientation. Yet the evidence on network agency problems shows a few intriguing patterns. First, these problems can emerge without any intention to oppose organizational objectives. Pursuing too many ties, weak existing ties, solidifying brokerage, and becoming a hub are local choices that individuals may pursue without intentional organizational disloyalty, even if these choices have negative organizational effects in aggregate. At the same time, though, individuals with classical agency-theoretic motivations that are contrary to organizational interests can pursue problematic network states that facilitate private interests that are opposed to current organizational objectives, whether consciously or unconsciously. In short, network agency theory and classical agency theory have a complicated relationship, as they propose only partially overlapping motivational states, even if the negative effects of both agency theories are predictable.

DIGITAL TECHNOLOGIES AND
NETWORK AGENCY PROBLEMS

Considering the above, the following are key questions in organizational analysis: What enables network agency problems? Why are we seeing so many social capital pathologies now? Why are network misalignments more prominent in modern, technology-enabled organizations? Traditional agency theory accounts often focus on individuals shirking their jobs, opportunism of some type, or the pursuit of private objectives. As the political motivations discussed in the previous section indicate, misalignments due to individual dispositions and orientations can occur in conjunction with network pathologies. Yet network agency problems are more organizationally fundamental in the sense that they are endogenous to the network: network structures generate local incentives and inducements to improve social capital that drive agentic action and the sorting into structures that reinforce it.[3] Whether it is too many ties, weak ties, inertial brokers, or hubs, these structures often produce incentives that lead others to reproduce them.

If there is any exogenous factor that seems to amplify this endogenous dynamic, it is the organization's adoption of digital technologies. Many types of digital technology are used for communication, productivity, and collaboration. The case data indicates a simple, base-level impact: amplifying network agency problems. Across multiple cases, I observed that a network of moderate ties, some strong and weak ties, a few brokers, and low inequality of hubs could be transformed after adoption of new digital technologies. Individuals used technology affordances to enact their network agency. Whether these were top-down enterprise software installations or bottom-up consumer software use by employees, the new networks often became vast networks of digital relationships, or this trend accelerated, after the adoption of digital technologies.

An irony is that the pernicious impact of digital technologies unfolds because it enhances individual networking in ways that amplify network agency problems. First, digital technologies enable individuals to form and maintain more ties and so are deeply related to the first network pathology I described, possessing too many ties. In particular, I found messaging tools such as email, WhatsApp, and Slack to be most implicated here. Messaging applications were the key tool enabling sufficient interactions underlying vast portfolios of ties. However, these applications created some obligation of interactions to maintain ties once formed. The fact that these ties were weak was partly a consequence of portfolio size expanding to meet the time and attention budgets of individuals. I also found that such social media platforms amplified the weakness of tie portfolios as individuals engaged in more minimal and virtual interactions online, often with people they had never met in real life.

Digital technologies also appear to reinforce the entrenchment of brokers and ossify their advantages. There is some evidence that this is functional: brokers use digital technologies to more effectively help alters, including sourcing information and facilitating interactions that are organizationally positive. Yet I also collected many examples of brokers using digital technologies to strategically erect entry barriers to brokerage or maintain brokerage cartels. Internal social media can be used to monitor behavior and informally sanction those who challenge brokerage positions.

Finally, the emergence of social network inequality appears to be intimately related to the capacity of some to attract a disproportionately large share of networking activity. Digital technologies are particularly useful for broadcasting the informal social status of various actors, leading to stronger preferences to make ties with those who have the highest status. Digital technologies that magnify status and expose social relationships, such as Twitter and LinkedIn, amplify distributional effects. Although high-status hubs can exist outside technological domains, there is usually a natural limit to this based on the time and attention they can dedicate to contacts. Even so, high-status actors access social networking tools to maintain vastly more relationships than most other members.

MANAGERIAL INTERVENTIONS TO RESOLVE NETWORK AGENCY PROBLEMS

When managers encounter network agency problems and understand their effects, they often attempt to directly intervene to change network structure, relational quality, or relationship content. There is some evidence that employees respond to the new incentives in tie formation.[4] Although there are many interventions, most are surprisingly ineffective in changing the network, sustaining the any change, or deriving the intended benefits of change. These results suggest that network agency problems are persistent organizational issues that are not always amenable to isolated managerial interventions.

Intervening to reduce the number of ties. Many of the interventions that managers I interviewed undertook were oriented toward reducing or limiting the number of ties that specific individuals were developing. Managers asked employees to not make specific new connections or to limit interactions in prior relationships. They sometimes backed this request with specific rewards or sanctions meant to induce compliance. In some cases, employees agreed to changes by discontinuing interactions and ties, only to restart them when managers were no longer exerting monitoring pressure. In other cases, they discontinued interactions as directed by managers, only to begin ties with others, producing a net effect of increasing ties. In some rare cases, employees directly resisted and refused managers' directives. The managers may have had very little influence or ability to monitor their employees, so the net effect was that employees kept their ties.

The broader finding is that interventions to reduce the number of network ties seem to fail when managerial attention toward monitoring and enforcement declines, or the full force of new incentives declines sufficiently such that employees realize that reconstituting new ties, creating substitute ties, or resisting tie interventions is permissible again. Networks are often observed to snap back to a prior or similar state after interventions, even if employees take some initial actions to comply with managerial directives. The blue-sky model indicates that this occurs because incentives to develop more ties increase as the number of ties falls away from the optimum. This suggests that a suboptimal number of ties exist in an unstable equilibrium that is difficult to maintain without exogenous effort. In organizations, this exogenous effort is provided by managers who mainly monitor employee networks, but as monitoring is expensive, managers may eventually turn their attention elsewhere, and employees resume tie formation.

Interventions to improve relational quality. Managers also attempt to intervene by mitigating the weakness of ties. Managers may create incentives for employees to invest in relational quality and tie strength, or create occasions to strengthen ties around new projects or recreational activities. In fact, managers may couple their prescription to avoid investing in too many ties with proscriptions to invest in a few strategic relationships to mobilize different resources. There is some evidence that these interventions increase the strength of some ties. However, in many cases there is a process similar to that described previously: once the initial interventions are over, employees have a tendency to reduce investment in strong ties and renew investments in many other ties, resulting in an overall weaker tie portfolio. Often, they believe that increasing investment in their strong ties risks overdependency on a few relationships, and the logic to diversify away those risks with weak ties returns. The time dynamics of tie monitoring is important here because generally monitoring by managers cannot last long enough to sustain their employees' relationships. Given enough time, presumably all relationships will decay without further investment. Although too many ties and tie weakness are related, even a static portfolio of the same ties will weaken in aggregate if employees choose to turn their attention elsewhere.

Interventions to mitigate entrenched positions. The scope of interventions managers use to address maladaptive network positions is broad only because those positions can have subtle differences in the incentives and capabilities they provide in networking. Since brokers have well-known information and control advantages, intervening to mitigate their influence is particularly challenging when they are entrenched in their positions. Interventions around brokers can be directing the broker to facilitate alters' ties, severing one (or both) of the broker's own ties with alters, encouraging alters to interact directly without assistance from the broker, encouraging the creation of new brokers who will mitigate the influence of older brokers whose advantages are entrenched, and, of course, reassigning or firing the broker so that the position is removed from the network.

Despite the great variety of interventions, I found that interventions to change the nature of brokerage is mostly likely to fail, so that the original structure snaps back. This may be mostly because the high information and control advantages of brokers gives them greater incentives and capabilities to resist managerial interventions. In fact, there is some evidence that management interventions may lead to the first strategic actions by brokers to reduce threats of disintermediation and raise entry barriers. Brokers often learn in response to managerial interventions to better employ strategic actions to sustain their positions. Such capability building further decreases the likelihood that these advantages will dissipate.

Of course, removing the broker through reassignment or dismissal is an intervention with a definite effect, as the bridging ties are then effectively removed from the network. However, in a few cases where I studied an organization for many years, I noted a surprising negative impact: although the original broker had departed, a new broker emerged who took strategic action to entrench his position all the same. This may reflect a combination of network memory on the part of organizational members to reconstitute network positions and alters who submit to being brokered by a new individual who fills the role. It is made possible by organizational incentives that remain unchanged so that entrenched brokers can maintain their advantages.

Interventions to equalize social capital. Managers also attempt to intervene to mitigate inequality in social capital by changing the distribution of ties. They do so with targeted interventions to encourage hubs with few ties to form more and hubs with many to form fewer or even reduce ties. As expected, these interventions have limited effect, as the underlying incentives that lead employees to prefer ties with hubs remain. Managers also attempt to shift the social dynamic so individuals rely less on status in choosing partners and more on formal assignments by their managers. Although these new collaborations may be formalized, employees still attempt to make connections to hubs to gain social support, resources, or reputational advantages, with a net effect of simply possessing too many ties.

Finally, some managers attempt to mitigate or remove hubs. Of course, hubs usually possess sufficient power to resist. Perhaps surprisingly, however, most resistance is from the hub's partners, who rely on the hub and do not want her to depart. Interventions to create minor hubs with a fraction of the ties seem to be somewhat more effective, as creating networking alternatives is useful. But even minor hubs usually connect to major hubs and defer to their advantages.

Viewing managerial interventions collectively, a clear pattern of ineffectiveness emerges in many cases. Direct interventions in a network either are difficult to implement or—if they are implemented—have little impact because employee networks snap back to prior states after managers cease monitoring. There are implications in this concerning the relative costs and benefits of network governance. In the case of network agency problems, the costs of network governance are often much higher than expected, as interventions encounter significant resistance and a long course of monitoring is necessary to make them stick. The benefits of governance through direct interventions in network agency problems can be less than expected, as networks can snap back quickly. Put another way, network agency problems persist because network system dynamics are quite robust to exogenous perturbations by management.

MANAGERIAL INTERVENTIONS WITH
DIGITAL TECHNOLOGIES

Digital technologies enable employees to express their agency in ways that amplify and accelerate the effects of network agency problems. It is therefore sensible to ask whether technology can be used by managers to improve their capacity to change employees' ties. There is an emerging stream of research on people analytics technologies that enable managers to monitor digitally. Although the bulk of this research is about big-tech companies that use surveillance as part of their business model with mass market consumers, some companies have developed surveillance-style tools for managing employees as well.[5]

While marketed primarily as collaboration and human resource management tools, people analytics systems give managers considerable visibility into employees' work activities which can be used for monitoring network interactions and their effects, including project assignment, internal communications, and performance outcomes. The adoption of these tools was just emerging across the companies that I studied, so a systematic exploration was not possible. Still, some initial insights emerged.

I found that surveillance-oriented enterprise software tools gave managers insights into employee networks that were useful for interventions. For instance, by observing email and messaging interactions, managers could estimate the total number of ties in the network and thus determine if a problem with excessive network density existed or was growing. At an individual level, managers could monitor individual relationships, discovering who was working with whom and how much investment was being put into each relationship by observing the number of emails or meetings on a calendar. With such information, managers could see not only who had too many ties but also which ties were weak. Interventions directed at strengthening individual relationships leveraged this information.

Information provided by people analytics systems can be used to identify maladaptive brokers and determine the level of intervention necessary, ranging from work directives to broker pruning. This information may also be useful for breaking up status orderings based on the distribution of ties. By graphing networks, managers can identify individuals who are hubs and those who lack sufficient ties to accomplish work objectives. In this way, digital surveillance technologies may promote efficient interventions, as they allow managers' attention and energies to be better targeted.

Although these digital tools may seem promising for network governance, it is not at all clear that people analytics have a net positive effect on network agency problems. I observed frequent and intense resistance by employees and managers to the adoption of surveillance technologies. Individuals are often deeply uncomfortable with surveillance precisely because of the power it affords managers to intervene in relationships. In some cases, employees' sense of violation makes the use of surveillance technologies untenable. Some managers even abandon them. The jury is out on whether this technology is effective in assisting managers in networking interventions.

It is possible that my initial findings are a sign that surveillance technologies will ultimately be viewed as immoral or distasteful in most organizations. Individual managers and employees have always negotiated about the role of new technologies in the wider context of work norms that are developing in society. Yet another possibility is that these technologies will see wide diffusion and come to be accepted by managers and employees alike. Without predicting the exact future, it is reasonable to assume that technology will play a role in future network interventions.

ORGANIZATIONAL FACTORS UNDERLYING THE PERSISTENCE OF NETWORK AGENCY PROBLEMS

This chapter mostly focuses on the internal structural dynamics of networks that determine whether network agency problems persist. In my fieldwork, I noted deep persistence of network agency problems precisely because the networking behaviors that led to them served individual employee's interests. This meant that any managerial intervention would be met with resistance or the network would return to a prior state without constant managerial attention and energy.[6] Yet, as some examples have illustrated, there are additional organizational factors that reinforce persistence.

In further work, I explore additional organizational roots of persistence—namely, why typical network designs and interventions that organizations use rarely generate lasting change in network system dynamics. I identify three interrelated reasons—design resistance, network ignorance, and managerial misattribution—and I document their effects.

First, employees may actively resist attempts to design networks, especially managerial efforts to reduce the number, strength, and content of relationships. An asymmetry exists: employees concede to prescriptive interventions that increase network size, but proscriptive interventions that aim to diminish networks and decrease networking often lead to resistance or subversion. Multiple participants respond to proscription with hidden tie formation, reconstitution, or other reassertions of individual control over networking. To be clear, resistance to network designs may be different from misaligned interests—employees may agree that a new network structure is optimal but resist changing their own ties.

The second cause of persistence is at the root of managerial ineffectiveness—network ignorance. Many managers are unaware that too many ties, weak ties, ossified bridges, and hub-and-spoke structures are present in their networks.[7] Or, if they are aware, they have difficulty identifying key positions, individuals, or roles on which they should spend their limited intervention budget of time and attention. Network ignorance is highly related to bounded rationality and our natural cognitive constraints on understanding others' social relationships.[8] In fact, understanding the organizational network may be the hardest task for a manager to undertake, as it is constantly changing and is difficult to codify and teach to new employees.

Network ignorance is highly related to a third cause of persistence: managers' errors about the link between network pathology and performance.[9] Since managers are forced to use employee satisfaction and "self-report" as proxies for progress in network intervention, they often misjudge the impact of fruitful network design efforts and stop them prematurely. Design resistance, network ignorance, and misattribution are related because knowledge about networks is a by-product of data-gathered about allocentric networks that are not completely observable by management and may be resisted by employees.

Ultimately, these designs and interventions fail because they do not shift the motivational structure of networking in the long run. Many interventions are not comprehensive because of hidden pockets of resistance or unseen pathological positions. Or short-run performance improvements may ensue, but they do not last when managers redirect their efforts elsewhere on the assumption that the interventions will stick. To increase or maintain impact, organizations seem to require significant, constant energy expenditure to maintain displacement from the suboptimal critical point or else there could be snapback.

In fact, it is possible that these three factors may affect any organizational change that requires appropriate networking, such as responding to disruptive innovations, reengineering efforts, and alliances and M&As. Network agency problems may be the root problem, sustained through network dynamics and a broader resistance to design, ignorance of networks, and managerial misattribution of the causes of network agency problems.

Agentic Function of the Executive

STRATEGIC SOCIAL CAPITAL AND THE
WORK-FROM-HOME EXPERIMENT

This chapter describes how executives can have a broader effect on organization-wide changes that mitigate the development and impact of network agency problems. The use of managerial digital technologies such as people analytics are discussed, and the rampant adoption of remote work digital technologies used as a natural experiment to better understand their impact. The development of strategic social capital practices to complement strategic human capital practices that are emerging are sketched throughout. A new function of the executive focuses on creating organizational environments that mitigate network agency problems.

SEARCHING FOR ORGANIZATION-WIDE REMEDIES
TO NETWORK AGENCY PROBLEMS

Network agency problems create suboptimal network structures for organizational functioning. As explained in earlier chapters, digital technologies have amplified and accelerated these problems. Worse, they are persistent and resistant to intervention by individual managers. After targeted interventions that seem to momentarily resolve the issue, networks and networking behaviors do appear to change for the better. Yet since the underlying networking incentives and opportunities do not fundamentally change, these networks often snap back to their original dysfunctional states when managers direct their attention elsewhere.

A general feature of network agency problems appears to be that they span levels of analysis. They are microfoundational in that they concern individual behavior and outcomes, but this behavior is shaped by organization-wide incentives and corporate adoption of technology. Therefore, one reason these problems are so persistent is that the directed microlevel managerial interventions described in Chapter 6—for instance, directing employees to break up ties—do not span levels and address the macroorganizational problem. Like water in the moats of a sandcastle, network agency problems eventually find their way to every part of the organization where individual and organizational interests may be misaligned.

Given such difficulties, an organizational analyst will typically search for ways to effect broader and lasting changes. Individual managerial interventions may temporarily ameliorate specific issues; however, more significant and lasting transformation may require organization-wide changes instituted by those with the highest authority, executives.

Typically, executives concern themselves with strategy content, broader organizational processes to achieve objectives, and communication with the outside world about the organization's activities. However, are there any broader organization-wide activities, processes, or programs they can implement, resources they can invest in, or capabilities they can develop to mitigate network agency problems? What is the function of the executive in light of network agency problems? This chapter explores various answers to these questions.

DIGITAL RELATIONSHIPS IN THE WORK-FROM-HOME EXPERIMENT

To begin with, we recall that network problems are amplified by digital technology; thus, it is reasonable to expect that executives will seek technological mitigation of their effects. Executives control the purse strings of an organization and are responsible for large-scale IT purchases in established enterprises.[1] The role of a chief information officer (CIO), in particular, focuses on large-scale IT procurement, installation, and maintenance, and the CIO often works directly with others in the C-suite to formulate IT procurement strategy.

Since network agency problems emerge in the social environment of organizations, executives seek out technological solutions to monitor and control social networks. Some tools have emerged to make it easier to intervene and structure the social environment. These include enterprise software solutions for monitoring email patterns, project management and workflow analysis, and even physical tracking. Additionally, executives can leverage consumer technologies, such as messaging and social media, which give them a window into employees' social interactions. Finally, data analytics, especially in the category of "people analytics,", can be used to extract patterns in employee behaviors and performance that may be a result of social interaction.[2]

Certainly, the increasingly accurate knowledge that these software tools generate can be used to undertake more effective, targeted managerial interventions. However, the broader applicability of this data is in informing an organization's structures and policies that determine which interactions are possible or how they are rewarded.

Methodological problems in studying technology and networks. In fact, a field of scholarship has emerged to analyze the impact of technologies on organizational behavior. As noted by many of scholars in this field, it is actually difficult to disentangle the effects of technology because they are twofold. On the one hand, technology can impact work and social interactions. On the other, executives choose to implement technology to achieve desired outcomes for which their organizations may already be prepared. A question always arises whether technology is responsible for that impact or whether the organization can effect the outcome without it.

The impact of technology on networks and work may be examined in small samples, as I have done. With a few cases, one can trace how a particular software tool enables network expansion, for instance. Moreover, most of the examples of network agency problems involve employees choosing to use consumer technologies in the workplace and their effect on the organization. It is even possible to note the organizational impact when management chooses to adopt enterprise technologies, especially when they have unintended consequences, as I note using several examples from earlier chapters.

What is harder to uncover is the impact of organization-wide technologies chosen by executives in larger samples of employees. Many scholars have noted the difficulty of empirical endogeneity, which is to say technology adoption may appear to change organizational states, but these states may have been caused by external conditions and in fact may have led to adoption of the enabling technology. Now, endogeneity is less of an issue in qualitative research because causal logics can be painstakingly traced in time through extensive field research in a small sample, but it remains a thorny problem in large-scale empirical research, where collecting qualitative data is difficult. Often, to disentangle these effects, empirical researchers wait for an experimental condition in which the technology changes but the organizational objectives do not. Indeed, such an experimental condition may aid qualitative inductive research as well if only because the effect might be dramatic and facilitate the exploration of multiple mechanisms.

There is something similar to a natural experiment, and that is the COVID-19 pandemic, which forced large numbers of employees to work from home. During the pandemic, a vast number of organizations supported their employees in their efforts to work from home by purchasing and supporting their use of digital technology. The most prominent of these were video conferencing packages such as Zoom, Skype, and Microsoft Teams. However, it is also true that the use of messaging software such as email, WhatsApp, and Slack increased dramatically, as did other project management and collaboration tools such as Trello and Microsoft Project. All at once, great numbers of organizations found themselves supporting a fully digitized version of work, distributing tasks among employees in their homes. What is useful for our inquiry is to explore this rampant technology adoption's impact on networking behavior, the resulting networks, and performance outcomes.

Network findings in the COVID-19 natural experiment. I explored the use of technology through the COVID-19 work-from-home experiment. Like other analysts, I originally assumed that the pandemic would create a massive sense of isolation as employees could no longer interact at the office.[3] Because employees were cut off from colleagues, they were forced into virtual interactions. In fact, I observed many who had previously resisted Zoom and Slack being asked by their managers to take up these platforms. This appeared to have a dramatic effect on networks and networking that went beyond just removing the sense of isolation.

I found employees of all types connecting and interacting with *more* people *more* often because of video conferencing technology. This was initially a purely internal phenomenon, but it quickly extended to more outside meetings with clients, customers, suppliers, and other partners. Many Zoom calls, Slack chats, and WhatsApp groups formed, and there were many more faces, messages, and people to keep track of over time.

The impact on networking and networks was the creation of many more ties; unfortunately, in most cases these ties were weak, like the "digital relationships" I described in earlier chapters. Moreover, I found that some preexisting strong ties became weak as attention was split among multiple new relationships. Many employees reported strained interactions, misunderstandings, and erosion of trust in these weak relationships. Of course, the pandemic saw some layoffs in the companies I studied, which were in fact associated with the weakest of ties, as might be expected.

It was also interesting to observe the impact of video conferencing on structure. Existing brokers seemed to stay in place as brokers, even though networks were growing around them. Many brokers came to serve many more alters, but their brokerage role remained intact. While difficult to measure, both alters and brokers perceived that the brokers were extracting a greater share of the value from intermediation. Similarly, hubs became even stronger and were often observed to be the biggest promoters of technology—hubs were often the ones calling for Zoom meetings, and members found it difficult to resist their requests.

I observed that the feeling of isolation remained very real during this time. This is ironic, given the greater connectivity. Isolation did not stem only from a lack of face-to-face interaction or fewer ties. It also stemmed from having time and attention split among more, weak ties, with stilted relationships dependent on brokers and hubs to remain connected. Overall, I saw a link between isolation and the acceleration of digital relationships during the work-from-home experiment. In this case, the rampant, forced adoption of digital interaction appears to have actually diminished meaningful social connection and fruitful collaborations.

There have been significant studies of social networks during the COVID-19 pandemic.[4] Some have suggested that many employees became substantially more connected to their colleagues thanks to Zoom, Teams, Slack, WhatsApp, among others.[5] There is also evidence that consumer social network sites like Facebook, Instagram, and LinkedIn were used more during the pandemic, which may have broadened the reach of networks as investment in a smaller number of in-person relationships diminished.[6] In organizational contexts, only teams that developed new interaction patterns to intentionally strengthen a few ties seemed to avoid problems of too much interaction. Bosses were essential to providing a structure to limit the downsides of remote work. Some teams merely reported fatigue due to the interactions, which affected their overall productivity.

Many researchers have speculated that remote or hybrid work will continue even after the pandemic; while this working style may be preferred by some employees, one hopes that the effects of rampant digital relationships will be mitigated by management. It may not be all bad news. Scholarship on technology and organization often suggests that new technologies lead to a combination of positive and negative impacts that create a new equilibrium. Technologies create many affordances for individuals, both employees and managers.[7]

Additionally, I investigated managerial technology systems such as corporate social broadcast tools and people analytics, which promise to give managers high-level transparency, influence, and control over organizational networks. Yet, consistent with the IT literature, I found that attempts to exert technological control over employees are rarely effective. Employees seem to be winning a technological arms race with their companies as they increasingly adopt their own tools to expand their networks even while their managers are using tools to monitor them. In fact, this has played out repeatedly in the history of corporate IT adoption, most recently in the case of consumer software technologies such as social media and smartphones, which have proven much more successful in enabling interactions than company-funded enterprise software is in controlling them. The scale and scope of connections, ideas, and technologies beyond the purview of an organization may always be greater than that of the coercive potential in any single organization, no matter how digitally enabled it may be. In short, employees resist social control by technology with technology.

If it is true that technology is insufficient to resolve the problems that it creates, then administrators must look elsewhere for solutions, typically in their own practices and roles in organizational life. The earlier insight, that organizations can be pulled away from suboptimal critical points with the input of constant managerial attention and energy, forms the basis for what may be the more effective solution to network pathology. How can organizations ensure that managerial energies are expended in an efficient manner? In fact, this issue underpins one of the most fundamental questions in organizational theory: What is the function of the executive (or any other manager) in light of recalcitrant individual efforts to subvert organizational objectives?

LOCATING THE AGENTIC FUNCTION OF THE EXECUTIVE IN NETWORKS

Technology is only one set of choices that executives can make. Organization theory suggests that executives serve a much broader function, which is to shape organizational purpose, vision, and culture. Purpose, vision, and culture are indeed more abstract and diffuse than strategic objectives and tactical organizational goals. Some have suggested that a broad common purpose is essential in long-standing organizations, as it can remain the same even when specific environmental disruptions require changing specific strategic objectives.[8] The vision of what the organization can be and its place in the world is often a unifying force even if it is never achieved. Further, organization culture—the values, norms, and ways of thinking that most members share—is often more enduring than specific organizational routines or policies.

The idea that executives are primarily responsible for these broader issues is pervasive in organizational theory. One of the most prominent early theorists in this vein was Chester Barnard. Barnard, whose conception of formal organization focused on why disparate individuals willingly cooperate in the first place. Viewing organizations as fundamentally hierarchical, he postulated that the key to proper organizational functioning is a question of whether or not employees make voluntary decisions to comply with authority. From a motivational standpoint, he suggested that employees usually comply if the organizational inducements exceed employees' contributions. That is, individuals will act in their self-interest in the long run and adjust their efforts in line with the organizational context.

According to Barnard, while the role of managers is to motivate individual employees, the role of executives is to set the broader context and the policies with which managers can create specific inducements. Of course, direct financial incentives can be helpful, but often they are insufficient for anything more than perfunctory contributions. One solution to the problem of inducement, Barnard thought, is to enact a higher purpose that employees can believe in to induce contributions and consolidate disparate organizational interests. To the extent that employees believe in a higher purpose, some unity in action can be achieved.

A key to Barnard's theory is the realization that executive orders by managerial fiat often fail to work because they do not fundamentally change underlying inducements while they demand increased contributions, leading to employee unwillingness to comply or lack of enthusiasm to take proper action. In Barnard's view, the proper function of executives is to develop noble or attractive higher purposes for the organization so that inducements naturally increase in a way that does not require constant managerial intervention.

Barnard's theory influenced a great many scholars and scholarly traditions, such as Selznick and institutionalism, Simon and the Carnegie school, and Perrow and bureaucracy theorizing. Although some criticized his neglect of top-down strategic action, he is most often remembered for highlighting the informal and social side of motivation behind voluntary employee action in an organizational context.[9]

Barnard's theorizing painted a world of administrative action that focused not just on developing routines, rules, and standard operating procedures for what should be done and how but also on why it should be willingly done by organizational members. Focusing on the employee motivational structure created by managers is a useful framework for analyzing network agency problems. What organizational activities or structures can executives put in place to induce employees to voluntarily align their network interests with the organization's?

In the search for long-term changes to networking behaviors, we are inevitably led to the microfoundational aspect of what individuals think and do. This involves seeking both cultural and behavioral change. One way is to change cultural beliefs and values based on the theory that changing how individuals think changes their networking behavior. A good example of this is Netflix. The company has become famous for a performance-oriented culture that focuses on providing "autonomy and power to get things done." This occurs in an environment in which employees are always competing for recognition. The famous Netflix "culture deck" is a document that encodes its meritocratic ethos. Seeking this sort of cultural and behavioral change has an underlying network implication: usually it involves changing employees' beliefs about what relationships are acceptable and what will be rewarded/sanctioned, with some influence granted to executives to shape the preferred type of networks.

In fact, this is synonymous with the broader behavioral approach to organizations, which suggests that several factors operate on employees to nudge their behavior in a more aligned manner.[10] Some take the view that modifying the behavior itself in establishing a new routine is the key to long-lasting change. For example, noted organizational behavior researcher Herminia Ibarra has recently argued that the essence of leadership development is to act like a leader in order to learn how to lead.[11] A broader lesson of the behavioral approach is that patterns of effective action often involve a learning-by-doing process that cannot be avoided.

Based on the behavioral and cultural approaches just described, one way to solve network agency problems more effectively may be to develop broader organizational processes that enable more aligned networking without constant managerial intervention or scrutiny. Organizational processes directly affect behavior and are often supported by the prevailing culture. The advantages of organizational processes are that they can be stored in organizational memory, provided they are routinized and institutionalized. In this way, network organizational processes become independent of specific individuals and can be passed down to new members and performed efficiently over time.[12]

There are several examples of network organizational processes. For instance, Obstfeld (2005) notes that some individuals come to occupy *Tertius Iungens* roles, in which they act as "connectors". New connections enable knowledge to be combined in innovative ways. Network processes are often more visible at the interorganizational level. Davis and Eisenhardt (2011) found that most innovative alliances use a rotating leadership approach, in which they alternate control so that each makes her own contributions. Further, Davis (2016) found that the most innovative triads engage in a group cycling, in which certain dyadic alliances are arranged in a series and proceed in time. Such processes align the interests of the parties, as they each have their "turn" to shift goals and lead development. There are likely many such network processes that may be discovered with further study.

THE NEW STRATEGIC SOCIAL CAPITAL FUNCTION OF HUMAN RESOURCES

One key question in organization science is how to change maladaptive cultures and generate new processes that are more effective in mitigating network agency problems. The key issue is that any approach must have a direct effect both on people and on how they interact with the organization. Since agency-theoretic problems happen at the individual level, it is reasonable to believe that microfoundational solutions are the most likely to be effective. By microfoundational, I mean mechanisms that focus on populations of individuals—who they are, what they think, what they do. Executives may be able to change how managers deal with people with respect to networking, by instituting better practices for people management concerning networking behavior and performance.

In fact, a new field has emerged that studies individual-level management from the perspective of organizational objectives. This is strategic human resources (HR) research. Strategic HR is defined as practices that operate to achieve organizational goals, including the development of competitive advantage. Traditional HR is tasked with performance management, succession management, compensation, employee relations, career development, and talent management. Strategic HR is different in that its core concern is organizational performance, including whether the organization enables competitive advantages when compared to rivals.

Research and a better understanding of strategic HR practices have generated a transformation in the HR function over the past ten years, making it much more focused on talent development and how people are managed.[13] Another insight of the HR literature is that, to make these practices truly strategic (useful for the organization), they must be performed not just by HR professionals but also by commercial line managers. Only then can employee inducements be changed in a way that improves organizational commitment, job satisfaction, career development, and socialization to fit into a new culture.[14]

Because strategic HR practices seem to be a good fit for the resolution of network agency problems, I explored them with an eye to the resolution or management of issues stemming from conflicting interests involving networking. I begin with hiring.

HIRING

The hiring interface is the first element of HR development with which individuals interact when they join an organization. Even at this point, differences in networking interests may emerge. New hires have just left the job market, which is often a highly socialized activity where they leverage individual social capital to find a job. The process of obtaining referrals to companies may require intensive networking. The hiring manager must judge if the new hire's networking interests can be aligned with organizational objectives.

It is important to note the hire's typical interests at the point of hiring. While on the surface those may simply be to get the job and fit into the organization, there is in fact heterogeneity in these interests. New hires are not yet loyal to the organization and may have conflicting interests. This is particularly true with high-potential employees who may have higher social capital and extensive networks. They may bring the attention constraints from those networks with them in ways that make them less effective, at least in the short term. A broader and longer-term risk is that they may bring an overactive networking approach into the organization and disrupt its culture. Such networking practices can easily diffuse to others.

Research on social factors in hiring reveals challenges.[15] For instance, hiring managers may wish to minimize bias in the selection of candidates, whether racial, gender, or cultural. It is often in the organization's interest to promote diversity, but this is generally not in an individual manager's interest—typically, social network–based hiring generates homophily, which means that those hired tend to resemble those who hire them. Some homophily can beget more homophily as members seek to hire others who are like them, whether consciously or unconsciously. In this case, a network agency problem emerges where the HR function should intervene to ensure diversity but does not so.

A large part of the solution is in the job design itself. A position with which a candidate is a good fit may decrease the likelihood that a new hire will engage in misaligned networking activities, such as forming many weak ties to insure against job loss. Moreover, jobs can be designed where some network diversity is required, so that homophily is less likely to be effective. In other words, the organization can create work contexts where networking is aligned.

Another important consideration is the interests of the candidate's advocates. Hiring is often plagued with personal lobbying for candidates by managers with misaligned interests, which can range from outside personal friendship ties to the desire to build an empire in the organization. Empire building is highly related to the network agency problems described in earlier chapters, especially concerning the possession of too many ties and the existence of hubs. A job offer is suspect if a private motivation in hiring is to increase a manager's ties or status as a hub, leaving very little value to be captured by the organization.

To combat network agency problems at the hiring interface, organizations can implement fair and transparent processes using selection committees formed by individuals from several organizational areas. In this manner, private interests that do not serve broader organizational mandates can be monitored by others and so partially mitigated. Professional hiring managers can also focus their efforts on analyzing a candidate's networking interests and engaging in productive job design to ensure that misaligned interests are not imported into the organization with each hire.

Ultimately, hiring is a sorting and matching process. Executives can clarify the organization's networking norms so that candidates unwilling to abide by them may drop out. Technology may make this task easier. External hiring is now supported by executive search firms, online job platforms, and social media sites such as LinkedIn, Instagram, and Twitter. These are valuable ways to observe the candidate's networking activity, from which hiring managers can infer their interests, but they should be supplemented by interviews and observations through which private interests may be more thoroughly revealed.

SOCIALIZATION

After hiring, the single most important process for the strategic development of employees is their socialization into the organization. Socialization is a process in which individuals learn "how things work", including the particular activities, routines, and behaviors that are effective.[16] It is also how the deeper purposes, values, norms, rules, and policies of an organization are learned. In the early days after joining, new employees appear to be in a critical period in which it is easy for them to absorb lessons. Employees learn much about their job activities, and there is evidence that values taught early are stickier than those taught later. As time passes, we should expect that fresh attempts to inculcate new learning will be less likely to be successfully adopted by employees.

Socialization comes in various guises. Managers can organize training events where new employees learn about standard routines and deeper purposes can be explained. Similarly, HR professionals may hold induction meetings. However, most socialization may actually come from a new employee's earliest interactions with colleagues. In fact, the most impactful role managers may play in socialization is in shaping the cohort of employees the new hire will encounter, for example through desk assignment and job design. In this context, the selection of "good" over "bad" influences is essential.

When applied to network agency, socialization may take several forms. First, it is a time when management has the largest sway over the network ties that employees form, including the specific collaborators and interactions that are aligned with organizational interests. The network ties that hiring managers facilitate for the new employee can serve as a model for "the types of relationships that we form here." This modeling is essential, since the manager will not have the time and energy to facilitate all of the employees' ties in the future. At some point, managers have to leave employees to their own devices.

Proper networking role models are critical. For instance, the first partners that a manager chooses for the new employee will ideally have aligned networking behaviors and networks that contain a moderate number of ties, with some strong ties focusing on important work assignments. New employees may better absorb the preferred socialization lessons through early role models rather than later interventions, as previously indicated.

What is most important is clearly communicating the norms of networking and providing a proper rationale for them. The employee should be able to answer the following: Which relationships should I be invested in? How much time is appropriate to spend on networking versus work? Which technologies are a good foundation for networking? What is the proper role of social media? Sometimes norms can be communicated by joint role models, but the telling of stories may be equally effective, including which networking strategies work and which do not. Such stories can reveal the risks and incentives that new employees may not be aware of, including cases of multiple employees leaving the company because of inappropriate networking. Discussing networking behaviors that are rewarded versus sanctioned is of particular importance, as this is how new employees construct their own mental models of appropriate networking.

As indicated in earlier chapters, the key is linking aligned networking behaviors—building moderate networks, investing in strong ties, being a helpful broker, and not attempting to become hub—and organizational, team, and career success. Perhaps the largest risk in socialization is that it is a time of enormous path dependence: if "bad" socialization routines are set forth, they can become very difficult to dislodge. Thus, managers responsible for socialization should be on the lookout for savvy organizational members who may try to use the socialization process for private gain at the expense of organizational interests. As this is the critical period, these early encounters may determine future networking behavior.

PERFORMANCE MANAGEMENT

After initial socialization in the organization's values, purposes, and procedures, perhaps the most important task in strategic HR is performance management. Individual organization members must perform at demanding levels such that they can contribute to achieving organizational goals. Of course, HR functions engage in performance management: job performance can be monitored, supported, and rewarded in a variety of ways.

However, the network is a dimension often neglected by HR professionals and bosses. As I argue in this book, networking may be one of the most critical factors in job performance and the achievement of organizational goals. I documented in earlier chapters that managers and HR professionals can be quite reluctant to interfere or even attempt to influence employee networks. However, it is becoming increasingly clear that networking is a significant component of employee performance. Thus, we should expect network performance management to become more common.

I observed some basic network management activities that may gain increasing acceptance. For instance, I noted that managers who visualize networks accurately are better able to intervene in them. However, this is only the first step. From a performance management perspective, the more important task is to communicate these network metrics to employees and ensure their alignment with specific network goals. I expect many companies will design networking scorecards that managers and employees will use to align and target specific network metrics.

Performance criteria for the number of ties generally, strong and weak ties, brokerage age, and the relative number of ties compared with that of the group can be constructed. In fact, tracking and managing these metrics may create greater awareness of the link between proper networking and high performance if employees observe that aligning their networks generates better personal performance. This can in turn further reinforce aligned networking. As with all performance scorecards, these metrics may not be perfectly measured, and employees might "game the system" by fulfilling their letter but not their spirit., and in these cases unaligned behavior will continue. Nonetheless, performance-oriented discussion of networking will yield some benefits.

COMPENSATION, RETENTION, AND TURNOVER

Like all elements of the HR system, performance management should be carefully tied to compensation to achieve the best results. There is debate on whether "pay-for-performance" schemes, which reward employees based on job achievement, are effective motivators.[17]Some evidence suggests that tactical changes in pay structure meant to reward employees can backfire and decrease motivation if they commoditize employees' efforts, create inequity, or focus the workforce excessively on extrinsic rewards. Such challenges can affect retention and turnover,[18] especially with work that requires tacit knowledge or hard-won expertise tied to a professional identity, where intrinsic motivation is necessary and the monitoring of task performance before project completion is difficult.[19]

Nonetheless, having some linkage between compensation and overall performance does appear to be an important and ideal practice for high-performing organizations. Often, the key is to reward employees based on long-term performance over multiple projects. Managers must properly attribute improvements (or declines) in performance to underlying efforts or skills versus uncontrollable environmental factors. Indeed, compensation is often driven by the external market for employees and their skills, and any compensation system must be sensitive to external compensation levels so that managers will be willing to make counteroffers to acquire and retain key talent.

I found that compensation can also be tied to the network performance management systems described earlier. Sometimes, particularly egregious antisocial and disloyal network misalignments emerge, and interventions to address them can be designed. More often than not, however, network performance management should proceed at a more cautious pace. It must be admitted that network ties are often formed randomly, and a momentary surge in too many ties or weak ties does not always signal a definitive and intentional misalignment in networking activity. However, with the use of networking-monitoring tools, a more long-term pattern can often be discerned and rewarded appropriately. Accordingly, employees can be given the benefit of the doubt in the short term, with compensation tied to long-term networking patterns. Negative compensation can be used in cases of extreme misalignment, while positive compensation such as bonuses, raises, and promotions can be used more liberally.

In fact, a good deal of HR research supports the idea that much of the variation in compensation is explained by social networks themselves.[20] Being well liked by bosses and other stakeholders predicts wages and promotions. Political networking for career gain is common in organizations, and many of the ties created do not serve—or actively thwart—organizational purposes. In fact, high potentials may be a particularly risky employee category in this regard, as they often have greater social skills and higher aspirations and so engage in political networking more often. This makes them more effective at misalignment should they choose it. Having some clarity about the pay and bonus schedule and its link to objectively measured performance can reduce inducements to game the system by developing connections with internal stakeholders who influence this process.

CAREER DEVELOPMENT

For new and old employees alike, performing at high levels may require skill acquisition to meet the demands of their roles. This is especially important in highly dynamic environments in which roles continually change to meet new organizational objectives. New skills can be of a functional or technical nature, such as learning new accounting rules or a new database. However, they may also be related to working with or leading others. As organizational objectives change, new and different intraorganizational collaborations may be required.

Certainly, learning new skills takes time and cannot be sacrificed to short-term pressure. Assuming a management team can make these investments, some career and talent development practices should promote appropriate networking behaviors. For instance, career development often involves carefully crafting mentorship and collegial relationships from which employees can acquire skills. This can be done judiciously by enabling employees to work with other employees but perhaps not too many. Often, career and talent development opportunities come in the guise of the job design itself. Of course, jobs are usually designed with organizational goals in mind, but an additional function may be to involve employees in appropriate networking role models and experiences.

In fact, research in strategic HR and talent development has identified some high-performance HR practices that might be viewed in light of network agency as well. For instance, routine job rotation, where early employees intentionally take on a series of job experiences, can accelerate learning. In fact, in many well-performing organizations, job rotation has become an important part of career progression. This, too, may be viewed from a network agency perspective. Job rotation can lead to political tie formation and empire building if taken too far, but if done conscientiously, job rotation can be used to engineer an appropriately diverse social network that does not veer into pathology. The key is to have managerial involvement in monitoring and in influencing networking behaviors that employees are learning and the resulting networks.

This exploration of HR practices is only the tip of the iceberg. The field of strategic resource management has highlighted several organization-wide practices that have an effect on the deeper culture and purposes of organizations and that might engender a more aligned organization. Further research might productively focus on strategic social capital management—how individuals develop networks in light of organizational objectives—to go along with the renewed interest in strategic human capital management.

A broader insight is that intervention to mitigate network agency problems may happen at multiple levels. Line managers of all types—product managers, program managers, unit heads—will continue to undertake specific interventions when network agency problems emerge. As noted in earlier chapters, we might expect some positive effects, but they may not persist if networking incentives remain in place. A snapback to the prior networking state might be expected if continual managerial attention and energy are not applied to the problem.

Instead, it is the function of the executive to effect broader organizational changes around network agency problems. Executives manage the organization's top managers and sometimes need to intervene in their maladaptive networking. However, executives have a greater responsibility—and capability—to create lasting organizational activities, policies, routines, programs, and practices that may have a broader effect on the organization's culture and purpose. These may involve leveraging novel organizational functions such as the HR group to institutionalize these practices. In fact, there is some indication that changes to broader organizational design may be the executive's ultimate lever in mitigating the impact of network agency problems. These changes may go far beyond the HR function and involve business units or even the C-suite itself. Chapter 8 focuses on these broader organizational design issues.

Network Governance

REINTERPRETING ORGANIZATIONAL
DESIGN AND BOUNDARIES

This chapter develops implications of network agency theory for organization design and boundary choices in network governance. Network agency issues underlying classic design problems like silos, conflicting coalitions, and inadequate matrix structures are developed. Network agency problems are developed as a novel theory of the firm - that is, firms exist and thrive because they better mitigate misalignments in networking incentives than some market forms.

ORGANIZATION DESIGN THROUGH
THE NETWORK AGENCY LENS

A key feature of well-functioning organizations is that they comprise individuals who are able to achieve complex goals requiring members to exhibit exceptional command of their specializations and coordinate among themselves. Since many of these goals pertain to long-standing and repeatable organizational objectives, the manner of arrangement of the individuals coalesces around a common organizational structure that can be shaped by management over time. Coordinated arrangements of individuals in specialized roles are the domain of organization design.[1]

Much of the research on organization design centers on organizational hierarchy and the span of control that managers exert over employees or on the clustering of individuals into divisions, units, or teams.[2] Hierarchy and units are under the formal control of managers, who can design and redesign these elements in order to better fulfill organizational objectives. In fact, reorganization efforts often focus on creating new roles with new reporting relationships or on combining units to achieve rationalization. Managers achieve these new designs by fiat, as hierarchical authority and unit divisions are under their formal control. Organization design scholars have effectively quantified such measures as the concentration of managers' span of control and the centralization of decision making. Armed with these statistics, they can track the changes observable in different features of design and their associated outcomes.

For quite some time, social networks, too, have been a subject of interest in organization design. Social networks differ from reporting relationships in that they have social as well as work purposes, are horizontal as well as vertical, and are not under management's direct control. Although social networks differ from other elements of organization structure, managers may have some capacity to proscribe or prescribe interactions between individuals. This means that networks are in their sphere of influence. For instance, managers may ask employees not to connect to brokers or ask two employees to start working together. As I described in earlier chapters, these directives may impact the shaping of informal social relationships, at least for a limited time.

The literature on organizational design has demonstrated that informal social relationships matter at least as much as formal directives in shaping organization-wide outcomes. More specifically, external connectivity matters in achieving organizational goals.[3] In fact, some scholars have used network representations of design problems to improve understanding of how formal and informal mechanisms interact. For instance, reporting relationships can be represented using directed networks in which an employee may report to their boss and, of course, not vice versa. Moreover, task interdependencies in workflows can be represented in network design matrices—these task interdependencies often imply that social relationships must be facilitated between those who work together with specialized expertise. Such analyses can use network statistics, such as centrality and constraint, with similar logic in order to suggest that some designs are more effective than others.

Perhaps the largest difference between network analyses used in organizational design and those used in the assessment of social relationships in organizations is that the literature on organization design makes greater use of configurational thinking and does not solely concentrate on broader structural features. For instance, contingency theorists have often argued that specific configurations of people in different roles are necessary to leverage emerging market opportunities. That is, managers often require specific sets of people in different roles to achieve goals, not a generic team with the right adequate centralization or interdependence measures, for example. Although generic structural features such as degree of concentrated authority or centralized communication may be marginally more effective, specific opportunities require specific configurations irrespective of the current average statistical measure.

In fact, a very specific form of this logic underlies the mirroring hypothesis, which suggests that an organization design that mirrors the constraints of the market is best able to perform in it.[4] The mirroring hypothesis is quite crucial, as it can be extrapolated to visualize large organizations, hierarchy levels, or the number of specialized roles in the organization. Perhaps the most famous example of mirroring is the degree of interdependence between the technical elements of products that meet customer needs and the interdependency between people or units that produce each technical element in an organization. Proponents of the mirroring hypothesis suggest that, since considerable interdependence among technologies is necessary, there should be a greater degree of interdependence in communication and decision-making among the people who make decisions. Some evidence seems to support this view.

Equipped with both broad statistical measures of design features and with analyses of specific design configurations, organization design scholars have gathered compelling insights into how relatively stable structures shape organizations and the very process of organizing. In some of the most promising work exploring this idea, organization design scholars have identified various design problems, including the classical ones—silos, bottlenecks, competing coalitions—and have explored remedies for them. I outline some of these core design problems in this chapter. In this chapter, however, I offer a different interpretation based on the network agency theory developed here. I suggest that each of these classical organization design problems can be reinterpreted as a combination of persistent underlying problems of network agency. Many chronic organization-wide challenges associated with organization design failures are actually attributable to misaligned network incentives that can only be treated by a thorough reorientation of network interests and behavior.

REINTERPRETING ORGANIZATIONAL SILOS

Silos are a major problem in organizations. They are defined as groups of individuals isolated from other groups. Because silos rarely interact, valuable information, perspectives, and resources rarely flow between them. This creates problems when organizational objectives require more intensive collaboration and coordination across silo boundaries.

In fact, many organizational problems are blamed on silos, and employees and managers alike are quick to complain about them.[5] For instance, silos often act as an impediment to translating customer needs into products, largely because marketers, who might better understand customer requirements, rarely interact with engineers, who are responsible for generating solutions. Functional groups often create their own silos, as those with different professional expertise, and coming from different backgrounds, speak different professional languages and have few opportunities to interact. Silos make it harder for individuals in different functional groups to interact, and the limited possibilities of interaction and the difficulty of cross-specialization communication is responsible for many lost opportunities for collaboration.

Silos can also be geographic in nature, as employees from different physical locations, such as those in different regions of a multinational company, can sometimes fail to work together to serve customers who span geographies. The difficulty of communicating and building trust across geographical distance is often to blame in such cases. Silos can also span hierarchies or different business units; for example, executives can act as a silo and not communicate well with groups below (e.g., middle managers) or above (e.g., boards of directors) or lateral to them (e.g., adjacent divisions).

Organization design offers an intuitive network-based explanation for these and other silo phenomena. Its central argument is that each silo can be thought of as a networked cluster of individuals, where members have too few connections with individuals in other clusters. Individuals in different clusters are more socially distant than individuals within clusters because they share fewer common connections. New, more socially distant relationships are harder to form, as they lack the social support of others in these fledgling relationships.[6]

In this view, the lack of connectivity between clusters explains their inability to collaborate, learn together, or trust each other sufficiently to achieve organizational goals. Clusters often form around formally designated groups such as functions, units, or locations. Formal boundaries are often cited as the reason that insufficient numbers of individuals interact, thereby creating boundaries. The argument is that silos reflect an equilibrium of too few boundary-spanning ties that inhibits effective intergroup collaboration.

As the lack of boundary-spanning ties is thought to be the core problem, the most recommended interventions often involve encouraging individuals to form these ties among clusters, perhaps by formalizing boundary-spanning roles. Joint projects, where cross-silo teams are formed, can engender new boundary-spanning relationships that may prove useful in the future. Also a complete redesign of the structure can formalize new relationships and create a broader culture of cooperation, all with the objective of rectifying the problem of too few boundary-spanning ties.

A network agency perspective offers an alternative explanation to the problem of silos. It regards silos as a result of different network interests. Individuals are interested in forming too many ties, leading to an unequal distribution of ties that does not reflect what is in the organization's interests. Rampant tie formation and the establishment of hubs have a higher likelihood of creating clusters that are disconnected—a hallmark of silos. In other words, the ultimate cause of organizational silos is not too few ties between clusters but too many ties that create clusters in the first place. As more ties are formed within clusters, less attention, energy, and resources are spent on creating ties outside them. That is, having too few boundary-spanning ties is an epiphenomenon to having too many within-group ties.

Clustering reflects path dependence: individuals who are indirectly connected are more likely to form direct ties and thus create a network cluster. When formal groupings such as units, functions, or locations are imposed on a network, the incentive to form ties within those units is increased, which exacerbates the clustering problem. Forming ties within group boundaries is easier and less risky, and individuals can afford to maintain weaker ties since the group boundary provides some reassurance that the ties are legitimate. Consequently, because of many easier, weaker ties in the group, individuals tend to experience less urgency to form riskier, more difficult ties outside the group. Although the more socially distant or boundary-spanning ties may have a higher value for the organization, since they are indeed riskier, individuals prefer to focus their networking specifically within their cluster. In many cases, then, the true cause of too few boundary-spanning ties may be network agency problems, which lead individuals to form ties only within their own cluster.

To be clear, the argument here is not that socially distant ties between clusters or boundary-spanning ties are unnecessary.[7] According to the network agency theory, insufficient distant and boundary-spanning ties are the proximate cause of silo problems, whereas misaligned networking interests that create silos are the ultimate cause. The theory has numerous practical implications. It suggests that attempts to cajole employees to form those ties are likely to be met with resistance and snapback unless the core problem is resolved. Changing networking interests that form clusters of ties should likely precede distant tie and boundary-spanning tie facilitation by managers. Network agency theory's focus on economic and political interests differs from prior silo theories that tended to emphasize the information-processing perspective. Issues such as inefficiency and learning that appear to be simple information-processing dilemmas resulting from the challenges of socially distant and boundary-spanning ties may have a deeper cost in terms of misaligned incentives.

CONFLICTING COALITIONS

Another organizational problem related to network clustering is conflict between organizational coalitions. Conflicting coalitions and silos bear some resemblance, as they both involve relational clusters of densely interconnected individuals as their network representation. However, conflicting coalitions differ from silos in that they often act as a group with common interests and goals. However, similar to silos they tend to have more internal connectivity within coalitions rather than external connectivity across coalitions. Coalitions often find themselves in competition with other coalitions if their goals conflict.[8]

Sometimes competition among groups can be productive. A classic example is the design of multidivisional firms, where different divisions compete to secure resources from an overarching corporate group by showcasing their growth prospects and divisional charters. As resources are limited, resource-seeking coalitions find themselves in conflict, although it is sometimes productive if constructive conflicts generate better resource allocation for the firm.

Yet, in many cases competition between coalitions can be unhealthy as it can turn emotional, acrimonious, and destructive, resulting in a net negative for the organization. When individuals complain of excessive organizational politics, what they are often referring to is the destructive pressure of maintaining membership in one coalition and eschewing affiliation with a competing coalition. One hallmark of this destructive competition is that organizational members wish for other coalitions' interests to fail and may, in fact, put more active energy into ensuring their failure than into advancing organizational interests.

Like silos, competing coalitions have an organizational explanation related to conflicting networking interests. Although too few ties between competing coalitions may be a proximate cause of conflict, too many ties may be its ultimate cause. Usually, organizational interests prevent competitive coalitions from forming around separate tightly linked clusters. However, individual interests may point in the opposite direction. A large number of ties within a coalition can signal group membership that mitigates risk for individuals. Nevertheless, too many ties can create a highly coercive environment, where defections from coalitional interests are harshly sanctioned. Creating ties with others in a competing coalition can be one of the most visible defections. If intergroup competition emerges, it may result in destructive actions such as deliberate sabotage or the undermining of the opposing group's activities.

AMBIDEXTERITY AND STRUCTURAL DECOUPLING

Another important organizational design issue is the capacity of organization members to explore their environment for new opportunities. Typically, this problem is framed as a tension between organizational needs around both exploitation and exploration. The exploitation of existing resources and potentialities is, of course, a necessary aspect of well-functioning organizations. More often than not, though, effective exploitation can be taken for granted, as it occurs as a result of existing organizational routines and structures. The greater challenge lies in ensuring sufficient exploration to respond to discontinuities and disruptions in the environment.

Exploration requires new behaviors, new thinking, and new resources to be assembled in ways that are not obvious. Exploration projects may also be riskier for both organizations and the individual members involved because the cost of failure can be high. Since ongoing exploitation is necessary for survival, exploration is sacrificed in times of crisis. The literature suggests that a real trade-off exists between exploitation and exploration, as the two activities are qualitatively different. Learning to be effective at both exploration and exploitation can be extremely difficult, and individuals and groups that must do both are often less effective at both. Given the asymmetric risks in this trade-off, we might expect exploration to be more neglected and underinvested relative to exploitation.

Organization design research has dedicated significant time to understanding structures and routines that enable sufficient exploration. A key metaphor is "ambidexterity"—the idea that organizations should be capable of using both hands—that is, both exploration and exploitation. Similar to ambidextrous individuals who use both hands with great skill, a few ambidextrous organizations sustain sufficient exploitation and exploration in order to survive and even thrive.[9]

The literature on ambidexterity suggests that the core solution to the problems of exploration and exploitation is structural decoupling. Structural decoupling separates the activities and routines associated with exploration and exploitation by creating separate organizational structures for them. A separate exploration unit is often formed to house activities promoting innovation and capturing new opportunities. Since learning to be effective at both exploration and exploitation is challenging, members of the organization may be specialized in one activity. With structural decoupling, these individuals can be grouped according to their area of specialization and thereby enjoy the benefits of collaborating with similarly oriented individuals. The central argument in structural decoupling is that a separation of exploration and exploitation activities is critical for achieving objectives, since it helps gather the expertise and focus to be directed at each. There is evidence to indicate that structural decoupling produces enhanced exploration, although those gains may dissipate over time as the exploration group becomes more inertial.

Network agency theory suggests a perspective that focuses on conflicts of interest in the formation and maintenance of ties in different organizational structures. It accepts some basic tenets of the ambidexterity theory, such as that organizations often struggle with exploration and that structural decoupling appears to help. A different explanation is provided for this dysfunction, with a different manner of resolution. As noted throughout the book, many network agency problems such as too many ties, weak ties, and entrenched brokers tend to have negative effects. Many of these structural features are in fact associated with difficulties in generating exploration. Too many ties create obligations for interaction and attentional deficits, which in turn curtail the higher resource needs of exploration. Weak ties form an inadequate foundation for riskier projects that require assembling diverse and heterogeneous resources, as exploration often does. Moreover, entrenched brokers often resist new bridging ties that are necessary for exploration. In other words, insufficient exploration can be explained by underlying network agency mechanisms.

The utility of structural decoupling can also be explained by network agency theory. The creation of separate exploration units typically entails the severing of existing ties and the facilitation of new ones. Many older, weak ties and entrenched brokers may be disrupted in the process as they are reassigned to new units. The structure of these smaller groups may accommodate easier monitoring and intervention in their networks, such that a smaller number of stronger ties can be created. That is, structural decoupling may succeed precisely because it mitigates the network agency problems that had inhibited innovation.

Network agency theory may also explain the eventual decline in exploration with the aging of separate exploration units. This phenomenon is sometimes noted by ambidexterity research. Over time, structurally separate exploration units are likely to have networks that rapidly increase ties and become weaker. Indeed, some entrenched brokers may emerge as well. Successful new groupings in fact often grow, which can compound problems of unchecked network growth. Eventually, new units can have network problems as severe as those of old units. Network agency theory can explain the eventual decline in exploration through new units as a form of snapback to network pathologies in the parent organization.

GENERALIZING ORGANIZATIONAL DESIGN PROBLEMS: INFORMATION BOTTLENECKS, MATRIX STRUCTURES, AND ADHOCRACY

The discussion just concluded provides some indication of how the major problems in organization design research can be interpreted through the network agency theory. Indeed, it is possible that many other organization design issues can be productively interpreted through this lens. For instance, decision and information bottlenecks often plague organizations. Bottlenecks emerge when one individual or group has so much authority or control that they delay decisions or information flow due either to the limited attention they offer or to conflicting interests.[10] In fact, many bottlenecks are actually entrenched brokers who have networking interests that conflict with organizational imperatives to pass along information or facilitate interactions that can eliminate the bottleneck.

A common organization design is the matrix. Matrix structures, which were popular in the 1990s, combine formal "vertical" lines of authority with formal "horizontal" connections between individuals in different teams, units, and divisions. Typically, horizontal connections involve consultation and other interactions, and have the objective of sharing information and enhancing boundary-spanning interactions that can lead to innovation. The challenge, however, is that matrix organizations have been found to decelerate innovation and consume the organization in interactions.[11] A network agency interpretation may be applicable if these formal connections give rise to long-standing social relationships that constitute "too many ties." The network agency mechanisms stemming from too many ties related to split attention and lack of learning can underpin the decline of organizational innovation associated with matrix structures.

Some have suggested that organizations should do away with formal structure altogether and implement an "adhocracy," or "holacracy", which has no formal authority figures and employees figure things out on their own. This structure was made popular by the electronic shoe seller Zappos[12], who attempted to implement adhocracy before the company was acquired by Amazon. Research reveals that, although a formal structure is missing from an adhocracy, an informal structure quickly emerges. As predicted by network agency theory, with no managers to intervene in networks, the social capital pathologies from before will be generated, including too many ties, ties that are too weak, and so on. Although no precise network measures were taken with Zappos, there is some indication that this occurred as employees formed entrenched clusters that may have decelerated growth. We will return later to the case of little or no formal structure.

Finally, network agency theory may help explain some organizational designs that appear to be functional. For example, Podolny and Hansen's (2020) research on Apple's organization design noted some unique features

that support innovation.[13] One is the overall functional organization structure, which differs from that of many technology companies organized by
business unit. Another is the proliferation of many small teams of experts.
Finally, there are very few professional or middle managers; rather, tech-
nologists take on management roles so that experts lead experts. These
unique structures may support innovation by diminishing network agency
problems. By eschewing business units and low-skill professional managers, greater alignment around technology goals is created and nontechnical
networking activity is reduced. An emphasis on small teams can diminish
entrenched brokerage and network inequality.

Of course, these interpretations are merely speculations, but it appears
that both positive and negative organization designs may be better understood with the help of network agency mechanisms. In fact, it is not surprising that agency problems related to the informal social network may be
an underlying cause of the effects of organization design, since the formal
features are more amenable to intervention. As observed before, network
agency problems can be persistent, even in the face of managerial interventions. At the least, this suggests that empirical studies of organization design
should measure network features to note if underlying networking interests
are an alternative explanation or a mediating mechanism.

ORGANIZATIONAL BOUNDARIES IN A NETWORKED
FIRM: TOWARD NETWORK GOVERNANCE

This book has focused on networks within organizations, including both the
value that they add and the problems inherent in them. It documents how
individual interests drive networking behavior in organizations. Yet many
studies on social capital illustrate how similar interests are more broadly
constituted, as individuals form ties outside of organizations—in markets,
communities, or society as a whole. In other words, networks are pervasive:
they exist within, outside, and across organizational boundaries. They overlap organizations and vice versa. This implies that networks and organizations are two separate social facts that share the same actors—individuals—
who are key to their functioning and existence. Thus, it is reasonable to ask
how organizations and networks interact.

This question can be viewed from a variety of angles, since individuals
undoubtedly use networks to compete and collaborate within, outside, and

across organizations. The most prominent strand of research on network and organizational interactions is also related to the interface of organizations and their environment, especially organizational boundaries. Organizational boundaries can be understood in many different ways to determine what exactly constitutes the organization. Typically, organizational boundaries delimit the people, activities, and resources employed to achieve organizational objectives.[14] Consequently, boundaries have become a critical object of study.

Theories in organizational economics and organizational sociology have much to say about what people, activities, and resources come to reside *inside* versus *outside* organizational boundaries. While organizational economics emphasize efficiency rationales for why an organization should internalize some activities but externalize others, organizational sociology focuses on social causes of organizational boundaries, including social network influences such as the dependence of hiring decisions on network referrals. Yet what these theories have in common is the consequentiality of organizational boundaries to shape a wide variety of outcomes. These outcomes include what activities the organization will perform, whether products or services should be made or bought, whether forward or backward integration into the value chain should be carried out, what knowledge is integrated into the whole, who can count themselves a member, and the identity of the organization and its members.

THEORIES OF THE FIRM: FROM DISPARATE PROXIMATE
CAUSES TO COMMON NETWORK ULTIMATE CAUSE

While all these organizational topics have used networks and boundaries in their theorizing, it is possible that the line of inquiry falling under the rubric "theory of the firm" is the most fundamental. This research asks a fundamental question: Why are there firms at all? Why do individuals not interact on their own without an organization? Underlying this question is the basic notion that individuals have sufficient capabilities to transact in markets on their own, in some cases even using complex coordination without the need for formal organizational boundaries to delimit membership and activities. If organizations exist, they must offer some functional value to some of the parties involved to maintain it. Otherwise, participants would not bear the additional cost of organizational establishment, continuation, and membership. In other words, if they had no useful function, firms would not exist. So, why do firms exist?[15]

There are various theories of the firm. The most prominent stem from organizational economics, with a focus on the costs incurred between individuals as they engage in economic exchange—transaction costs. Although transaction costs between any two individuals may be small, the sum of these costs across collections of individuals—small groups, communities, or societies—may be sufficiently large to hold it back from achieving goals that would benefit the organization and its members. In transaction cost theories of the firm, firms exist because some transactions are carried out at a lower cost when they are within the boundaries of a stable organization. Thus, firms exist because they serve a useful function of transaction cost reduction.

The boundaries and structures of formal organizations help groups reduce transaction costs if individual members are more effective than doing the same activities in the market, thereby supporting the rationale for the firm's continued existence. The original treatments of transaction cost theory argued that firms internalize activities under various conditions whereby transaction costs are minimized, including asset specificity, high frequency, uncertainty, and the possibility for opportunistic market behavior. Other theories suggest that the uniqueness of knowledge-based resources underlies the existence of organizations, since formal organizations are well suited to sustaining tacit knowledge, producing joint knowledge, and coordinating different knowledge bases.

Some theories are even more deeply socialized. For example, voice theory suggests that formal organizations function to preserve voice rights, which determine who is allowed to speak on behalf of the group. Moreover, identity can be a powerful driver of organizational substance, as internal members and external audiences come to expect useful identity-congruent responses from a firm, leading to the firm's sustainability.

NETWORKS UNDERLYING ECONOMIC AND SOCIAL THEORIES OF THE FIRM

Theories of the firm usually take very little consideration of social networks. However, given the ubiquity of networks in almost all social contexts, it is reasonable to regard them as a fundamental social fact, or at least more so than formal organizations, which are a more historically bounded phenomenon. That is, social networks have existed as long as the human species has, whereas large-scale, bureaucratized formal organizations are a recent civilizational fact.

In fact, network mechanisms might underlie the core concerns of many theories of the firm. For example, network rationales are already well linked with the knowledge-based view and theory of the firm. The knowledge required to achieve complex objectives is often widely distributed among individuals. Networks enable information to flow via knowledge transfer mechanisms, to be shared through collaboration, and to be recombined in order to generate innovation. Without networks, knowledge may not constitute a rationale for the existence of firms.

Networks may also underlie transaction costs in organizations and markets. For instance, although the rationale in make-or-buy decisions concerns whether it is cheaper to internalize or externalize transaction costs, it is often the network itself that determines these costs.[16] Well-functioning networks with strong ties, for instance, are necessary to reduce transaction costs related to the mistrust or miscommunication that often occurs in market transactions. Moreover, as this book has argued elsewhere, the effectiveness of networks may be the key variable in determining which organization should take on certain activities. For example, if one organization's network is less effective at producing components than another's, the most efficient vertical integration decision may be to place component production in the hands of the latter firm, with all else equal.

One of the most famous examples in the literature on make-or-buy decisions is General Motor's acquisition of its supplier, Fisher Body.[17] The case is often used to illustrate the consequence of holdup by a key supplier and how internalization may be one of the few solutions to this problem. There is some debate about the specific cause of the acquisition, whether it was related to Fisher Body demanding better terms for its components and creating an intolerable situation for GM or it was a disagreement between the two parties about the location of the Fisher Body assembly plant. GM wanted the body plant to be closer to its new manufacturing capabilities, whereas Fisher Body preferred to maintain its location to serve not only GM but its other customers that were nearby. Whatever the proximate cause, it became clear that Fisher Body's management team had intense fortitude in its long resistance to GM's demands before ultimately relenting and accepting its high acquisition offer.

A network account can be found in this famous case related to the theory of the firm. What enabled Fisher Body to resist so effectively? What is often unsaid but clear in the case details is that a tight cadre of managers, the Fisher family, and their longstanding investors, the Mendelssohns, were united. Certainly, these long-standing and strong relationships between the operators and a small group of investors were a vital factor in their capacity to resist the entreaties of their largest exchange partner for so long. Of course, this is but one case where the counterfactual data is not available to fully test these ideas. But it would not be surprising if many more network mechanisms underlie other economic theories of the firm.

Moreover, the more highly socialized theories of the firm, including theories emphasizing organizational voice and identity, may be dependent on network processes as well.[18] In fact, it is networks that allow individuals to converge on a common identifying frame and point of view of who is best positioned to speak for a group. In fact, identity and voice may be particularly powerful forces that vary across industries precisely because their underlying network conditions also vary. For example, a positive identity and a unified voice may be harder to establish in the typical Silicon Valley high-technology firm because of the effect of high turnover on its networks. This may offer an alternative explanation for why new-organization churn differs from the typical product-oriented explanations of organizational disruption.

The broader argument here is that, although prior theories of the firm may postulate disparate proximate causes for the existence of firms (e.g., transaction costs, knowledge, identity, voice), networks may be the ultimate factor behind these dynamics. They may be the largest driver of transaction cost reduction, knowledge preservation, identity construction, and voice rights. This is not to say that networks account for all variation in these concepts, but given the apparent stability of this common cause, it is suggested that networks can be thought of as a metatheory of the firm. In fact, this idea has some scholarly precedents. The research presented in Chapter 7 adds a network agency perspective: the major barrier to constructing optimal networks for firms to flourish appears to be conflicts of interest in networking, which allow social capital pathologies to flourish. Network agency problems may be the key mechanism connecting networks with the existence of firms and their variable performance. One aspect adding to the attractiveness of a network theory of the firm is that network visibility is enacted consciously every day through interactions and is therefore at least partially susceptible to managerial intervention, as observed in Chapter 7. It is sometimes more difficult to intervene directly in processes involving knowledge, transaction cost, identity, and voice constructs.

The view just expressed is consistent with sociological perspectives on organizational boundaries, which view individual networks as the backdrop against which organizations are formed. In this view, the appropriate counterfactual argument for the existence of firms involves not some anonymous, undersocialized individuals transacting in a market but rather a network of individuals with a history of relations. Put precisely, we should consider how networked individuals interacting in organizations provide benefits to those individuals interacting in networks outside organizations. What advantages do networks embedded in organizations offer over networks in markets? The theory of the firm can be reframed to give primacy to networks: How does a network of individuals differ from an organization? Why do organizations exist at all if a network can serve as an adequate substitute? Reframing the theory of the firm as a network agency issue may be a productive way to proceed.

What has been challenging in constructing a network theory of the firm is that most research and theorizing have adopted an individual unit of analysis, with models focusing on variation in individual outcomes due to social capital. Network agency theory shows promise in forming a detailed network theory of the firm itself, as its view of network effectiveness is organizational, with firm-level dependent variables being a natural analytical construct stemming from its predictions. Differing individual and organizational interests in networking can underlie a variety of agency costs that shape make-or-buy decisions or the prospects of firm sustainability. While the sketch presented does not count as a fully fleshed-out theory of the firm, it does suggest that network agency problems may be at the heart of some future investigations.

Network Agency over the Life Cycle

ENTREPRENEURSHIP AND INNOVATION ECOSYSTEMS

This chapter develops implications of network agency theory for different types
of organizations as they evolve over the lifecycle, namely entrepreneurial and
established organization. Heterogeneity in different agency costs related to
bonding, monitoring, and intervention is used to explain typical organizational
lifecycle differences. Network agency ideas are used to explain fundamental
differences in organizational forms for innovation, namely closed innovation
leveraging corporate structures and open innovation as in open source
communities.

NETWORK AGENCY COSTS IN ENTREPRENEURIAL
VERSUS ESTABLISHED ORGANIZATIONS

One of the clearest applications of a network agency perspective is consideration of how network agency problems change over the life cycle of an organization. In fact, organization theorists have accumulated significant evidence on how organizations generally proceed along the life cycle. Although organizations have substantial heterogeneity in terms of their structure and functions, a consistent pattern of organizational aging is observed in many studies. When organizations are founded, they usually start small,

with only a few employees outside of the founders themselves. These nascent organizations may be effective in meeting niche market demands or
developing new technologies, yet they face the liability of newness, which
is associated with a lack of resources, low market power, and insufficient
organizational routines and structures to accomplish goals. They also suffer
from insufficiently developed identity, reputation, and legitimacy. The ones
fortunate enough to survive and grow typically do so by adding members
in order to broaden their reach in the activities the new members perform.
Yet as organizations become more established, their growth may slow and
innovation declines. This is sometimes called the liability of aging or obsolescence, and it results from inertial pressures, as resource commitments are
difficult to unwind, routines and structures are too complex and unrespon-
sive to stakeholder needs, and organizational identity is mismatched with
what is valued in the market.[1]

Networks have always had some role to play in explanations of organizational life-cycle impact. For instance, forming entrepreneurial networks
may be the key to overcoming the liabilities of newness associated with
inadequate resource acquisition or failures of industrial coordination. Although it is difficult and costly to form new network ties, evidence suggests
that entrepreneurial firms that do so enhance their path to profitability and
growth. On the other hand, networks may also be a key element of inertia
because they are difficult to change. Stable relationships may constitute the
core activities of an organization, but as networks grow, the large number of
ties makes it difficult to change.[2]

An agency theory perspective enables analysts to dig deeper into life-
cycle mechanisms. The key is to identify prominent sources of interest conflict, which are usually organizational circumstances that lead to incentive
misalignment, the unfolding that takes place as an organization ages and
grows. The resulting negative impacts that the organization absorbs are
referred to as "agency costs." In a similar vein, we can label negative impacts on the organization due to network interest misalignment as "network
agency costs." Agency costs can be measured, typically as the costs of managerial resources, since effort must be expended to mitigate costs or lost profit
potential due to misaligned agency behavior when it does occur. A key task
of governance is to find ways of realigning interests, changing behavior, and
thereby minimizing agency costs.[3]

Agency costs change over the life cycle of an organization. In the early days, the founders bear what are often called "bonding costs"—costs associated with aligning the initial interests of founders, partners, and other stakeholders in establishing the organization. In fact, many of these bonding costs are associated with networks. For instance, the founder's trust and agreement is crucial, and securing them may entail deep relational investment on the founder's part. Establishing an organization may involve severing some ties as well. For example, stakeholder divestment from other organizations leads to a conflict of interest. Of course, an organization can engage in reorganization, in which case it incurs rebounding costs. Arguably, these costs are much higher than the original costs for familiar reasons of organizational inertia. Networks are a part of inertia as well: compared with founding, reorganization often involves more dissolution, which is often more attention- and resource-intensive than formation.

Once the organization is established, the key costs associated with running it pertain to the effort, attention, and energy managers invest in monitoring and assessing agent behavior and its impact on performance. These costs also pertain to subsequently dealing with the consequences. Many of the network interventions described in this book are attempts to govern based on the ideas of network monitoring. For example, when managers attempt to sever ties associated with agency problems or facilitate new ones, they are implicitly engaging in network governance.

The agency cost that is seemingly most relevant for organizations in highly dynamic industries is "residual loss" in activities and opportunities that are foregone if agents pursue interests that obviate them. Perhaps the simplest way to think of these is as business opportunities not pursued because the organization is embroiled in conflict or has shifted to pursue the narrow private interests of a coalition of managers. As Williamson (1996) notes, residual loss is often the largest component of agency cost, and, perhaps not surprising the largest component of network agency as well, as many opportunities in the modern economy demand an appropriate network to pursue. High-risk opportunities are foregone when networks have many weak ties when it is strong ties that are needed. And many opportunities are not pursued if nonhubs choose not to collaborate in favor of maintaining connections with hubs.

A general argument can be made. In the early days of an entrepreneurial organization, bonding costs dominate other agency costs. Forming the initial connections between founders and early stakeholders is critical. Monitoring is less important, as the small set of stakeholders are already mostly aligned. Additionally, intervention may be unnecessary except in the specific cases of replacing a CEO or adding a new investor. Residual loss is negligible because the organization has been designed to capture specific opportunities, rendering others beyond the organizational scope by definition. This expectation for entrepreneurial organizations can be expressed with the following general inequalities:

Bonding costs $\gg$ Monitoring costs $>$ Intervention costs $\gg$ Residual loss

After some time, as the organization ages and becomes established, bonding costs are no longer or rarely incurred, but monitoring is necessary and extremely costly, as observing networks can be difficult. Taking action on network agency problems is usually much more taxing than observing them, which is why the intervention cost exceeds the monitoring cost. Yet residual loss is potentially greater than all other losses, which provides a window for the economic application of network governance because residual loss should be avoided if possible. The liability of obsolescence may be a state in which residual loss is so high that it can destroy value, defying mitigation through extensive monitoring and intervention. Thus, for established organizations, we may expect

Bonding costs $\ll$ Monitoring costs $<$ Intervention costs $\ll$ Residual loss

A network agency perspective may underlie the essential challenges associated with entrepreneurial and established organizations as well as the manner in which they differ. What is essential is the relative size of the costs at various stages. The preceding arguments suggest that the most established organizations in dynamic environments—for example, the big-tech firms discussed in this book—face a predictable ordering of network agency costs, whereby the governance involved in monitoring and intervention seeks to avoid large residual losses of social capital pathologies. Startups have a unique advantage in that they focus nearly all their resources on bonding costs and eschew governance until it becomes necessary.

This ordering explains the reason executives allocate some managerial resources to monitoring and intervention through network governance. Bonding costs are mostly incurred in the past and therefore constitute sunk costs that cannot be mitigated. Some rebonding may, however, occur in any restructuring or fundamental reorganization. This may explain why corporate entrepreneurs are often in search of opportunities to "start from scratch," whether in greenfield projects, corporate venturing, acquisition integration, joint ventures, or new alliances. Corporate entrepreneurship is an activity that prefers lower bonding costs over higher monitoring and intervention costs in the pursuit of new opportunities.

For example, managers I spoke with often said that they conducted technology collaborations in the same marketspace as their business units because doing so allowed them to "avoid internal politics," "act like entrepreneurs," and "make a new network." Each perspective involves bonding costs to create a new, albeit temporary, organizational configuration—one that is customized to the business opportunity at hand. In other words, the core rationale for both venture and corporate entrepreneurship can be explained with the help of network agency theory.

Network agency theory may also shed light on the way digital technologies are shifting the core challenges of entrepreneurial firms as opposed to established firms. The blue-sky model (Chapter 2) shows that digital technologies may have a more positive effect on entrepreneurial organizations than on established ones. As the adoption of digital technologies increases, the cost of networking falls. The effect is initially positive in smaller organizations, as digital technologies make it easier for startups to pass the threshold of network viability. This may explain why digital technologies enable some entrepreneurial organizations to operate very thinly staffed ventures and grow quickly, passing the unstable critical point that the model predicts. Thus, network growth may be a fundamental factor in explaining entrepreneurial scaling over time.

By contrast, the blue-sky model indicates that established organizations with networks that are already larger may be pulled toward a suboptimal critical point that is stable. It thus becomes difficult to dislodge the organizational system from a position of too much connectivity. Attempts to do so via managerial intervention may be temporarily effective but are not persistent; therefore, snapback to suboptimal levels may occur. The performance implications of the model are paradoxical: although digital technologies increase potential performance, most established organizations see diminished actual performance.

The allocation of network governance effort across time is an interesting subject of study. One can imagine how new ventures might face a difficult choice of when they should invest in network governance. While the venture tries to find its product and market fit, it may have a suboptimal number of ties, so it is essential for it to grow and enhance connectivity. Founder-managers may focus their effort there. After passing the critical point, however, networks may grow endogenously, without any necessity of external managerial energy. The key task then is to prevent rapid-scaling organizations from passing the optimum and becoming entrenched established organizations. This may be the ultimate "network pivot" that successful ventures make: moving from encouraging ties to discouraging ties.

In established, static organizations, managers discourage ties and thus constantly "pull back" from the suboptimal critical point and push toward the optimum. Yet, this may indeed be unrealistic, as continued monitoring and intervention may overoccupy managers. Managers, it must be remembered, have other tasks besides networking. A more optimal dynamic pattern may be oscillations of managerial effort to prune and refocus networks, allowing them to grow unchecked and then pruning and refocusing them. Some low monitoring cost can be borne to trigger higher intervention costs when they become necessary. Of course, these ideas are simply implications of the model and of arguments that came before. Other, superior strategies for managing network agency costs in different types of organizations must be discovered. This will likely depend on the environmental context and core activities if they shape networking interest and behavior.

OPEN VERSUS CLOSED INNOVATION: LINKING NETWORK AGENCY TO INNOVATION MANAGEMENT

The theory of the firm is related to an important issue in high-tech industries—the problem of open source. The open-source movement is made up of communities of individual software developers who voluntarily build computing systems together. Open source is usually organized in a distributed and decentralized fashion, and can be conceptualized as a virtual network of members who voluntarily contribute to an evolving codebase. This software is often free to use, and the contributors are uncompensated, at least in a direct manner. They may enjoy the reputational benefits they build in this public forum and derive satisfaction by contributing to open-source projects, which are usually intended for the public good.[4]

The open-source scenario is complicated by the many for-profit firms that use open source for their own advantage, to run back-end enterprise operations with servers and the corporate intranet. Many successful cloud-based companies such as Amazon and Microsoft use open-source software as part of their core systems, which they complement with proprietary offerings. Taking into account these full use cases of open software, upward of 50 percent of the software running systems today is actually open source, suggesting a real strength in this model.

Inspired by open-source software as a core example but widening the logic, some scholars have advanced a broader categorization of innovation systems. Many argue that open innovation, defined as individuals contributing freely to projects without organizational sanction or support, can be an effective generator of high-value innovations, and not only in the software sector. Individuals in an open-innovation ecosystem may contribute components to movements or content to blogs or video platforms.[5] This is in contrast to a closed-innovation ecosystem, which is enclosed within the boundaries of firms. Closed innovation enjoys the support of corporate management and the advantages of resource acquisition, but often lacks the crowd-sourcing element that drives novelty and creativity during innovation.

To be fair, organizations reached beyond their boundaries in order to innovate long before the advent of open-source software or the development of research on open innovation. Usually, this innovation developed through contracts and alliances around licensing or joint efforts with other firms.[6] Whether these should be classified as open or closed is a semantic designation, however. Sometimes, technology-focused alliances are labeled "collaborative innovation" in order to distinguish them from open and closed innovation.

It is clear that organizations engage in technology collaborations in order to access ideas, knowledge, and resources beyond their boundaries, even if they do so with an intent to appropriate the collaboration's value within their own boundaries, for the firm. In other words, collaborative innovation shares both advantages of openness in sourcing knowledge, ideas, and talent from beyond organizational boundaries and advantages of corporate control and resources.

The past decades have seen a newer organizational form emerge, the platform ecosystem, in which an organization develops a technology or a product platform on which many other organizations collaborate and compete through use of that technology or platform. This is sometimes called "eco-system innovation." As the theory goes, complementarities between organizations increase the value created in their ecosystems. Platform ecosystems, like alliances, can have open aspects in terms of knowledge sharing and spillover but organizational boundaries are sustained.

In fact, the emergence of an even newer organizational form of innovation, the blockchain ecosystem, suggests that open-source logic has broader implications. Blockchains enable entrepreneurs to compensate developers in a decentralized software system without the need for organizational boundaries.[7] Blockchain is perhaps open-source software's answer to venture capital in aligning incentives for early contributors. It is a form of open innovation that may have a network structure at its core.

Managers of large organizations face the dilemma of whether they should embrace open innovation. Although many of the best innovation ideas, knowledge, and resources can be generated outside the firm, open innovation often entails loss of control and difficulty in capturing the value of the innovation product. Although collaborative and ecosystem innovation offers relatively more control, it must ultimately be negotiated with ecosystem partners or complementors. Entrepreneurs and investors in startups face a similar dilemma of whether to invest in open-innovation projects, including those in blockchain ecosystems. The lack of control over project scope makes it difficult for individual investors to be confident of securing returns.

What the proliferation of open and closed elements in organizational forms makes clear is the importance of considering the attributes associated with their success. It would be useful to understand which form, open or closed, performs better and under what circumstances. Since the two share a network structure of some sort, the network agency theory developed here may have something to offer in viewing open-innovation ecosystems (open-source software, blockchains) and closed-innovation ecosystems (groups of firms, platform ecosystems) as networks.

For example, it may actually be a mystery that we do not see more open innovation, such as open source, given its apparent advantages over closed innovation. One can imagine the open form of production in many industries, and, indeed, it may be surprising that it has yet to take over software production. Open innovation offers great advantages in engendering ideas and broadening diversity; yet evidence suggests that its effectiveness may not be as strong as its proponents would like it to be. There are few empirical ways of testing whether any innovation project is better served by an open or closed approach, but we can ask some intriguing questions:. If open-source software is so powerful in mobilizing and sharing knowledge across broad networks, why do closed networks of firms continue to exist and create so much value and wealth? Open innovation is new; closed innovation is old. Why, then, has the former not completely replaced the latter?

This puzzle can partially be explained by the features of organizational networks that make them unique, including hierarchy, incentives, and managers. However, it appears that only the last of these may be truly unique. Hierarchy is observed in open source, particularly in terms of expertise, reputation, and status. For example, in the Linux open-source project, many individuals defer to Linus Torvalds, the project founder. Although he has no authority to make unilateral decisions for Linux, his opinion carries great weight. In addition, high-powered incentives are prominent in open blockchain communities, as described previously. Tokens give contributors direct incentives to improve a project. Yet most blockchains do not have centralized authority, by design.

In fact, it is the managerial role that is exclusive to closed organizations, as many proponents of open innovation are quick to point out. Managers can be viewed as the legitimate representatives of an organization, carrying the license and mandate to make important decisions regarding projects, resources, and people. Of interest in previous chapters were managerial interventions in individual relationships. Are managers playing any useful roles that open ecosystems lack? Do they give closed organizations any advantages?

It is useful to see these questions in light of network agency problems, which may exist in both closed and open ecosystems. The direct managerial interventions described in previous chapters often have some positive effect, even if temporary, thereby improving organizational outcomes. This in fact may be the agentic function of executives and management: to exert constant energy in mitigating these problems lest network dynamics turn pernicious. More sustainable interventions are meant to enhance strategic human resource capabilities in hiring, socialization, and culture that pay longer-run dividends in discouraging network agency problems.

Open-innovation systems may have many advantages, but they lack these managerial benefits. Networks growing without administrative limits can easily develop a preponderance of weak ties, entrenched brokers, and a few dominant hubs. In fact, these issues may explain why open innovation has been mainly confined to open-source software projects. Usually, these projects are focused on smaller, less complex systems with more modularity, meaning that individual contributors do not need extensive coordination, which limits the interdependent coordination problems that require managerial intervention.

The few successful large platforms generated by open source, such as the Linux operating system, have benefited from extreme modularity. Modularity requires standardized interfaces between components so that small groups or individuals can innovate on different elements of one system without affecting elements of other systems. In other words, it limits interdependencies that demand intervention for effective coordination.

This leaves a vast space of market opportunities that require broader coordination of rampant interdependencies, usually requiring strategic commitments in some areas that forestall commitments in other areas. That is, there are real, irreversible conflicts, organizations must commit to one path or the other in order to be successful. One manager told me he believed that the key to management was to "kick some butt and get people to focus for a higher goal." Yet the key question is: Focus on what? What is required to achieve that higher goal?

As detailed in previous chapters, a central difficulty in overcoming the conflicts and making strategic commitments is often the networks themselves. Network ties revolve around conflicting strategies, with the cultivation of networks itself becoming a strategy for many employees. Individuals focus on their own network objectives more than on the organization's, and relationships may be more entrenched than even ideas, strategies, or knowledge itself. Another view on closed organizational innovation is that it benefits from managerial mobilization of attention, the ability to direct rewards, and assignment of roles to counter natural individual tendencies that lead to unchecked network growth. This suggests that understanding different organizational forms of innovation may aid the resolution of network agency problems.

A Research Agenda

MORE CASES, MORE MODELS, MORE EXPERIMENTS

This chapter outlines a research agenda for network agency theory, including central questions to be answered about behavioral antecedents of network agency theory and the impact of misalignment between individual and organizational networking interests. I argue for the most fruitful application of inductive research methods such as case methods, simulation and analytical modeling, and experimentation.

The chapters that make up Part II of this book focused on the implications of network agency problems discussed in the first half. Their emphasis was whether the impact of network agency issues affect managerial and executive roles, the functioning of teams while working from home, the influence of human resource functions on social capital, the broader design and structuring of organizations, and whether organizations are sustainable and innovative enterprises. It is useful to review these issues before discussing a way for research.

Chapter 6 focused on the persistence of network agency problems. These problems exist in a dynamic equilibrium in which digital technologies amplify the misalignment of interests between organizations and individuals. Managerial interventions have positive effects but are not long-lasting, as pernicious social dynamics reemerge when managerial attention and energy are directed elsewhere.

Typically, digital technologies enable resistance to intervention more than they support it. That is, although managers may believe that the use of people analytics or surveillance technologies will assist in managerial intervention in network agency problems, they often find that employees adopt consumer technologies more fervently and use them to develop networks to serve their own interests more readily. At least in this study, these enterprise technologies supporting managerial interventions seemed to be less effective than the consumer technologies employees used to resist them.

Finally, various organizational factors that explain the persistence of network agency problems were found. First is a general resistance to organizational design efforts involving networks—a factor that seems to vary to some degree among people and across organizations. Network ignorance on the part of managers is another factor because lack of awareness of structural issues makes it difficult to diagnose and intervene in problems. Finally, managers often do not attribute negative outcomes to network agency issues as they should—this ironically leads them to overinvest in network growth, which exacerbates network agency problems.

Chapter 7 focused on how executives can have a broader mitigative effect on the impact of network agency problems faced by their organizations. The chapter identified the network function of the executive as being responsible for organization-wide changes that minimize conflicts of interest between individuals and the organization. One major challenge in exploring which interventions may work is fundamentally methodological. As executive action is often determined by organizational conditions, it is difficult to know if it is a true cause of organizational change.

The pandemic created a unique opportunity to examine causal changes to work practices, particularly those associated with technologies that enable remote work. Like some researchers, I found that the adoption of remote-work technology often had a negative effect on work outcomes. My investigation focused on network agency problems that appeared to cause these outcomes. These technologies dramatically increased the size of networks, the predominance of weaker digital relationships, and the ossification of brokerage positions as hubs. Although adoption of these technologies

Table 2: Organizational implications of network agency theory: persistence, organization design, and methods

Core issue	Findings and implications	Role of digital technology	Application areas
Network agency problem persistence and managerial interventions	Network agency problems persist if individual interests continue to outweigh organizational inducements Organizational Factors—design resistance, network ignorance, attribution errors—reinforce persistence Managerial interventions may have temporary positive impact Organizations snap back to network agency problems after managerial attention is removed	Digital technologies accelerate and amplify network agency problems Digital technologies may enable resistance to managerial intervention more than support it	Persistent performance differences Managerial effectiveness
Broader executive role in digital environments	Agentic function of the executive: broader organization design choices shaping culture, structure, and technology Strategic social capital functions—hiring, socialization, performance management, compensation—to mitigate network agency problems	Work-from-home experiment suggests remote/virtual technologies amplify network agency problems, along with isolation found by other researchers	Executive roles Organization culture, structure, and technology Strategic social capital function
Network governance through organization design and boundary management	Classic organization design problems—silos, coalitions, matrix, ambidexterity—may have underlying network agency explanations Organization boundary decisions to "make, buy, or partner" and avoid holdup may be shaped by network agency problems Network agency problems may explain why firms survive and thrive vs. market forms	Digital technologies that amplify network agency problems may be responsible for the re-emergence of organization design issues in companies	Organization design Boundary governance (e.g., "make or buy") Theory of the Firm

Core issue	Findings and implications	Role of digital technology	Application areas
Entrepreneur-ship and innovation over the life cycle	Differences in innovative capacity over the organiza-tional life cycle due to net-work agency cost differences Governance of organization forms—closed vs. open—have different forms of network agency governance	Digital technology that amplifies network agency problems may be responsible for shifting value of closed vs. open innovation approaches	Organizational life cycle Organization forms for closed vs. open innovation
Network agency research agenda: questions and methods	Fundamental questions in network agency theoriz-ing: microfoundations of network interest misalign-ments, structural factors shaping network interests, further research on man-agerial interventions and executive roles Methodological preferences in network agency research: inductive multiple cases, formal and simulation mod-eling, and organizational experiments	Digital technology is likely useful in data collection and analysis of network agency problems	Network agency theory

was necessary in many cases, it seemed to lead to some negative outcomes caused by increased network misalignment.

On a more positive note, new human resource practices were identified that seem to mitigate network agency problems. New strategic social capital practices related to hiring, socialization, performance management, and compensation can be designed from a network agency perspective that complement strategic human capital practices that have been emerging in the past few decades. The key is to use the human resource function and the hiring interface as an opportunity to mitigate future network agency problems.

Chapter 8 focused on the implications of network agency theory for organization design. Various organizational design problems, such as silos, conflicting coalitions, and inadequate matrix structures were shown to have a network agency interpretation. Many organization structures fail to perform adequately because they enable employees to form maladaptive network structures. This produces a useful conclusion that such design issues can be resolved if network agency mechanisms are managed.

Organizational implications are also explored for the so-called boundary choices that determine whether activities should naturally be performed within the organization itself or outside, in the market or another organization. These make-or-buy decisions are often at the core of organizational governance processes. A network agency approach suggests that agency costs associated with networks might underlie many core problems in network governance, such as strategic holdup by suppliers. The chapter ended with discussion of a network agency approach to the theory of the firm which asks, "Why do firms exist versus transactions in a market?" Viewing both organizations and markets as groups of individuals with potentially conflicting interests suggests a new perspective: firms exist and thrive because they mitigate misalignments in networking incentives better than market forms in certain circumstances.

Finally, Chapter 9 focused on how organizations age over their life cycle, as they grow from new startups to large, established organizations. In this chapter, typical problems with entrepreneurial venturing and innovative inertia as organizations age were interpreted via network agency theory. Different costs in the agency theory literature, such as bonding costs, monitoring costs, intervention costs, and residual loss were used to explain typical organizational life-cycle differences such as increasing inertia with age.

Network agency ideas are also used to explain fundamental differences in organizational forms for innovation: closed innovation leveraging corporate structures and open innovation leveraging communities. Viewing both closed and open forms as having a network structure at their center reframes the choice of innovation mode to be about which system is more effective at mitigating network agency problems. Despite the persistence of these problems, closed innovation can mobilize managerial agents to some positive effect over long periods of time, which is a significant advantage over open forms, which lack managers to make those interventions.

When taken together, the chapters in Part II indicate several fruitful avenues for examining the implications of network agency problems from a broader perspective of an organization's functioning beyond the direct impact of those problems on generalized performance. Sometimes indirect impacts on organizational outcomes derive from specific critical activities, such as technology adoption, the human resource function, organization design, and the innovation process. Of course, the ideas developed by case research were merely sketched and not presented in as much detail as would be preferred, yet they do indicate a broader agenda for future research, to which I now turn.

FUNDAMENTAL QUESTIONS IN NETWORK AGENCY THEORY

In this book, I have outlined a network agency theory that considers how misalignments among networking interests and behavior may generate social capital pathologies that cause broader organizational failures. However, if network agency theory is to evolve and thrive, it should address many critical questions in organizational life. In what follows, I pose a few questions that can be addressed in future research. The link that unites these questions is the idea of misalignments in networking interests and behavior between individuals and organizations.

Perhaps the most fundamental question in network agency theory is how networking misalignments arise in the first place. Some research may have assumed that social capital theory offers a guide for organizations when choosing networking approaches and what individual employees will actually enact. Yet once these assumptions are abandoned, it becomes clear that misalignments are at least as likely to occur as are alignments because individual and organizational interests may not be the same and individual employees will pursue their own networking interests even when those interests do not align with the organization's.

When and why do these network misalignments arise? This book examined a variety of causes, starting with the fundamental differences in risk profiles and preferences of individuals and organizations, and heterogeneity in the functions that networks perform for these actors at the micro- and macrolevels. Further research into the behavioral factors driving misalignment will be useful, whether these factors are cognitive biases shaping behavior or behavioral predilections that shape organizational routines regarding networks. A better understanding of behavioral tendencies will give greater clarity to how microfoundational networking choices aggregate to the macroorganizational level.[1]

Another category of research should investigate structural factors that generate network agency problems. This book investigated structural factors related to network density, relational quality, position, and degree inequality. More work can certainly be done in these areas. In addition, it may be fruitful to explore other organizing structures for their effect on misalignment, whether they are organizational structures such as hierarchy or social structures such as status or identity formation. Both certainly have a network interpretation as well.

Of course, this book also explored technological factors underlying network agency problems. One imagines that other material factors may be related to network agency, such as financial resources, business activities, and even industry conditions. In short, although the endogenous network factors described in this book may be primary causes of the network misalignments that maintain them, myriad other factors may be supportive and causal in network agency.

An important question relates to the social and behavioral aspects of network agency issues. When investigating patterns of incentive misalignment, it is easy to forget that human beings must choose to act on differences in interests for them to have any effect. I investigated several cases in some qualitative detail, but I must admit that this merely scratches the surface of the wide variety of ways in which network agency can be enacted: How are network agency problems acted upon by different agents in organizations? How do employees, managers, and owners differ in their responses? Such questions might need a performativity lens to identify the many different responses. What behaviors are typical when misalignments occur? In fact, this line of questioning may be more fundamental, as individuals can take a variety of stances on specific networking situations. Disposition, specific social context, and broader social context probably play some role in explaining networking responses.

Ironically, networking behavior and its causes may be the key to unlocking a more specific understanding of its performance consequences and its persistence. As this book illustrates through several network agency problems, behavior and performance are often in dynamic equilibrium. Behavior and outcomes are endogenous, so understanding performance is not really possible without understanding the behavioral inclinations that underlie it.

A complication with this or any other agency-theoretic research is that it is necessarily multilevel, even if only implicitly. To develop the theory presented here, I built on decades of individual-level social capital research. Although this research primarily focused on the consequences of social capital, it was most useful for understanding its antecedent inducements. If certain network features are shown to be beneficial, then it is a natural next step to view them as inducements to networking, even if this is mostly inferential. Further organizational research into the performance implications of larger networks will provide a foundation for understanding optimal network structures for organizations themselves.

Both strands of research deserve further work, but by far the organizational level is more lacking, perhaps because of the difficulty of obtaining comparable individual-network data from multiple organizations. It may be that the greatest opportunity will be to examine the interplay of organization and individual network choices, particularly across the typical organizational roles of employee, manager, executive, and owner. When managers are aware of the inducements of social capital, how do they shape their responses, including in incentive design? What equilibria emerge? Should we expect that the actual network will always be decoupled from the optimal organizational network structure? Are some supposedly useful network structures simply unachievable given current network agency costs? If so, can we discover which departures or suboptimal equilibria are preferred over others? Research on the "interplay" of organizational and individual factors may provide the most insightful and pragmatic lessons about network agency.

RESEARCH AGENDA BY ANALOGY: LEARNING FROM ENTREPRENEURIAL NETWORK EVOLUTION

There is one thriving branch of literature that considers both individual and organizational issues simultaneously—including behavioral and performance outcomes—and that is entrepreneurial network evolution, perhaps because of its tight link between individual entrepreneurial actions and organizational venture outcomes.[2] This research takes a network approach to understanding new ventures along a variety of micro- and macronetwork perspectives, including the social networks of the individual founders of new ventures; interorganizational network ties, such as when new ventures develop relationships with corporate partners or venture capital firms; and the social networks of employees within and beyond the boundaries of organizations as they grow.

Because entrepreneurship is a complicated phenomenon, interdisciplinary literature has the virtue of considering networks from a variety of perspectives: organizational, sociological, economic, and psychological. One of the most important issues is entrepreneurial agency. Yet this highlights an important distinction and broadens the term *agency* to include its more sociological dimensions. Very little of this literature focuses on principal-agent issues, which is perhaps not surprising given the small size of these ventures, in which ownership and management are more aligned and interorganizational relationships often comprise just the founder's ties to outsiders.

The idea of agency in this literature is the broader notion of behavioral agency in which individual entrepreneurs take network actions to benefit themselves and their organizations. A recent paper I co-authored (Halen, Murray, and Davis 2020) reviewed this literature and found that entrepreneurial network evolution seems to be progressing in two directions with distinct perspectives. In one perspective, labeled *structural localism*, individual entrepreneurs are seen to exhibit less variety in their networking behaviors. Network evolution is mostly path-dependent, with new ties that are local to entrepreneurial network, hierarchical, and geographic positions. This view suggests a "rich get richer" process of accumulative advantage in which those with effective networks and positions build on their advantages and amplify them over time. By contrast, those with disadvantageous networks find themselves stuck in their positions.

An alternative perspective, *agentic network change*, emphasizes much more variety in network evolution, in which future networks are much less constrained by current networks. This view is more consistent with path creation in explaining the formation of new and distant ties that may have higher potential but also be higher risk for participants. These broader, more distant network changes may be necessary to mobilize complex combinations of resources that are necessary during innovation or new venture formation. Of these two perspectives, the agentic network change approach appears to be emerging rapidly while the structural localism perspective continues in a normal science vein.

Research on network agency problems may combine similar perspectives and thus mirror literature on entrepreneurial network evolution in some respects. Indeed, structural approaches to network agency problems that emphasize exogenous features or prior network structures may prove fruitful. The theorizing in this book about digital technology adoption and the impact of network features on future networks may be examples of this approach. A structural localism perspective bears some resemblance to arguments about the persistence of network agency problems in which network misalignments grow as a small number of advantaged actors increase their advantages through networking.

With its emphasis on a wide variety of networking behaviors and distant-tie formation, an agentic network change perspective may be most useful in network agency theory because the responses to networking incentives can be quite heterogeneous. One of the most interesting ideas is that of networking trajectories, which proposes that network structure does shape and constrain action but that courses of actions may have their own economic logic. That is, engaging in a series of networking events, even if they are contrary to local network structures, may be economical if the final objective is reached. Ironically, the agentic network change perspective may apply more to managerial network interventions in network agency problems than employees because managerial interventions are often concerned with finding efficient ways to affect network change.

The entrepreneurial network evolution literature may also offer guidance on how an interdisciplinary field can develop a thriving and interesting body of research on a critical topic. A hallmark of this literature, consonant with its interdisciplinarity, is its methodological diversity. While the majority of work has been in the traditional quantitative and deductive vein, the field has had consistent threads of other types of research ranging from inductive using qualitative, ethnographic, and case methods to experimental designs and computer simulations. This may be an important factor underlying the momentum behind entrepreneurial network research.

A METHODOLOGICAL PERSPECTIVE ON NETWORK AGENCY RESEARCH

Ultimately, the mix of methodologies in a new research stream must match the state of science around those methodologies, including the research questions that are at the forefront. This book has presented some testable propositions about likely network agency problems and the role of digital technologies in exacerbating them. As a result, we imagine some productive empirical tests on large samples of networks and organizations to discover evidence for these ideas. Large sample tests are the gold standard of deductive research. I encourage such efforts to test the ideas presented here.

However, it is also likely that further inductive and abductive research is needed to develop additional network agency theories.[3] In fact, just as the entrepreneurial network evolution literature proceeded in somewhat parallel but different directions, with one pursuing a mostly deductive agenda with empirical tests on large samples and another pursuing a more inductive agenda with a wider variety of methods and data; so, too, might deductive and inductive approaches proceed in parallel. In fact, some interplay of these approaches may be highly productive, as inductive research produces greater insights that can be tested with deductive research and deductive efforts can confirm or disconfirm specific assumptions and thereby lead to deeper, more accurate, and new inductive theorizing.

Because of the inherently behavioral, complex, and multilevel nature of network agency phenomena, I have come to see that, although large-sample empirical work may be the most direct route to theoretical validation of the propositions presented here, a collection of other methods—case methods, modeling, and experiments—may be most fruitful for the inductive agenda of developing network agency theory. I outline this perspective next.

First, I am of the view that more research using case methods is needed to reveal more examples and mechanisms related to network agency theory in its organizational context. Network agency problems arise in organizations of various types and can often only be seen across multiple examples. As a result, the replication logic of the multiple-case method is ideally suited to inducing generalizable network processes. Comparative case methods are also appropriate for examining boundary conditions to see when and where mechanisms may operate, whether they lie in different types of networks, organizations, or industries.

The multilevel nature of network agency theory often lends itself to embedded units of analysis (individual, team, unit, organization, industry, etc.) in multiple-case research. That is, when case researchers enter an organization, they often, naturally, probe many issues at once, including the individual motivations and behavior of the organization's members; the different roles, memberships, and actions of its teams; the guiding structure of its divisions and organizational structures; and its incentive structure. Case researchers should follow an inductive approach that does not privilege any one level of analysis over another so that the most novel theory will be developed.

Second, as part of the inductive toolkit, formal modeling and simulation modeling seem to be of great use for network agency theory. Modeling is most useful when some basic theory exists but extensions and what-if experiments are also useful. As modeling requires internal consistency, it is often helpful in examining unforeseen implications of assumptions.

The most insightful models can generate new predictions or explain surprising results using social mechanisms. Because network agency theory is sometimes surprising in its effects, modeling can also bring clarity to theoretical efforts. As the type of case data required to explore every counterfactual is usually not available, models can supplement primary data collection efforts.

Third, organizational experiments may be of great use to network agency theory. Recently, randomized controlled trials in natural contexts have become popular in looking for causal effects. Given the multimechanisms of network agency theory, experiments may best control and isolate the right mechanisms—for example, typical experiments using individuals or teams at the behavioral level.

Perhaps the most applicable experiments are at a higher level of social complexity: the division, unit, or organization itself. Randomized controlled trials, or RCTs, involving different organizations or divisions are the most desirable, as different groups can be compared for differences between treatment and control. Although RCTs seem new, they are actually in consonance with older sociological literature on scientific intervention in cases or the type of "stimulations" that microsociologists like Erving Goffman performed in a variety of social contexts. In this vein, experiments need not be purely deductive. Organizational experimentation can be inductive if analysts diligently observe the consequences of carefully designed experiments across different groups.

CONCLUSION

Leveraging some of the unique comparative case data and the modeling described previously, this book has attempted to develop a first sketch of a network agency theory that goes beyond social capital theorizing to better understand how individual and organizational networking interests can become misaligned and generate dysfunction. An agency-theoretic lens was developed to explain how an individual's behavior can become decoupled from organizational interests and cause profound effects that culminate in agency costs high enough to prevent the organization from achieving its performance goals.

Four primary network agency problems—too many ties, ties that are too weak, entrenched brokerage, and a scale that is too free—were described to explain how the pursuit of individual social capital goals can become pathological for the organization. Digital technologies were found to be a primary driver and amplifier of these negative effects as they enable individuals to more efficiently pursue unchecked network growth that is difficult to monitor and in which it is difficult for managers to intervene to produce persistent improvements in networks.

Broader implications of network agency problems were found to shape many of the core issues related to the theory of the firm and broader organization functioning. Indeed, in the presence of network agency problems, the role of the executive itself shifts to reinterpreting typical functions such as HR, hiring, socialization, and talent development in light of network misalignment. Classical organization design problems, such as silos and matrices, are found to be caused by network agency problems. And the boundaries of the firm and its innovative activities were found to be, at least partially, determined by network agency issues. When taken together, this suggest that many of the critical inquiries of macroorganization theory can be examined from a network agency perspective.

Future research might productively explore a wide variety of network agency questions, using either a traditional deductive approach or a variety of methods from the inductive toolkit. If the network agency theories presented here are expanded and validated, they might go a long way toward explaining why some organizations succeed and some fail in achieving their most critical goals with innovations and other forms of value creation.

Afterword

This book is the outcome of twenty years of intensive research on the relationship between technological innovation and networking activities in modern organizations. It began with a multiple-case dissertation project during my doctoral studies at Stanford University. I was particularly interested in how newly emerging big-tech companies like Google and Amazon were using distributed organizational arrangements such as alliances to innovate collaboratively. When the opportunity to focus my dissertation on this issue arose, I did not hesitate.

I have benefited greatly from my network of mentors and colleagues. Over the course of my doctoral studies, I was fortunate to learn from many top researchers. From Kathy Eisenhardt, I learned the craft of inductive research, including the high bar that "replication logic" imposes to ensure that insights emerge from the data. Kathy protected me from distraction and taught me how to write research papers. She always pushed me to focus on the biggest insights in my data, for which I am grateful. From Riitta Katila, I learned how to communicate with the broader community of innovation scholars, most of whom are deductive researchers. Woody Powell nurtured my passion for organization theory, including about interorganizational relationships and innovation. Finally, from Mark Granovetter, I learned much about networks, and how little we knew about networking. He pushed me to see what was general and true and to pursue what was puzzling and novel.

Armed with this training, support, and inspiration, I entered the field and pursued my research on the use of interorganizational collaborations by large companies in the computer industry to develop platform innovations, many of which have become fundamental to the digital revolution that has come to fruition. These innovations include web services, VPNs, deep learning, spam filters, people analytics, online marketplaces, and smartphones. I was fortunate to gain access to nearly all of the companies I was interested in, and I conducted more than a hundred interviews at large high-tech organizations in Silicon Valley. I preserved the pseudonyms of individual informants to protect the identities of the brave souls who were willing to tell me about their networking successes and failures.

Beginning with a focus on technological collaboration was useful for two reasons. First and foremost, R&D alliances are a difficult strategic activity that only sometimes achieves its innovative objectives, so my informants were interested in supporting doctoral research on this topic and learn the results in order to improve their practice. Second, the boundary-spanning nature of new alliance projects exposes networks and networking activity to study in ways that internal projects do not. My interviewees were eager to talk about relationships and nonrelationships, including what "could have been" if various people had collaborated more effectively. I alternated between reading the literature and collecting and analyzing data, trying to come up with new ideas—typically failing but hopefully sometimes succeeding.

As an assistant professor at MIT Sloan, I continued to explore other aspects of networking at these companies, including how they managed larger, multipartner alliances of three or more companies that enabled entire platforms and ecosystems. I benefited greatly from a multidisciplinary department and a "high-diversity" network of senior scholars, including Rebecca Henderson, Ezra Zuckerman, and Michael Cusumano, who pushed me to up my game. It was like being in graduate school a second time. While painstakingly developing inductive research papers (published in the *Administrative Science Quarterly* (*ASQ*) in 2011 and 2016), I engaged in what Bob Sutton called "closet qualitative research" on strange social anomalies or issues not related to alliances. In many cases, I was able to explore these side questions at the end of semistructured interviews or when interviewing anyone who was willing to talk to me as I wandered the halls of company headquarters. My research at this point included some ethnographic observations when I was on staff for several months at the R&D labs of Intel Corporation. This was a valuable experience that allowed to me to participate in the alliance formation and boundary-spanning management process.

During these experiences, I became concerned that some of the network dynamics I was observing might be confined to high-tech companies on the West Coast or to a few European tech firms I studied. A move to INSEAD and Asia allowed me to investigate this issue. I am eternally grateful to have benefited from scholars such as Phil Anderson, Henrich Greve, Martin Gargiulo, and Bala Vissa, who exposed me to the INSEAD perspective on networks. Working with many non-technology-focused multinational companies in Asia and Europe has been particularly eye-opening. It has forced me to generalize my findings and abandon a few culturally specific insights in favor of the more generalizable dynamics that were unfolding in all these companies. I am especially grateful to various company leaders in Singapore, Indonesia, Malaysia, India, and China. Taking together my research in the US and Asia, I am enormously grateful to many informants from companies such as Apple, Amazon, Checkpoint, Cisco, eBay, Google, Intel, Microsoft, Nokia, RIM, SAP, Sun Microsystems, Lenovo, Citibank, Bank Indonesia, Prudential, Axiata, Natixis, CIMB, JG Summit, Jardines, Aviva, Vale, Pertamina, Frasers, Starhub, Go-Jek, Colonial, Astra Life, BCA, ICICI, TCS, Accenture, Public Bank, as well as many participants in INSEAD's MBA program and the Digital Transformation Open Enrollment program.

This book is unique for an "inductive/qualitative" book in its occasional use of simulation modeling. I have constructed models of key networking dynamics that I observed in the field in order to deepen my understanding, uncover unforeseen implications and boundary conditions, and better generalize insights beyond the high-tech firm context. My approach has been to build models from the ground up to capture mechanisms I observe in the field. Although the results have sometimes been well cited and seemingly influential (my 2009 *ASQ* paper won that journal's Scholarly Achievement award), the outputs have tended to be slower and more problem-focused than those using canonical models that elaborate highly general theories such as learning, evolution, and search. However, the intellectual value of modeling middle-range theories is still high: it lies in forcing rigor into a theoretical effort, particularly in making assumptions explicit, ensuring internal consistency, and (sometimes) generating surprising implications and predictions that may not have been apparent ex ante. This approach is particularly useful as a complement to generalizing qualitative research where not all counterfactuals can be explored in the data.

In this book, I construct simple models to illustrate the minimum assumptions necessary to produce results that contrast with earlier network logics used in organizational studies. The models tend to be simple by construction—interconnected individuals transfer and recombine knowledge and strengthen and form new ties endogenously within a dynamic process—but complex in their effects. I measure diffusion and innovation outcomes at the organizational level to interrogate the impact of structural, relational, positional, and topographic network features on organizational success.

As a result of my inductive research, I have come to a different perspective about how networks and networking activity are shaping organizational dynamics. At first, I thought that my qualitative research might simply fill in the gaps around relatively unexplored network processes and explain some of the variation in outcomes not explained by the structure itself. Over time, however, I began to believe that the structural theories are themselves incomplete, unrealistic, and incorrect when applied indiscriminately to modern organizations. Because of organizational social capital inducements, networks in organizations are fundamentally different from networks "in the wild" studied by social capital researchers. Thus, making indiscriminate inferences about organizational outcomes from individual measures becomes profoundly misguided. If this book makes a broader contribution than merely highlighting and explaining this difference, it is in taking an agentic view of the allocentric networking activity of managers, as well as their responsibility to shape the self-interested networking activities of individual employees for the greater good. I suggest that the failures to explore, innovate, and change that are endemic to modern organizations have a root cause in the networking activities of employees, which we previously thought were mainly the solution to these failures. Without an active, agentic, and occasionally intrusive role for managers in employee networks, I expect these failures to continue.

APPENDIX

Blue-Sky Model of Organizational Networking

In the blue-sky model of organizational networking, performance depends on ties in two different ways.

First, performance is proportional to the number of ties, as these relationship is assumed to be necessary to get things done, yielding ax where x is the number of ties. Second, there are costs associated with using ties that depend on the number of ties, represented by cx. Yet some investment in baseline capabilities not having to do with network ties reduces costs, b, represented by $-(cx - b)$. This yields $y = ax^*(b - cx)$, representing the impact of ties on performance, y. Thus, we compute the optimal number of ties, $x' = b/2c$.

But how do ties change over time? Organizations must rely on individual efforts to form and maintain them. Of course, the costs of forming and maintaining ties shape individual choices about whether to form ties in the first place, as does the likelihood of success in their future use. Let us assume there is some baseline level of change that is exogenously driven through turnover due to hiring/firing and births/deaths, d—that is, a constant rate. Then the cost of forming/maintaining ties reduces this level of change, $-c$.

Because individual success in using ties depends on how many other ties are present in an organization, the expectation of success depends on how far away the organization is from that performance optimum. That is to say, the amount of change critically depends on the number of ties already formed. The likelihood that a new tie will be useful depends on how far away the current number of ties is from the optimal number of ties, so the effect on change can be depicted as where e is a parameter modulating individuals' sensitivity to how far away from the optimum they are. This aggregates to the firm level to give an expected rate of change in the number of ties:

$$dx/dt = d - c - e(x - x')$$

The resulting equation can be subjected to stability analysis for nondynamical systems. The goal in stability analysis is to identify critical points where the system comes into equilibrium and the trajectories that exist around them. Setting $dx/dt = 0$, we find critical points

$$= \pm\sqrt{[(d - c)/e]} + x' \Longrightarrow = \pm\sqrt{[(d - c)/e]} + b/2c$$

This seemingly inelegant equation generates substantial insight into how ties change over time.

It is useful to understand the baseline dynamics of the model. At very high $c = d$, where the cost of forming ties, c, equals the baseline rate for forming ties, d, the overall effect of tie formation depends completely on the distance from the optimal number of ties and the distance between the actual number of ties and the optimum. In this case, there is only one critical point and the organization reaches the optimum.

Consider a more realistic scenario, $c > d$, where the costs of forming and maintaining ties to achieve strategic objectives are a more salient consideration relative to the baseline demographic forces leading to turnover through births and deaths. In this case, an additional critical point emerges in what mathematicians call a "blue-sky bifurcation" in which the system approaches one of two equilibria depending on its initial state—that is, how many ties the organization currently possesses and where it finds itself on the inverted-U curve.

The lower critical point, $\dot{x}_1$, is unstable in that small perturbations on either side send the system away from this point. In other words, organizations with a number of ties somewhat less than this point ($x < \dot{x}_1$) are likely to decrease their ties whereas those with a number of ties somewhat above ($x > \dot{x}_1$) are likely to increase theirs. This may resemble an entrepreneurial startup forming ties from scratch: although some startups succeed in successfully scaling ties and becoming established organizations in which incentives to form new ties dominate, many remain in a region of diminished tie formation incentives and eventually disappear. Such events may represent prototypical preestablishment organizations that rarely appear in cross-sectional analyses, generating a sampling bias that is well known among entrepreneurship researchers.

The higher critical point is more informative. Since dx/dt is positive at values lower than $\dot{x}_2$ and negative at values higher than $\dot{x}_2$, it is a stable critical point that is generally above the optimal number of ties, x'. As I illustrate with qualitative evidence, this equilibrium describes the state of affairs in many modern organizations, where individuals seek a greater number of ties than are optimal for organizational performance, generating inertia, lower innovation, frustrated organizational change, and suboptimal performance as a result. The stability analysis is also useful: we expect insufficient attempts to decrease (or increase) the number of ties to return to equilibrium after some time.

The blue-sky model enables us to examine the impact of digital technologies. Digital technologies like email, enterprise software, and social media are assumed to to straightforwardly reduce the cost of forming and maintaining network ties, c. As a result, they affect both performance and the number of ties in the system. The first effect on performance is simple: as c decreases because of improvements in digital technology, organization performance $y = ax(b - cx)$ increases at all network levels, x. Optimal performance $x' = b/2c$ increases as well. The result is an expanding inverted-U curve with a higher peak.

The effects of digital technologies on network dynamics are informative. As the costs of digital information decrease, the effects on small and large organizations diverge in a manner dictated by the blue-sky bifurcation. For small organizations possessing few ties, the number of ties that must be formed before passing the scale threshold decreases. In such a world, it is arguably easier to become "established" in the population—witness the proliferation of new organizations in technology ecosystems. For larger organizations, however, the number of ties sought by the system increases, taking it further from the optimum. Large stable but mediocre established organizations are a consequence.

An intriguing paradox arises that may explain the current state of many modern organizations: as digital technologies reduce the costs of networking, they increase potential performance at the optimum. At the same time, the number of ties the organization is creating actually diverges further from this optimum. The paradox is that digital technologies engender higher potential performance, but at the same time may actually diminish performance. This helps to explain the puzzlement of many senior executives who see tremendous potential from investments in digital transformation but actually experience substandard or even diminishing performance as the digital age progresses.

NOTES

Chapter 1

1. The debate over organization ecology and adaptation focused on sources of heterogeneity in organization forms—one interesting thread concerned whether heterogeneity was due to selection (Hannan and Freeman 1989; Hannan and Carroll 1995) or adaptation of organizations (DiMaggio and Powell 1983; DiMaggio 1988; Baum and Powell 1995).

2. Research on managerial practices that are linked to effectiveness, adaptability, and innovation flourished in the 1990s and the 2000s in various corners of the interdisciplinary field of organization science, ranging from organizational behavior (Perlow, Okhuysen, and Repenning 2002; Galunic and Eisenhardt 1996) to organization science (Miner, Bassoff, and Moorman 2001; Brown and Eisenhardt 1997), technology change (Anderson and Tushman 1990; Henderson and Clark 1990), and strategic management (Mintzberg 2002; Burgelman 1994; Rindova and Kotha 2001).

3. Indeed, prior relationships and repeated communication patterns were often linked to positive organizational outcomes such as innovation, effectiveness, and successful organization change (Brown and Eisenhardt 1997; Ancona and Caldwell 1992; Tushman 1977; Tushman and Katz 1980; Katz and Tushman 1979; Adler 1995; Hargadon and Sutton 1997) even though these scholars may not have used an explicit network theory framework.

4. Older research repeatedly emphasized the primacy of relations between individuals in organizations and markets. See Granovetter and Swedberg (2011) for a summary and a collection of these readings.

5. Social capital has been an important object of study since at least Coleman's (1998) article linking it to the creation of valuable human capital, along with other

important early works (Mizruchi 1989; Burt 1997; Frank and Yasumoto 1998; Coleman 1988), which launched a thriving research stream in sociology and management on social capital issues (Tsai and Ghoshal 1998; Nahapiet and Goshal 1998; Baker and Obstfeld 1999; Gargiulo and Benassi 1999; Hansen, Podolny, and Pfeffer 1999; Uzzi 1999; Burt 2000; Reagans and Zuckerman 2001).

6. Social capital has been repeatedly linked to positive individual outcomes outside of organizations, specifically achievement in socioeconomic status and in the labor market (Granovetter 1995; Fernandez and Fernandez-Mateo 2006; Rubineau and Fernandez 2015) or in entrepreneurship (Stam, Arzlanian, and Elfring 2014).

7. Network diversity became a large topic of study near the turn of the millennium as various statistical techniques for measuring diversity in larger network datasets emerged (Ibarra 1995; Reagans, Zuckerman, and McEvily 2004; Beckman and Haunschild 2002; Beckman, Burton, and O'Reilly 2007; Beckman et al. 2014a).

8. Despite decades of research linking network structure to individual performance, research on what is sometimes called "network effectiveness"—how network structure shapes organizational performance—is thinner than is ideal—although a recent conference session addressed this (Coutinho et al. 2019). A few useful strands exist from the analysis of group network structure and performance, and public administration (Tsai 2002; Oh, Chung, and Labianca 2004; Milward and Provan 1998; Bavelas 1950; Leavitt 1989; Provan and Kenis 2008). However, it should be cautioned that modern studies of network effectiveness with strong empirics are in their early days, and some studies are finding contradictory or null conclusions. For instance, a large sample study of more than a million email messages found no clear association between network structure and firm age and performance (Jacobs and Watts 2021). Using email to infer network structure does appear to be a fruitful way forward (Kleinbaum, Stuart, and Tushman 2013).

9. Although organizational politics used to be a popular topic in management research (Pfeffer 1978; Pfeffer 1992; Gargiulo 1993; Kilduff and Krackhardt 1994; Krackhardt 1999; March and Olsen 1984), it seems to have fallen off before the turn of the millennium. A resurgence of interest has occurred (Stern and Westphal 2010; Kellogg 2012; Ocasio, Pozner, and Milner 2020), so this topic may be reemerging in organization studies.

10. Some organization researchers have long called for more research on individual social capital in an organization context, particularly its effect on organizational outcomes, mechanisms, and behavior (Ibarra, Kilduff, and Tsai 2005; Kilduff and Tsai 2003; Brass et al. 2004; Salancik 1995).

11. Examining a smattering of recent HBR and SMR articles on networking and social capital reveals that most focus on forming more ties (Uzzi and Dunlap 2006; Ibarra and Hunter 2007; Casciaro, Gino, and Kouchaki 2016; Fleming and Juda 2004; Dyer 2004; Baker 2000).

12. Following on the original statement (Granovetter 1985), research on embeddedness has explored multiple dimensions of social structure and its effect on multiple individual, team, and organizational outcomes (Mauskapf et al. 2017; Haveman et al. 2017; Lazzarini, Miller, and Zenger 2006; Rogan 2014; Rowley, Behrens, and Krackhardt 2000; Tatarynowicz 2008; Uzzi 1996, 1999; Uzzi and Lancaster 2003;

Vasudeva, Zaheer, and Hernandez 2013; Polidoro, Ahuja, and Mitchell 2011; Azoulay, Repenning, and Zuckerman 2010).

13. There are a few notable exceptions in research on tie dissolution (Broschak 2004; Broschak and Block 2014; Clough and Piezunka 2020; Rogan 2014; Seabright, Levinthal, and Fichman 1992; Hernandez, Sanders, and Tuschke 2015; Davis 2008; Palmer 1983; Hernandez and Menon 2018), often driven by rationales of organizational or market turbulence.

14. There is some research on the downsides of networks, although it is limited (Uzzi 1996; Uzzi and Spiro 2005; Gargiulo and Benassi 1999; Beckman et al. 2014a; Yenkey 2018; Li 2021; Holloway and Parmigiani 2016; Diestre and Rajagopalan 2012; Jonsson, Greve, and Fujiwara-Greve 2009). For instance, Gargiulo and Benassi (1999) described a type of inability to break from ties that lose their utility. Holloway and Parmigiani (2016) demonstrated an inability to make adjustments in partnerships with old friends. Jonsson et al (2009) demonstrated a reputational concern that prevents network members from enforcing norms. Diestre and Rajagopalan (2012) illustrated the significant time and resources required to maintain existing networks.

15. Research on the size of typical premodern networks often centers on Dunbar's number (Hill and Dunbar 2003; Dunbar 1992), some of it arguing that migration actually resulted in significantly larger networks (Bird et al. 2019). Other research demonstrates that interactions become substantially more complicated when collaborations become exceedingly complex, at five or more members (Krems and Wilkes 2019), and that long-standing relationships with three or more members may generate instability because of third-party interactions (Simmel 1950; Li and Piezunka 2020; Davis 2016; Sosa, Gargiulo, and Rowles 2015).

16. This research is inspired by earlier research on agency problems that focused on interest misalignment between principals and agents in organizations. This earlier research was itself inspired by managerial and behavioral accounts of organizations in which managers and employees often seem to depart from the perfect assumptions of "economic man" (Simon 1965; Cyert and March 1963; Williamson 1975a). In the models of several early agency theorists, the firm was productively viewed as a nexus of contracts that limit the discretion of organizational members, a rubric sometimes referred to as "property rights." (Alchian and Demsetz 1972; Jensen and Meckling 1976; Fama 1980). This contractual view of the firm produced many useful models that seemed to explain profits and losses of firms with agency problems (Foss, Lando, and Thomsen 2000). As Foss et al (2000) described, early perspectives ranged from those that viewed further contracting as a potential optimal solution to these problems and those that suggested that contracting may always be incomplete in the face of some agentic behavior, suggesting persistent losses or a space for useful managerial intervention. The research presented in this book is broadly consistent with the latter view, which suggests that the relational and behavioral aspects of agency are essential in any study of network agency problems.

17. There is an emerging stream of research in economics that examines incentives in social networks (Jackson 2008). Although it tends not to focus on organizational issues, this research has generated a variety of intriguing microeconomic models of networking choice and outcomes in which equilibria are identified (Golub

and Jackson 2012a; Golub and Jackson 2012c, 2012b; Jackson and Yariv 2009). The organizations field could take inspiration from this one in developing similar models of organizational networking.

18. There is a long-standing sociological debate over the relative role of structural constraint versus agentic choice in social life, including in the development of network ties (Emirbayer and Mische 1998; Fligstein 2001; Giddens 1984; Hallen, Davis, and Murray 2020; Sewell 1992; Wrong 1961). This tension can be found in managerial research on network agency (Kleinbaum and Stuart 2014b; Obstfeld, Borgatti, and Davis 2013) and relational styles (Canales and Greenberg 2016; Vissa 2012) as well. Network agency theory highlights both incentive structure and social capital inducements to networking as well as motivational states and technical facilitation elements of choice.

19. As Williamson (1988) noted, residual loss is often the largest component of agency cost—it is perhaps not surprising that this is true for network agency as well, as many opportunities in the modern economy demand an appropriate network to be pursued.

20. In fact, some economic agency theorists intuited that network ties may be related to agency problems as, for instance, when Fama (1980) described limits to managerial discretion—including monitoring of managers and employees and its effectiveness—as being based on familiarity. Yet these studies put little emphasis on network agency problems per se.

21. This model is described at the end of the chapter; its mathematical details are provided in the Appendix.

22. A literature stream has quickly emerged that analyzes the effects of the pandemic, including the rapid adoption of new IT tools, like Zoom and Slack, and its impact on employment, organization behavior, productivity, and networks (Yang et al. 2022; Zuzul et al. 2021; Brynjolfsson and Raymond 2022; Bloom 2022; DeFilippis et al. 2020).

23. A debate has raged over whether open or closed forms are more conducive to innovation, with multiple attempts at resolution (Ter Wal et al. 2016; Alexy, Henkel, and Wallin 2013; Felin and Zenger 2014; O'Mahony 2003; Dahlander and Piezunka 2014; Shaw and Nagel 2020; DeJordy et al. 2020).

Chapter 2

1. The literature on social capital and its management is vast, with a long history ranging from early storied developments (Coleman 1988; Burt 1997; Baker and Obstfeld 1999; Gargiulo and Benassi 1999; Watts and Strogatz 1998; Milgram 1967) to more modern applications (Dokko and Rosenkopf 2010; Alexy et al. 2012; Sorenson and Rogan 2014; Stam, Arzlanian, and Elfring 2014; Clough et al. 2019; Fonti and Maoret 2016; Phelps, Heidl, and Wadhwa 2012).

2. Studies on the benefits of ties are too numerous to cite here, although it quickly becomes clear that network ties generate benefits in many contexts, including labor markets and within and across organizations (Granovetter 1995; Podolny and Baron 1997; Uzzi 1999; Botelho 2018; Brass 1984). A useful summary of organizational social capital is provided by Brass et al. (2004).

3. Sometimes managers seek to develop organizational capabilities around social capital (Sorenson and Rogan 2014; Obstfeld 2013; Pollock, Porac, and Wade 2004; Zollo, Reuer, and Singh 2002; Vissa 2012; Hasan and Koning 2020; Kleinbaum and Stuart 2014a), suggesting an approach that focuses on proactively influencing or designing agents' networks.

4. Emerging literature and popular accounts suggest that the problem of overcommunication and overinteraction plagues many organizations (Van Zandt 2004; Repenning 2001; Dodge, Kieffer, and Repenning 2018; Gerber 2018; Cross, Rebele, and Grant 2016; Cross and Carboni 2020; Newport 2016a; Bernstein, Shore, and Lazer 2018).

5. Much literature has suggested a network component to overcommitment and overinteraction problems if relationships require some obligation for interaction, investment, and maintenance (Uzzi 1996; Li 2021; Ter Wal et al. 2016).

6. Research on digital tools in organizations and work has long noted how communications and social media technologies facilitate work through various affordances for more efficient networking (Leonardi 2014; Treem and Leonardi 2013; Mazmanian, Orlikowski, and Yates 2013; Orlikowski et al. 1995; Aven 2015; Kleinbaum, Stuart, and Tushman 2013; Piskorski 2014; Neeley and Leonardi 2018).

7. An emerging trend in managerial publications and some research is the suggestion of a link between the adoption of digital technologies in organizations—whether by traditional IT tools like email and databases, by newer social media platforms like Facebook, Twitter, and Slack, or by video conferencing technologies like Zoom and Skype—and decreased individual productivity and diminished work and organizational performance (Newport 2016b; Molla 2019; Hoffman 2019; Beck 2019; Parise, Whelan, and Todd 2015; Becker et al. 2021; Neeley and Leonardi 2018). Some of this research emerged during the pandemic, which produced a large upsurge in digital technology adoption often in work-from-home arrangements (DeFilippis et al. 2020; Bernstein et al. 2020; Dahlander et al. 2021).

8. Some accounts have suggested that internal messaging software like Slack is the most pernicious generator of overinteraction (Hoffman 2019; Molla 2019), although it is difficult to carry out comparative research on the topic. While communication platforms like Slack mainly present all messages equally, it can be challenging to carry out algorithmic sorting of information on platforms like Facebook (Kellogg, Valentine, and Christin 2020; Rahman 2021), as they bias human perception and cognition in unforeseen ways.

9. Some research has focused on the downsides of managerial attention that becomes too distributed to effectively mobilize resources or achieve project results (Huy 2016; Ocasio 1997; Ocasio and Joseph 2005). For instance, one study concluded that sources supplying too much information may lead to less attention dedicated to their information because it is discounted by organizational members (Hansen and Haas 2001). Various communication strategies can be used to focus attention and mobilize support (Kahl and Grodal 2016; Vaara, Sonenshein, and Boje 2016).

10. The network diagrams presented here are conceptual. They are an amalgam of various sociograms and network structural dynamics that I have observed across many organizations.

11. Research on networks has shown some downsides or decreasing returns from acquiring social capital (McFadyen and Albert A. Cannella 2004), consistent with broader research on embeddneddness (Granovetter, 1985; Uzzi, 1996).

12. A growing research stream on multiplex ties indicates that the different dimensions of relationships can shape how they are enacted and their performance outcomes in different ways (Shipilov et al. 2014; Shipilov 2012; Li and Piezunka 2020; Kuwabara, Luo, and Sheldon 2010; Shipilov and Li 2012). A related study on idiosyncratic and particularistic relationships illustrates the specialization of relationships and their nonfungible nature (Luo and Chung 2005).

13. In times of crisis or change, network ties may become even more important (Gargiulo 1993).

14. There is growing research on bad bosses (Sutton 2012; Gupta, Nadkarni, and Mariam 2019; Tang et al. 2015; Weber and Wiersema 2017), including psychological traits and contextual factors leading to their emergence and dismissal.

15. Intriguing new research has found evidence for the "Peter Principle," which is the idea that employees are promoted to their level of incompetence (Benson, Li, and Shue 2019). The argument is that when employees are promoted based on past performance, their promotion potential often stalls when their performance does, leading them to stagnate in positions where they are lower performing. Strong evidence for lower performance of sales managers who were high performing as salespeople exists. Ironically, lower-performing salespeople add more value than high performers when they are promoted to management (Benson, Li, and Shue 2019).

16. Those with more network ties are more likely to be promoted and occupy leadership positions (Jonczyk et al. 2016; Westphal and Stern 2007).

17. Prior relationships outside of an individual's organization can often be a predictor of employee mobility and entrepreneurship (Byun, Raffiee, and Ganco 2019; Agarwal et al. 2004; Agarwal, Gambardella, and Olson 2016).

18. Organizational politics often have a network basis, with highly connected subgroups allied against each other.

19. Although most of the literature is on tie formation or passive decay, some work has suggested a more active process for tie dissolution (Zhang and King 2021; Clough and Piezunka 2020; Davis 2008; Hallen, Davis, and Murray 2020; Davis 2007; Hernandez, Sanders, and Tuschke 2015).

Chapter 3

1. Research on strong ties has noted their utility in difficult, complex, and uncertain tasks involving attitudinal change or coordination (Battilana and Casciaro 2012, 2013; Ruef 2002; Gargiulo 1993; Ruef, Aldrich, and Carter 2003; Krackhardt 1992).

2. Several studies have linked bringing together specialized knowledge and resources in different combinations with greater creativity and innovation (Teodoridis, Bikard, and Vakili 2019; Davis and Eisenhardt 2011; Galunic and Rodan 1998; Karim and Kaul 2015; Hargadon and Sutton 1997; Katila and Ahuja 2002; Conti and Liu 2015).

3. The original findings on weak ties were developed in the context of job search (Granovetter 1995, 1983) and have seen consistent support since then (Yakubovich

2005). Yet research on investment in strong and weak ties suggesting that actors economize on investments in relational quality has a longer history (Boorman 1975).

4. Some research on weak ties has sought to bound the application of weak ties within contexts requiring network diversity (Brashears and Quintane 2018), or it has suggested that strong ties are important for creativity (Sosa 2011).

5. Research on network diversity examines various contexts such as R&D teams, alliances, and other innovative contexts (Reagans and Zuckerman 2001; Corritore, Goldberg, and Srivastava 2020; Beckman et al. 2014b; Beckman, Burton, and O'Reilly 2007; Briscoe and Rogan 2016; Beckman and Haunschild 2002).

6. I examine network agency problems related to network structure in later chapters. However, it should be noted here that some literature on network diversity and innovation suggests that excess diversity may not be useful in some cases (Su et al. 2019; Lungeanu and Contractor 2014). For instance, homophily in country of residence has been found to be more useful than knowledge diversity in scientific innovation (Lungeanu and Contractor 2014).

7. Research on network activation is emerging, but with some exceptions it has not focused on when individuals choose to put their social capital at the service of the organization's goals (Davis and Eisenhardt 2011).

8. A long stream of research suggests that mobilizing knowledge outside the firm involves more investment and a more elaborate process than mobilizing knowledge inside the firm (Monteiro and Birkinshaw 2017).

9. An intriguing example of firm-specific motivations is a new analysis of business school professors which found that high performers tend to resist firm-specific roles more than low performers, suggesting that employees may be aware of their market value and use that to decide their firm specificity (Dyer et al. 2021).

10. The notion of firm specificity has been applied to many resource types in literature about competitive advantage. Regarding individuals, though, it has mostly been applied to an organization's human capital (Galunic and Anderson 2000; Benner and Veloso 2008; Helfat 1994; Makadok and Barney 2001; Mayer, Somaya, and Williamson 2012; Szulanski 1996; Sakhartov and Folta 2014). However, some scholars have begun to think about firm control of social capital as well (Dyer and Singh 1998; Gulati, Lavie, and Singh 2009; Sorenson and Rogan 2014; Aven, Morse, and Iorio 2019).

Chapter 4

1. Although research on networks has looked at a wide variety of positions generated by network structure, it tends to focus on either central or brokerage positions (Zaheer and Bell 2005; Hallen 2008; Tsai 2001; Ibarra 1993; Burt 1992).

2. The literature on brokerage and structural holes is large, ranging from early efforts to understand brokerage (Marsden 1982; Fernandez and Gould 1994) to accounts of the social capital of brokerage across structural holes (Hahl, Kacperczyk, and Davis 2016; Burt 2005, 1992) to newer research on brokerage processes used to create and capture value across structural holes (Obstfeld, Borgatti, and Davis 2013; Lingo and O'Mahony 2009; Davis 2016).

3. Brokerage research has productively used the threat of disintermediation as a key construct to understand returns to brokerage (Bidwell and Fernandez-Mateo 2010; Fernandez-Mateo 2007; Hahl, Kacperczyk, and Davis 2016; Soda, Tortoriello, and Iorio 2018; Rider 2009).

4. Not many studies have explored organizational performance implications of individual brokerage, but a few intriguing studies have noted some externalities of brokers on other individuals in the network with whom they are connected.(Clement, Shipilov, and Galunic 2018; Galunic, Ertug, and Gargiulo 2012; Davis 2007, 2008).

5. Research is emerging around cultural factors in brokerage and networking that considers how values and norms shape networking and network structures (Xiao and Tsui 2007; Li and Piezunka 2020; O'Reilly and Chatman 1996; Emirbayer and Goodwin 1994; Pachucki and Breiger 2010; Goldberg et al. 2016; Vaisey and Lizardo 2010; Godart and Claes 2017; Seong and Godart 2018).

6. These brokerage orientations have a long history, starting with Simmel (1950), although they were clarified in modern scholarship by Obstfeld and others (Obstfeld 2005; Obstfeld, Borgatti, and Davis 2013; Grosser et al. 2019; Kauppila, Bizzi, and Obstfeld 2018; Quintane and Carnabuci 2016; Shi, Markoczy, and Dess 2009; Simmel 1950).

7. Although the literature suggests that brokers may accrue enough benefits to occupy important formal positions in organizations, they may also choose other roles (Kleinbaum 2012).

8. Research on brokerage processes has progressed substantially; see Obstfeld et al (2013) for a review.

9. This literature is consonant with a broader literature on relational style and agency in networks which illustrates that network ties may leave some latitude for variation in behavior (Canales and Greenberg 2016; Hallen, Davis, and Murray 2020; Vissa 2012). Also, research on personality features such as self-monitoring has indicated some heterogeneity of behavior within network structures (Mehra, Kilduff, and Brass 2001; Flynn et al. 2006; Kleinbaum, Jordan, and Audia 2015; Sasovova et al. 2010; Kuwabara, Hildebrand, and Zou 2018).

10. Industrial organization research on monopolies indicates that barriers to entry maintain profits for incumbent monopolists. Recent research has noted a coalitional approach to value capture that may have some applications in brokerage monopolies (Asmussen et al. 2021). Notions of value appropriation have also been productively applied to employees in organizations (Laursen and Salter 2020; Call and Ployhart 2020), even as competition has been shown to be a driver of collaboration (Toh and Polidoro 2013).

11. In fact, there has been recent discussion about technology companies like Amazon primarily using their monopsony power to maintain profits.

12. The distinction between natural and unnatural monopolies has been present for some time in the literature on industrial organization, with collusion and cartels being the key examples of unnatural or strategic monopolistic behavior. There is a related stream on cooperation and competition in and across groups in the organization theory literature (Ingram and Qingyuan Yue 2008; Rowley et al. 2004; Rowley et al. 2005; Davis 2016).

Chapter 5

1. Although there are few studies of social capital inequality, some lines of research relate to studies of core and periphery; macrotopological research indicates that heterogeneity in social capital can be substantial (Cattani and Ferriani 2008; Cattani, Ferriani, and Allison 2014; Tomaskovic-Devey and Avent-Holt 2019).

2. Research on political action often has an implicit network representation in mind, as differing coalitions usually form around highly interconnected subgroups and cliques (Cyert and March 1963). Some research suggests that negative ties may be particularly important in political formation (Labianca, Brass, and Gray 1998; Sytch and Tatarynowicz 2014; Labianca and Brass 2006).

3. Small-world theory as developed by Milgram (1967) and Watts and Strogatz (1998) has had some application in organizational research, with prominent studies at the alliance network level (Baum, Shipilov, and Rowley 2003; Fleming, King III, and Juda 2007; Gulati, Sytch, and Tatarynowicz 2012; Schilling and Phelps 2007; Watts and Strogatz 1998).

4. An emerging stream of literature followed Barabasi and Albert's (1999) paper on scale-free networks, much of which tested the scale invariance hypothesis, with mixed results (Albert, Jeong, and Barabasi 2000; Barabasi 2003; Barabasi and Albert 1999; Jeong, Neda, and Barabasi 2001; Yook, Jeong, and Barabasi 2002).

5. Research on stars reveals their link to status and networks (Chen and Garg 2018; Groysberg, Polzer, and Elfenbein 2011; Prato and Ferraro 2018), suggesting that status within and conferred by organizations can enable individuals to capture value (Bidwell et al. 2015).

6. The rich-get-richer effect is sometimes associated with literature on the Matthew effect, which has implications not just for networks but also for status and reputation (Askin and Bothner 2016; Bothner et al. 2010; Bothner, Podolny, and Smith 2011; Piezunka et al. 2018; Hallen, Davis, and Murray 2020; Zhelyazkov and Tatarynowicz 2021; Sharkey 2018; Malter 2014; Cao and Smith 2020). In fact, there is some research that Matthew, rich-get-richer, wealth inequality, preferential attachment, and scale-free dynamics may all stem from a common underlying Yule process (Clauset 2021).

7. Research on celebrity CEOs and celebrity firms indicates that the dynamics of celebrity can be self-reinforcing in that celebrity status begets stronger celebrity status (Chatterjee and Pollock 2017; Hayward, Rindova, and Pollock 2004; Pfarrer, Pollock, and Rindova 2010; Rindova, Pollock, and Hayward 2006). An analogous literature on individual star performers in organizations also suggests that network-based status may underlie the creation, recognition, and maintenance of stars (Bothner, Podolny, and Smith 2011; Groysberg, Polzer, and Elfenbein 2011; Fonti and Maoret 2016; Prato and Ferraro 2018; Li et al. 2020; Lahiri et al. 2019).

8. In fact, robustness to turnover is a key advantage of scale-free networks (Albert, Jeong, and Barabasi 2000; Barabasi 2003; Barabasi and Albert 1999).

9. Some research has indicated that organizations may have a form of network memory, as individuals remember who possesses which ties, the content of those ties, and prior network composition (Jonczyk et al. 2016; Ren, Carley, and Argote 2006; Argote and Ren 2012; Krackhardt 1990; Krackhardt and Kildruff 1999).

10. In fact, simulation modeling has been used as a bridge from theory development with ethnographic or case data from the field to testing in large samples (Davis, Eisenhardt, and Bingham 2007). One of the core challenges is "docking" models to what is known from empirical reality, which involves the art of computational representation of phenomena in analytical form and computer code, which is crucial (Burton and Obel 2011 1995; Carley 2001; Baumann and Siggelkow 2013; Levinthal and Posen 2007; Repenning 2002; Zott 2003; Lant and Mezias 1990).

Chapter 6

1. The puzzling, apparently suboptimal organizations that persist in the long run are an instance of a broader social phenomenon in which suboptimal social structures persist (Granovetter 2017). As Granovetter (2017) argues, weak selection pressures and path-dependent evolution are sufficient to explain persistence. Arguments for the persistence of network agency problems share a family resemblance to these broader arguments.

2. Classical agency theory motivations tend to be focused on intentional shirking (Williamson 1996; Williamson, Winter, and Coase 1991). That is, individuals have knowledge of organizational interests and intentionally defy them (Flammer and Luo 2017; Jia, Huang, and Zhang 2019).

3. Endogenous network dynamics in which network outcomes cause individuals to select those very structures have been explored in multiple lines of research using methods like computational simulation or multicausal modeling (Lomi et al. 2011; Centola and Macy 2007; Davis 2013; Balazs and Stark 2010; Zaheer and Soda 2009).

4. For example, in one study in a Japanese electronics firm, performance-based incentives were found to cause employees to revise their goals and reconfigure networks to achieve them. This involved more closed and smaller networks and new ties with those who had similar expertise (Mitsuhashi and Nakamura 2022). Another intriguing study gives weight to the idea that incentives can shift collaborative and networking activity. A field experiment reveals that encouraging discussion of sales techniques and providing incentives for joint output improve sales (Sandvik et al. 2020).

5. Some research on technology-enabled surveillance has been emerging (Anteby and Chan 2018; Bernstein 2012, 2017), although it has focused less on networks.

6. The research is consonant with a broader literature on the stability of networks and the persistence of network outcomes which notes that network structures often tend to be more stable than many expect, seeming to outlive their apparent utility because both advantaged and disadvantaged actors maintain their current positions and different logics coexist (Gargiulo and Ertug 2015; Hallen, Davis, and Murray 2020; Kennedy and Fiss 2009; Dahlander and McFarland 2013). This is observed most prominently in the literature on diffusion, which often has a network representation underlying the theory (Naumovska, Gaba, and Greve 2021).

7. There is an important literature stream on network perception and cognitive social structures linking knowledge of networks with their effectiveness (Casciaro 1998; Hahl, Kacperczyk, and Davis 2016; Krackhardt 1987, 1990).

8. An important underpinning of interpersonal network research is the cognitive dimension. Research indicates that deep-seated views of networking—its appropriateness (Kuwabara et al. 2020; Kuwabara, Hildebrand, and Zou 2018), personality traits (Kleinbaum 2018; Sasovova et al. 2010; Mehra, Kilduff, and Brass 2001), and individuals' mental representations of network ties (Krackhardt 1990, 1987; Hahl, Kacperczyk, and Davis 2016; Moldoveanu and Baum 2014) and what nodes know (Argote, Aven, and Kush 2018; Argote and Ren 2012; Reagans, Argote, and Brooks 2005)—have a profound impact on how individuals network.

9. This is related to a tradition of research suggesting that managerial attribution around learning and performance is a key driver of future behavior (Repenning and Sterman 2002; Lee, Lee, and Kim 2021; Bingham and Davis 2012).

Chapter 7

1. The large and growing literature on IT adoption in organizations ranges from research on new affordances of digital technologies in the workplace (Zammuto et al. 2007; Birkinshaw, Gudka, and D'Amato 2021) to increases in productivity (Brynjolfsson and Raymond 2022; Bloom, Sadun, and Van Reenen 2012) to the impact of data on organizational knowledge (Alaimo and Kallinikos 2021, 2022; Cepa and Schildt 2022).

2. Research on digital tools that can be used for governance, including monitoring, intervention, and surveillance, has only recently begun (Zuboff 2019; Bernstein 2017). Some of it focuses on governance in platform economies where data on worker choice is readily available (Cameron 2021; Cameron and Rahman 2022; Karunakaran 2021).

3. A number of studies of organizations having work-from-home schemes during the pandemic focus on the role of technology (DeFilippis et al. 2020; Bernstein et al. 2020; Dahlander et al. 2021; Neeley 2021). Along with other research, they generally support the finding of increasing isolation with more geographically distributed work in virtual teams (Bartel, Wrzesniewski, and Wiesenfeld 2012; Hadley and Mortensen 2020; Hinds and Bailey 2003; Hinds and Mortensen 2005; Ancona, Bresman, and Mortensen 2021).

4. An emerging discipline focuses on the effect on social networks of working from home during the pandemic. Much of this research supports the idea of digital relationships having more interactions and more weak ties. For example, a study of Microsoft data showed that connections across silos were difficult to form but that connections within silos increased dramatically (Yang et al. 2022). Another large-scale study of four thousand organizations and billions of emails found that groups became more siloed with an increase in modularity and less stable membership. In this case, emails spiked and insular group communication intensified (Zuzul et al. 2021). Another study of 3 million email users found a dramatic increase in meetings and the number of people meeting but decreases in meeting length (DeFilippis et al. 2020). Yet another, a field experiment in Bangladesh, found that an intermediate number of days working remotely from home led to more emails sent (Choudhury et al. 2022). The absence of in-person encounters may limit encounters generally, narrowing the scope of communication to formal or essential (Yang et al. 2022). A

study of ten thousand IT professionals in Asia found that they worked more during the pandemic but average output did not go up because of increased time spent on coordinating and attending meetings, although there was less informal networking (Gibbs, Mengel, and Siemroth 2021). During virtual work, employees may become more task-oriented and neglect relationship building and tie strengthening (Birkinshaw, Gudka, and D'Amato 2021; Deal and Levenson 2021).

5. Some studies found increasing connectivity due to technology, even if that was not always the primary research question. Literature is emerging on the negative impact of digital interactions lacking face-to-face interactions (Gibbs, Mengel, and Siemroth 2021; DeFilippis et al. 2020; Brynjolfsson et al. 2020; Rahman 2021). For instance, Gibbs, Mengel, and Siemroth (2021) studied ten thousand workers and concluded that work from home generates two more hours of work per day but less productivity. DeFilippis et al. 2020 studied more than 3 million workers, finding that the pandemic has resulted in a longer workday, more meetings of shorter length, and more email.

6. Much research focuses on the impact on organizations, individuals, and social networks of social media sites like Myspace, Facebook, Instagram, and LinkedIn (Piskorski 2014; Boyd and Ellison 2007; Ellison, Steinfield, and Lampe 2007; Lampe, Ellison, and Steinfield 2006). Importantly, research indicates that social networking sites supplement in-person social networks (Ellison, Steinfield, and Lampe 2007; Lampe, Ellison, and Steinfield 2006; Haythornthwaite 2005). For instance, Facebook is used to maintain offline relationships or solidify offline connections (Ellison, Steinfield, and Lampe 2007). Users search for people with whom they have an offline connection more than they browse for complete strangers to meet (Lampe, Ellison, and Steinfield 2006). In other words, these sites help individuals access latent ties (Haythornthwaite 2005). They are usually public, which makes it easier to form ties as well (Acquisti and Gross 2006), particularly for youth (boyd 2007). This may result in larger networks of weak ties.

7. Technology and organization studies often note the dual nature of technology in enabling and constraining interactions (Orlikowski 1992; Barley 1990). Technology can both increase and decrease autonomy and flexibility as well as mediate resistance to and decommitment from organizations (Kellogg, Orlikowski, and Yates 2006; Mazmanian, Orlikowski, and Yates 2013; Karunakaran 2021; Cameron and Rahman 2022; Rauch and Ansari 2022; Beane 2019). Some research suggests that social media in particular may have positive benefits on work practices by engendering curiosity and knowledge sharing (Neeley and Leonardi 2018). Social media used by enterprises may enhance communication and the diversity of the knowledge shared (Leonardi, Huysman, and Steinfield 2013; Leonardi 2014). It provides unique affordances related to the social graph, tagging, and microblogging that may prove beneficial (Treem and Leonardi 2013).

8. Research on organizational culture indicates that defined purpose is a key factor leading to organizational identification and commitment (Chatman et al. 1998; O'Reilly and Chatman 1996; Albert, Ashforth, and Dutton 2000; Besharov 2014). In fact, identification and organizational climate influence whether individuals share knowledge with colleagues or competitors beyond organizational boundaries (Di Stefano and Micheli 2022).

9. Barnard's influence has been profound and broad (Barnard 1938), ranging from threads in more rationalistic accounts to threads in more naturalistic accounts of organization theory (Perrow 1972; March and Simon 1958; Selznick 1949).

10. Behavioral theory focuses on aspirations and change (Greve 1998; Cyert and March 1963), which have recently experienced a resurgence in organizational studies (Eggers and Kaul 2018; Gaba and Bhattacharya 2012; Joseph and Gaba 2015; Kacperczyk, Beckman, and Moliterno 2015; Audia and Greve 2020). One can imagine that differences in individual and organizational aspirations, and performance feedback, play a large role in network agency problems.

11. This work has ranged from considerations of identity to change in routines through practice (Ibarra and Barbulescu 2010; Ibarra and Petriglieri 2010).

12. The literature on network organizational processes has progressed steadily using primarily inductive methods involving multiple cases (Davis and Eisenhardt 2011; Hallen and Eisenhardt 2012; Ozcan and Eisenhardt 2008; Davis 2016) as well as ethnographic and field methods (Lingo and O'Mahony 2009; Obstfeld 2005, 2012, 2013; Klein et al. 2006).

13. Strategic HR research that explores human resource practices shaping firm performance and competitive advantage has become an important trend in the HR literature of the past few decades (Cappelli 2012; Bidwell et al. 2013; Carpenter, Sanders, and Gregersen 2001). At the same time, strategic management researchers have become more interested in individual factors, culminating in important research on strategic human capital (Call and Ployhart 2020; Felin, Foss, and Ployhart 2015; Coff 1997; Campbell, Coff, and Kryscynski 2012).

14. The literature on how much value employees capture from their work has so far been focused on either individual factors like job performance or macrolevel factors like labor markets (Call and Ployhart 2020), leaving some space for network explanations.

15. Research on hiring has considered many social factors, including network ties (Fernandez and Fernandez-Mateo 2006; Fernandez-Mateo and Fernandez 2016; Fernandez-Mateo and Kaplan 2018; Prato and Ferraro 2018; Yakubovich 2013; Yakubovich and Kozina 2000; Fernandez and Mors 2008; Fernandez, Castilla, and Moore 2000).

16. Research on socialization also links to research on organizational identification (Chatman 1989b, 1989a), where learning about the organization entails greater commitment in both the social (Albert, Ashforth, and Dutton 2000; Cable, Gino, and Staats 2013; Labianca, Brass, and Gray 1998; Pratt 1998) and the economic sense (Baker, Gibbons, and Murphy 2002a; Gibbons and Henderson 2012; Tsui, Egan, and O Reilly 1992; Williamson 1983).

17. Research here has centered on executive compensation and the pay-for-performance debate (Bidwell et al. 2013; Gibbons and Murphy 1990; Westphal and Zajac 1994, 1997; Beatty and Zajac 1994; Lee and Puranam 2017).

18. Recent research suggests that managers' social and people skills are a strong predictor of retention, and that managers themselves have higher subjective performance ratings, are promoted more, and receive larger salary increases (Hoffman and Tadelis 2020).

19. In fact, high performers who are internally hired for new jobs are highly likely to stay in firms for reasons of organizational identification (Benson and Rissing 2020).

20. The literature on networks and compensation forges a strong link between network position and pay (Mizruchi, Stearns, and Fleischer 2011; Mitsuhashi and Nakamura 2022). Newer studies have noted that relational and perceptual aspects of evaluation may also shape compensation (Castilla and Ranganathan 2020; Cameron 2021; Botelho and Abraham 2017).

Chapter 8

1. Research on organization design has a long history, with many review papers and books written to summarize its core theories (Puranam, Raveendran, and Knudsen 2012; Joseph et al. 2018b; Burton, Obel, and Hakonsson 2006; Puranam 2018; Galbraith 1973, 1974; Joseph et al. 2018a).

2. Modern research on hierarchy proceeds from similar notions (Levinthal and Workiewicz 2018; Williamson 1991; Siggelkow and Levinthal 2003).

3. Organization design literature has made connections to the informal side of design such as network ties (Kleinbaum 2018; Sosa, Gargiulo, and Rowles 2015; McEvily, Soda, and Tortoriello 2014; Mors, Lynch, and Lovas 2008; Puranam and Gulati 2008; Yakubovich and Burg 2019; Clement and Puranam 2018).

4. Although the mirroring hypothesis was originally explored in product and technology development (Colfer and Baldwin 2016; MacCormack, Baldwin, and Rusnak 2012), one can imagine its generality for other forms of material resources.

5. Research on silos is perhaps the most well-developed area of organization design, especially as it links to issues of exploration and exploitation and ambidexterity (Lessard and Zaheer 1996; Gulati, Puranam, and Tushman 2012; Benner and Tushman 2003; Kleinbaum and Tushman 2007; Lavie, Stettner, and Tushman 2010; Tushman and O'Reilly 1996; Gulati 2007) and to research on how interdependencies across silos leads to coordination challenges (Aggarwal and Wu 2015). This literature shares some links to literature on organizational hybridity, in which organizations balance competition tensions and values (Marquis, Besharov, and Thomason 2011; Smith and Besharov 2019; Smith, Gonin, and Besharov 2013; Birkinshaw et al. 2016; Lee and Jay 2015), or to those studies on adaptation where a balance of flexibility and efficiency is necessary (Davis, Eisenhardt, and Bingham 2009; Levinthal 1997; Nickerson and Silverman 2003; Posen and Levinthal 2012).

6. Clustering has played a large role in linking networks and group structure (Davis 1970; Shore, Bernstein, and Lazer 2015; Gibson and Vermeulen 2003; O'Leary and Mortensen 2010; O'Leary and Mortensen; Polzer et al. 2006; Sorenson 2005; Greve and Kim 2014), as highly connected individuals may form group boundaries around cohesive clusters. In turn these groups increase the likelihood of interaction within boundaries. This is consistent with interactionist perspectives in which structures emerge from interpersonal interactions (Soderstrom and Weber 2020; Barley 1986; Burton and Beckman 2007).

7. Research on boundary-spanning ties has indicated their value both in accessing valuable information (Fleming and Waguespack 2006; Mors, Rogan, and

Lynch 2018; Tushman and Scanlan 1981) and in the potential for spillovers to competitors (Shipilov, Godart, and Clement 2017; Davis and Aggarwal 2020; Flammer and Kacperczyk 2019; Nelson 2009; Singh and Marx 2013; Aharonson, Baum, and Feldman 2007).

8. Research on coalitions dates back to at least Cyert and March's (1963) political view of organizations, although it continues to have some resonance as an explanation for organizational behavior (Asmussen et al. 2021; Eisenhardt and Bourgeois 1988; Kellogg 2012; Rogan and Greve 2015; Labianca, Brass, and Gray 1998; Sherif et al. 1961).

9. The literature on exploration and exploitation related to ambidexterity is vast (Csaszar 2013; Gupta, Smith, and Shalley 2006; Kleinbaum and Stuart 2014a; Reinecke and Ansari 2015; Rogan and Mors 2014; Rothaermel and Alexandre 2009; Stettner and Lavie 2014; Benner and Tushman 2003; Tushman and O'Reilly 1996; Gibson and Birkinshaw 2004), indeed with some connections to network theory (Lazer and Friedman 2007; Lazer et al. 2010; Lavie, Kang, and Rosenkopf 2011; Mors, Rogan, and Lynch 2018; Rogan and Mors 2014, 2017).

10. Bottlenecks have been studied from a variety of perspectives ranging from information processing to incentives (Ethiraj 2007; Van Zandt 2004; Hannah and Eisenhardt 2019; Puranam, Raveendran, and Knudsen 2012; Davis and Eisenhardt 2011).

11. Research on matrix structures has noted the challenges of collaboration with too much connectivity (Sytch, Wohlgezogen, and Zajac 2018).

12. Zappos' brand of self-organization became prominent as an exemplar (Askin, Petriglieri, and Lockard 2016) of a broader trend discussed and critiqued by scholars (Bernstein et al. 2016; Burton et al. 2017).

13. This research appears in *Harvard Business Review* (Podolny and Hansen 2020).

14. Although the traditional economic view of organizational boundaries has dominated (Williamson 1975b), there are various conceptions of boundaries ranging from identity to power (Santos and Eisenhardt 2005; Schilling and Steensma 2002).

15. Research on the theory of the firm arguably started with Coase (1937) but accelerated after Williamson (1975a, b) and continued over the next several decades (Baker, Gibbons, and Murphy 2002b; Conner and Pralahad 1996; Cyert and March 1963; Dyer and Singh 1998; Gibbons 2005; Grant 1996; Hart 1989; Jensen and Meckling 1976; Kim and Mahoney 2005; March 1992; Poppo and Zenger 1998; Coase 1937; Williamson, Winter, and Coase 1991; Vroom and Gimeno 2007).

16. Research on make-or-buy decisions became an important governance implication of theory of the firm, especially in transaction cost economics (Gatignon and Gatignon 2010; Jia 2018; Klein 2005; Poppo and Zenger 1998; Williamson 1996; Williamson 1975b; Bodner and Capron 2018; Capron and Mitchell 2013).

17. The Fisher Body story has become an important example in governance research (Freeland 2000; Klein 1988; Coase 2000; Williamson, Winter, and Coase 1991).

18. Some research links tie strength, number of ties, and network similarity to governance and monitoring (Aven, Morse, and Iorio 2019; Hernandez and Shaver 2019; Ranganathan and Rosenkopf 2014; Garg 2013).

Chapter 9

1. Research on organizational aging includes some classic studies (Stinchcombe 1965) and more modern studies of entrepreneurship and innovation (Sorensen and Stuart 2000; Freeman, Carroll, and Hannan 1983; Posen and Chen 2013; Sine, Mitsuhashi, and Kirsch 2006; Dushnitsky and Lenox 2005).

2. Network age is a key feature in many organizational analyses (Kim, Oh, and Swaminathan 2006; Li and Rowley 2002; Rider 2012; Stam, Arzlanian, and Elfring 2014; Hallen, Davis, and Murray 2020; Burt 2002).

3. Research on agency costs has been highly varied and includes relevant research in the field of finance (Chung and Luo 2008; Eisenhardt 1989; Jensen and Meckling 1976; Mahoney 1992; Berle and Means 1932; Fama and Jensen 1983).

4. Research on open-source and other communities often has a network metaphor implicitly or explicitly in mind (Dahlander and O'Mahony 2011; Ferraro and O'Mahony 2012; O'Mahony 2003; O'Mahony and Ferraro 2007; Boudreau and Lakhani 2014; Lakhani and von Hippel 2003; Tushman, Lakhani, and Lifshitz-Assaf 2012; Quintane et al. 2014; Alexy, Henkel, and Wallin 2013; Ansari, Munir, and Gregg 2012; Hargadon and Bechky 2006; O'Mahony and Bechky 2008). This literature often overlaps that on crowdsourcing and crowdfunding (Greenberg and Mollick 2017; Agrawal, Catalini, and Goldfarb 2014; Dahlander and Piezunka 2014), as it involves accessing resources beyond organizational boundaries. Recent research on innovation and platform ecosystems has leveraged network theory (Jacobides, Cennamo, and Gawer 2018; Shipilov and Gawer 2020; Burford, Shipilov, and Furr 2021; Adner and Kapoor 2009; Gawer and Cusumano 2002) to explain corporate innovation activity beyond organization boundaries.

5. Some have argued that open innovation should include a variety of activities ranging from open-source software to user-generated content to crowd-funding (Agrawal, Catalini, and Goldfarb 2014). In this section, I restrict my focus to innovative production.

6. Research on R&D alliances or technology collaborations in the computer and biotechnology industries has a long history (Owen-Smith and Powell 2003; Powell, Koput, and Smith-Doerr 1996; Hoang and Rothaermel 2005; Davis and Eisenhardt 2011; Davis 2007; Baum, Calabrese, and Silverman 2000; Diestre and Rajagopalan 2012; Piezunka and Grohsjean 2022).

7. Organizational research on blockchains is in its infancy, although see Seidel (2018), Catalini and Gans (2020), Felin and Lakhani (2018), and Luminaeu, Wang, and Schilke (2020) for promising exemplars.

Chapter 10

1. This study may join a growing body of research exploring microfoundations of macrolevel phenomena (Felin, Foss, and Ployhart 2015; Felin et al. 2012; Davis and Aggarwal 2020; Argote and Ren 2012; Barney and Felin 2013; Eisenhardt, Furr, and Bingham 2010; Camuffo et al. 2019; Gavetti 2005).

2. Research on entrepreneurial network evolution is broad and growing (Stam, Arzlanian, and Elfring 2014; Stuart, Hoang, and Hybels 1999; Ozcan and Eisenhardt 2008; Pahnke, Katila, and Eisenhardt 2015; Vissa 2011, 2012; Clough et al. 2019; Stuart

and Sorenson 2007; Hallen, Davis, and Murray 2020; Katila, Rosenberger, and Eisenhardt 2008; Bermiss et al. 2017; Eesley and Wang 2017; Pahnke et al. 2015) because network representations seem to capture key activities like fundraising and innovation that shape entrepreneurship.

3. Thinking about inductive and abductive methodologies has undergone a flourishing (Eisenhardt and Graebner 2007; Pratt 2008; Davis, Eisenhardt, and Bingham 2007; Gehman et al. 2018; Hannah, Tidhar, and Eisenhardt 2020) in the past few decades because they are useful in the multidisciplinary and complex world of organization and management theory.

REFERENCES

Acquisti, Alessandro, and Ralph Gross. 2006. *Imagined Communities: Awareness, Information Sharing, and Privacy on the Facebook* (New York: Springer).

Adler, Paul S. 1995. "Interdepartmental Interdependence and Coordination: The Case of the Design/Manufacturing Interface." *Organization Science*, 6: 147–67.

Adner, Ron, and R. Kapoor. 2009. "Value Creation in Innovation Ecosystems: How the Structure of Technological Interdependence Affects Firm Performance in New Technology Generations." *Strategic Management Journal*, 31: 306–33.

Agarwal, R., R. Echambadi, A. Franco, and M. B. Sarkar. 2004. "Knowledge transfer through inheritance: spin-out generation, development, and survival." *Academy of Management Journal*, 47: 905–17.

Agarwal, R., Alfonso Gambardella, and DM Olson. 2016. "Employee Mobility and Entrepreneurship: A Virutal Special Issue." *Strategic Management Journal*, 30: 1349–74.

Aggarwal, Vikas A., and Brian Wu. 2015. "Organizational Constraints to Adaptation: Intrafirm Asymmetry in the Locus of Coordination." *Organization Science* 26: 218–38.

Agrawal, Ajay, Christian Catalini, and Avi Goldfarb. 2014. "Some Simple Economics of Crowdfunding." *Innovation Policy and the Economy*, 14: 63–97.

Aharonson, Barak S., Joel A. C. Baum, and Maryann P. Feldman. 2007. "Desperately Seeking Spillovers? Increasing Returns, Industrial Organization and The Location of New Entrants in Geographic and Technological Space." *Industrial and Corporate Change*, 16: 89–130.

Alaimo, Cristina, and Jannis Kallinikos. 2021. "Managing by Data: Algorithmic Categories and Organizing." *Organization Studies*, 42: 1385–407.

———. 2022. "Organizations Decentered: Data Objects, Technology and Knowledge." *Organization Science*, 33: 19–37.

Albert, Reika, Hawoong Jeong, and Albert-Laszlo Barabasi. 2000. "Error and Attack Tolerance of Complex Networks." *Nature*, 406: 378–82.

Albert, Stuart, Blake E. Ashforth, and Jane E. Dutton. 2000. "Organizational Identity and Identification: Charting New Waters and Building New Bridges." *Academy of Management. Academy of Management Review* 25: 13–17.

Alchian, Armen, and Harold Demsetz. 1972. "Production, Information Costs, and Economic Organization." *American Economic Review*, 62: 777–95.

Alexy, Oliver, Joachim Henkel, and Martin W. Wallin. 2013. "From closed to open: Job role changes, individual predispositions, and the adoption of commercial open source software development." *Research Policy*, 42: 1325–40.

Alexy, Oliver T., Joern H. Block, Philipp Sandner, and Anne L. J. Ter Wal. 2012. "Social Capital of Venture Capitalists and Start-Up Funding." *Small Business Economics*, 39: 835–51.

Ancona, D., Henrik Bresman, and M Mortensen. 2021. "Shifting Team Research after COVID-19: Evolutionary and Revolutionary Change." *Journal of Management Studies*, 58.

Ancona, Deborah G., and David F. Caldwell. 1992. "Bridging the Boundary: External Activity and Performance in Organizational Teams." *Administrative Science Quarterly*, 37: 634–65.

Anderson, Philip, and Michael Tushman. 1990. "Technological Discontinuities and Dominant Designs: A Cyclical Model of Technological Change." *Administrative Science Quarterly*, 35: 604–33.

Ansari, Shahzad, Kamal Munir, and Tricia Gregg. 2012. "Impact at the 'Bottom of the Pyramid': The Role of Social Capital in Capability Development and Community Empowerment." *Journal of Management Studies*, 49: 813–42.

Anteby, Michel, and Curtis K. Chan. 2018. "A Self-Fulfilling Cycle of Coercive Surveillance: Workers' Invisibility Practices and Managerial Justification." *Organization Science* 29: 247–63.

Argote, Linda, Brandy L. Aven, and Jonathan Kush. 2018. "The Effects of Communication Networks and Turnover on Transactive Memory and Group Performance." *Organization Science* 29: 191–206.

Argote, Linda, and Yuqing Ren. 2012. "Transactive Memory Systems: A Microfoundation of Dynamic Capabilities." *Journal of Management Studies*, 49: 1375–82.

Askin, N., Gianpiero Petriglieri, and Joanna Lockard. 2016. *Tony Hsieh at Zappos: Structure, Culture and Radical Change* (Fontainebleau, France: INSEAD Publishing).

Askin, Noah, and Matthew S. Bothner. 2016. "Status-Aspirational Pricing: The "Chivas Regal" Strategy in U.S. Higher Education, 2006–2012." *Administrative Science Quarterly*, 61: 217–53.

Asmussen, Christian G., Kirsten Foss, Nicolai J. Foss, and Peter G. Klein. 2021. "Economizing and Strategizing: How Coalitions and Transaction Costs Shape Value Creation and Appropriation." *Strategic Management Journal*, 42: 413–34.

Audia, Pino G., and Henrich Greve. 2020. *Organizational Learning from Performance Feedback: A Behavioral Perspective on Multiple Goals* (Cambridge, UK: Cambridge University Press).

Aven, Brandy L. 2015. "The Paradox of Corrupt Networks: An Analysis of Organizational Crime at Enron." *Organization Science* 26: 980–96.

Aven, Brandy L., Lily Morse, and Alessandro Iorio. 2019. "The Valley of Trust: The Effect of Relational Strength on Monitoring Quality." *Organizational Behavior and Human Decision Processes.*

Azoulay, Pierre, Nelson P. Repenning, and Ezra W. Zuckerman. 2010. "Nasty, Brutish, and Long: Embeddedness Failure in the Pharmaceutical Industry." *Administrative Science Quarterly.*

Baker, George, Robert Gibbons, and Kevin J. Murphy. 2002a. "Relational Contracts and the Theory of the Firm." *Quarterly Journal of Economics*, 117: 39–83.

———. 2002b. "Relational Contracts and the Theory of the Firm." *Quarterly Journal of Economics*, 117: 39–84.

Baker, Wayne E. 2000. *Achieving Success Through Social Capital* (Ann Arbor: University of Michigan Ross Business School).

Baker, Wayne E., and David Obstfeld. 1999. "Social Capital by Design: Structures, Strategies, and Institutional Context." in R. T. Leenders and S. M. Gabbay (eds.), *Corporate Social Capital and Liability* (Boston: Kluwer Academic).

Balazs, Vedres, and David Stark. 2010. "Structural Folds: Generative Disruption in Overlapping Groups." *American Journal of Sociology*, 115: 1150–90.

Barabasi, Albert-Laszlo. 2003. *Linked: How Everything Is Connected to Everything Else and What It Means For Business, Science, and Everyday Life* (New York: Plume).

Barabasi, Albert-Laszlo, and Reika Albert. 1999. "Emergence of Scaling in Random Networks." *Science* 286: 509–12.

Barley, Stephen R. 1986. "Technology as an Occasion for Structuring: Evidence from Observations of CT Scanners and the Social Order of Radiology Departments." *Administrative Science Quarterly*, 31: 78–108.

———. 1990. "The Alignment of Technology and Structure through Roles and Networks." *Administrative Science Quarterly*, 35: 61–103.

Barnard, Chester I. 1938. *The Functions of the Executive* (Cambridge, MA: Harvard University Press).

Barney, Jay, and Teppo Felin. 2013. "What Are Microfoundations?" *Academy of Management Perspectives* 27: 138–55.

Bartel, Caroline A., Amy Wrzesniewski, and Batia M. Wiesenfeld. 2012. "Knowing Where You Stand: Physical Isolation, Perceived Respect, and Organizational Identification among Virtual Employees." *Organization Science* 23: 743–57.

Battilana, Julie, and Tiziana Casciaro. 2012. "Change Agents, Networks, and Institutions: A Contingency Theory of Organizational Change." *Academy of Management Journal*, 55: 381–98.

———. 2013. "Overcoming Resistance to Organizational Change: Strong Ties and Affective Cooptation." *Management Science*, 59: 819–36.

Baum, J. A. C., and W. W. Powell. 1995. "Cultivating an Institutional Ecology of Organizations: Comment on Hannan, Carroll, Dundon, and Torres." *American Sociological Review*, 60: 529–38.

Baum, Joel A. C., Tony Calabrese, and Brian R. Silverman. 2000. "Don't Go It Alone: Alliance Network Composition and Startups' Performance in Canadian Biotechnology." *Strategic Management Journal* 21: 267–94.

Baum, Joel A. C., Andrew V. Shipilov, and Tim J. Rowley. 2003. "Where Do Small Worlds Come from?." *Industrial and Corporate Change*, 12: 697–725.

Baumann, Oliver, and Nicolaj Siggelkow. 2013. "Dealing with Complexity: Integrated vs. Chunky Search Processes." *Organization Science* 24: 116–32.

Bavelas, Alex. 1950. "Communication Patterns in Task-Oriented Groups." *Journal of the Acoustical Society of America* 22.

Beane, Matthew. 2019. "Shadow Learning: Building Robotic Surgical Skill When Approved Means Fail." *Administrative Science Quarterly*, 64: 87–123.

Beatty, Randolph, and Edward J. Zajac. 1994. "Managerial Incentives, Monitoring, and Risk Bearing: A Study of Executive Compensation, Ownership, and Board Structure in Initial Public offerings." *Administrative Science Quarterly*, 39: 313–35.

Beck, Julie. 2019. "Facebook: Where Friendships Go to Never Quite Die." *Atlantic*, February 4.

Becker, William J., Liuba Y. Belkin, Samantha A. Conroy, and Sarah Tuskey. 2021. "Killing Me Softly: Organizational E-mail Monitoring Expectations' Impact on Employee and Significant Other Well-Being." *Journal of Management*, 47: 1024–52.

Beckman, Christine M, C. Schoonhoven, R. Rottner, and S. J. Kim. 2014a. "Relational Pluralism in De Novo Organizations: Boards of Directors as Bridges or Barriers?." *Academy of Management Journal*, 57: 460–83.

Beckman, Christine M., M. Diane Burton, and Charles O'Reilly. 2007. "Early Teams: The Impact of Team Demography on VC Financing and Going Public." *Journal of Business Venturing* 22: 147–73.

Beckman, Christine M., and P. R. Haunschild. 2002. "Network Learning: The Effects of Partners' Heterogeneity of Experience on Corporate Acquisitions." *Administrative Science Quarterly*, 47: 92–124.

Beckman, Christine M., Claudia Bird Schoonhoven, Renee M. Rottner, and Sang-Joon Kim. 2014b. "Relational Pluralism in De Novo Organizations: Boards of Directors as Bridges or Barriers to Diverse Alliance Portfolios?" *Academy of Management Journal*, 57: 460–83.

Benner, Mary J., and Michael L. Tushman. 2003. "Exploitation, Exploration, and Process Management: The Productivity Dilemma Revisited." *Academy of Management Review* 28: 238–56.

Benner, Mary J., and Francisco M. Veloso. 2008. "ISO 9000 practices and financial performance: A technology coherence perspective." *Journal of Operations Management* 26: 611–29.

Benson, Alan, Danielle Li, and Kelly Shue. 2019. "Promotions and the Peter Principle." *Quarterly Journal of Economics*, 134: 2085–134.

Benson, Alan, and Ben A. Rissing. 2020. "Strength from Within: Internal Mobility and the Retention of High Performers." *Organization Science*, 31: 1313–620.

Berle, Adolf Augustus, and Gardiner Coit Means. 1932. *The Modern Corporation and Private Property* (New York: Macmillan).

Bermiss, Y. Sekou, Benjamin L. Hallen, Rory McDonald, and Emily C. Pahnke. 2017. "Entrepreneurial Beacons: The Yale Endowment, Run-Ups, and the Growth of Venture Capital." *Strategic Management Journal*, 38: 545–65.

Bernstein, Ethan, Hayley Blunden, Andrew Brodsky, Wonbin Sohn, and Ben Waber. 2020. "The Implications of Working Without an office." Big Ideas Series. *Harvard Business Review* 97: 82–91.

Bernstein, Ethan, John Bunch, Niko Canner, and Michael Y. Lee. 2016. "Beyond the Hoacracy Hype: The Overwrought Claims—and Actual Promise—of Next Generation Self-Managed Teams." *Harvard Business Review*, 94: 38–49.

Bernstein, Ethan S. 2012. "The Transparency Paradox: A Role for Privacy in Organizational Learning and Operational Control." *Administrative Science Quarterly*, 57: 181–216.

———. 2017. "Making Transparency Transparent: The Evolution of Observation in Management Theory." *Academy of Management Annals*, 11: 217–66.

Bernstein, Ethan, Jesse Shore, and David Lazer. 2018. "How intermittent breaks in interaction improve collective intelligent." *Proceedings of the National Academy of Sciences*, 115: 8734–39.

Besharov, Marya L. 2014. "The Relational Ecology of Identification: How Organizational Identification Emerges When Individuals Hold Divergent Values." *Academy of Management Journal*, 57: 1485–512.

Bidwell, Matthew, Forrest Briscoe, Isabel Fernandez-Mateo, and Adina Sterling. 2013. "The Employment Relationship and Inequality: How and Why Changes in Employment Practices are Reshaping Rewards in Organizations." *Academy of Management Annals*, 7: 61–121.

Bidwell, Matthew, and Isabel Fernandez-Mateo. 2010. "Relationship Duration and Returns to Brokerage in the Staffing Sector." *Organization Science* 21: 1141–58.

Bidwell, Matthew, Shinjae Won Won, Roxana Barbulescu, and Ethan Mollick. 2015. "I Used to Work at Goldman Sachs! How Organizational Status Creates Rents in the Market for Human Capital." *Strategic Management Journal*, 36: 1164–73.

Bingham, Christopher B., and Jason P. Davis. 2012. "Learning Sequences: Their Existence, Effect, and Evolution." *Academy of Management Journal*, 55: 611–41.

Bird, Douglas W., Rebecca Bliege Bird, Brian F. Codding, and David W. Zeanah. 2019. "Variability in the Organization and Size of Hunter-Gatherer Groups: Foragers Do Not Live in Small-Scale Societies." *Journal of Human Evolution*, 131: 96–108.

Birkinshaw, Julian, Donal Crilly, Cyril Bouquet, and Sun Young Lee. 2016. "How Do Firms Manage Strategic Dualities? A Process Perspective." *Academy of Management Discoveries* 2: 51–78.

Birkinshaw, Julian, Maya Gudka, and Vittorio D'Amato. 2021. "The Blinkered Boss: How Has Managerial Behavior Changed with the Shift to Virtual Working?." *California Management Review*, 63: 5–26.

Bloom, Nicholas. 2022. "Efficiency of Working from Home Relative to Working on Business Premises." Working Paper.

Bloom, Nicholas, Raffaella Sadun, and John Van Reenen. 2012. "Americans Do IT Better: US Multinationals and the Productivity Miracle." *American Economic Review*, 102: 167–201.

Bodner, Julia, and Laurence Capron. 2018. "Post-Merger Integration." *Journal of Organization Design*, 7: 3.

Boorman, S. A. 1975. "A Combinatorial Optimization Model for Transmission of Job Information through Contact Networks." *Bell Journal of Economics*, 6: 216–49.

Botelho, Tristan L. 2018. "Here's an Opportunity: Knowledge Sharing among Competitors as a Response to Buy-In Uncertainty." *Organization Science* 29: 1033–55.

Botelho, Tristan L., and Mabel Abraham. 2017. "Pursuing Quality: How Search Costs and Uncertainty Magnify Gender-based Double Standards in a Multistage Evaluation Process." *Administrative Science Quarterly*, 62: 698–730.

Bothner, Matthew S., Richard Haynes, Wonjae Lee, and Edward Bishop Smith. 2010. "When Do Matthew Effects Occur?." *Journal of Mathematical Sociology*, 34: 80–114.

Bothner, Matthew S., Joel M. Podolny, and Edward Bishop Smith. 2011. "Organizing Contests for Status: The Matthew Effect vs. the Mark Effect." *Management Science*, 57: 439–57.

Boudreau, Kevin, and Karim Lakhani. 2014. "'Open' Disclosure of Innovations, Incentives and Follow-on Reuse: Theory on Processes of Cumulative Innovation and a Field Experiment in Computational Biology." *Research Policy*, 44: 4–19.

Boyd, Danah. 2007. "Why Youth (Heart) Social Network Sites: The Role of Networked Publics in Teenage Social Life." In *Youth, Identity, and Digital Media*. ed. David Buckingham (Cambridge, MA: MIT Press, Cambridge, MA, 2008

Boyd, Danah M., and Nicole B. Ellison. 2007. "Social Network Sites: Definition, History, and Scholarship." *Journal of Computer-Mediated Communication*, 13: 210–30.

Brashears, Matthew E., and Eric Quintane. 2018. "The weakness of tie strength." *Social Networks*, 55: 104–15.

Brass, D. J. 1984. "Being in the Right Place: A Structural Analysis of Individual Influence in an Organization." *Administrative Science Quarterly* 29.

Brass, Daniel J., Joseph Galaskiewicz, Henrich R. Greve, and Wenpin Tsai. 2004. "Taking Stock of Networks and Organizations: A Multilevel Perspective." *Academy of Management Journal*, 47: 795–817.

Briscoe, Forrest, and Michelle Rogan. 2016. "Coordinating Complex Work: Knowledge Networks, Partner Departures, and Client Relationship Performance in a Law Firm." *Management Science*, 62: 2392–411.

Broschak, Joseph P. 2004. "Managers' Mobility and Market Interface: The Effect of Managers' Career Mobility on the Dissolution of Market Ties." *Administrative Science Quarterly*, 49: 608–40.

Broschak, Joseph P., and Emily S. Block. 2014. "With or Without You: When Does Managerial Exit Matter for the Dissolution of Dyadic Market Ties?." *Academy of Management Journal*, 57: 743–65.

Brown, Shona L., and Kathleen M. Eisenhardt. 1997. "The Art of Continuous Change: Linking Complexity Theory and Time-Paced Evolution in Relentlessly Shifting Organizations." *Administrative Science Quarterly*, 42: 1–34.

Brynjolfsson, Erik, John J. Horton, Adam Ozimek, Daniel Rock, Garima Sharma, and Hong-Yi TuYe. 2020. "COVID-19 and Remote Work: an Early Look at US Data." NBER Working Paper.

Brynjolfsson, Erik, and Lindsey Raymond. 2022. "Augmented Intelligence: Effects of AI on Productivity and Work Practices." ASSA Working Paper.

Burford, Natalie, Andrew Shipilov, and Nathan Furr. 2021. "How Ecosystem Structure Affects Firm Performance in Response to a Negative Shock to Interdependencies." *Strategic Management Journal*, 43: 30–57.

Burgelman, Robert A. 1994. "Fading Memories: A Process Theory of Strategic Business Exit in Dynamic Environments." *Administrative Science Quarterly*, 39: 24–56.

Burt, Ronald S. 1992. *Structural Holes: The Social Structure of Competition* (Cambridge, MA: Harvard University Press).

———. 1997. "The Contingent Value of Social Capital." *Administrative Science Quarterly*, 42: 339–65.

———. 2000. "The Network Structure of Social Capital." *Research in Organizational Behavior* 22: 345–423.

———. 2002. "Bridge Decay." *Social Forces* 24: 333–63.

———. 2005. *Brokerage and Closure: an Introduction to Social Capital* (Oxford, UK: Oxford University Press).

Burton, M. Diane, and Christine M. Beckman. 2007. "Leaving a Legacy: Position Imprints and Successor Turnover in Young Firms." *American Sociological Review*, 72: 239–66.

Burton, Richard M., Dorthe Døjbak Håkonsson, Jackson Nickerson, Phanish Puranam, Maciej Workiewicz, and Todd Zenger. 2017. "GitHub: Exploring the Space between Boss-Less and Hierarchical Forms of Organizing." *Journal of Organization Design*, 6: 10.

Burton, Richard M., B. Obel, and Dorthe Dojbak Hakonsson. 2006. *Organization Design: A Step by Step Approach* (Cambridge, UK: Cambridge University Press).

Burton, Richard M., and Børge Obel. 1995. "The validity of Computational Models in Organization Science: From Model Realism to Purpose of the Model." *Computational & Mathematical Organization Theory*, 1: 57–71.

———. 2011. "Computational Modeling for What-Is, What-Might-Be, and What-Should-Be Studies—and Triangulation." *Organization Science* 22: 1195–202.

Byun, Heejung, Joseph Raffiee, and Martin Ganco. 2019. "Discontinuities in the Value of Relational Capital: The Effects on Employee Entrepreneurship and Mobility." *Organization Science*, 30: 1368–93.

Cable, Daniel M., Francesca Gino, and Bradley R. Staats. 2013. "Breaking Them in or Eliciting Their Best? Reframing Socialization around Newcomers' Authentic Self-Expression." *Administrative Science Quarterly*, 58: 1–36.

Call, Matthew L, and Robert E. Ployhart. 2021. "A Theory of Firm Value Capture from Employee Job Performance: A Multi-Disciplinary Perspective." *Academy of Management Review*, 46: 572–90.

Cameron, Lindsey. 2021. "'Making Out' while Driving: Relational and Efficiency Games in the Gig Economy." *Organization Science*, 33: 231–52.

Cameron, Lindsey D., and Hatim Rahman. 2022. "Expanding the Locus of Resistance: Understanding the Co-constitution of Control and Resistance in the Gig Economy." *Organization Science*, 33: 38–58.

Campbell, Benjamin A., Russel W. Coff, and David Kryscynski. 2012. "Rethinking sustained competitive advantage from human capital." *Academy of Management Review*, 37: 376–95.

Camuffo, Arnaldo, Alessandro Cordova, Alfonso Gambardella, and Chiara Spina. 2019. "A Scientific Approach to Entrepreneurial Decision Making: Evidence from a Randomized Control Trial." *Management Science*: 503–1004.

Canales, Rodrigo, and Jason Greenberg. 2016. "A Matter of (Relational) Style: Loan Officer Consistency and Exchange Continuity in Microfinance." *Management Science*, 62: 1202–24.

Cao, Jiyin, and Edward Smith. 2020. "Why Do High Status People Have Larger Social Networks? Belief in Status-Quality Coupling as a Driver of Social Networking Behavior.." *Organization Science*, 32: 111–32.

Cappelli, Peter. 2012. *Strategic Talent Management: Contemporary Issues in an International Context* (Cambridge, UK: Cambridge University Press).

Capron, Laurence, and Will Mitchell. 2013. *Build, Borrow, or Buy* (Cambridge, MA: Harvard Business Review Press).

Carley, Kathleen M. 2001. "Computational Approaches to Sociological Theorizing." In *Handbook of Sociological Theory* ed. J. Turner (New York: Kluwer Academic/Plenum).

Carpenter, Masson, W. G. Sanders, and Hal B. Gregersen. 2001. "Bundling Human Capital with Organizational Context: The Impact of International Assignment Experience on Multinational Firm Performance and Pay." *Academy of Management Journal*, 44:493–511.

Casciaro, Tiziana. 1998. "Seeing Things Clearly: Social Structure, Personality, and Accuracy in Social Network Perception." *Social Networks*. 20:331–51.

Casciaro, Tiziana, F. Gino, and Maryam Kouchaki. 2016. "Learn to Love Networking." *Harvard Business Review*. 2016:104–07.

Castilla, Emilio J., and Aruna Ranganathan. 2020. "The Production of Merit: How Managers Understand and Apply Merit in the Workplace." *Organization Science*, 31:909–35.

Catalini, Christian, and J. S. Gans. 2020. "Some Simple Economics of the Blockchain." *Communications of the ACM* J, 63: 80–90.

Cattani, Gino, and Simone Ferriani. 2008. "A Core/Periphery Perspective on Individual Creative Performance: Social Networks and Cinematic Achievements in the Hollywood Film Industry." *Organization Science*, 19:824–44.

Cattani, Gino, Simone Ferriani, and Paul D. Allison. 2014. "Insiders, Outsiders, and the Struggle for Consecration in Cultural Fields: A Core-Periphery Perspective." *American Sociological Review*, 79:258–81.

Centola, Damon, and Michael Macy. 2007. "Complex Contagions and the Weakness of Long Ties." *American Journal of Sociology*, 113:702–34.

Cepa, Katharina, and Henri Schildt. 2022. "Data-Induced Rationality and Unitary Spaces in Interfirm Collaboration." *Organization Science*, https://doi.org/10.1287/orsc.2021.1566.

Chatman, Jennifer A. 1989a. "Improving Interactional Organizational Research: A Model of Person-Organization Fit." *Academy of Management Review*, 14:333–49.

———. 1989b. "Matching People and Organizations: Selection and Socialization in Public Accounting Firms." *Academy of Management Proceedings*, 1989:199–203.

Chatman, Jennifer A., Jeffrey T. Polzer, Sigal G. Barsade, and Margaret A. Neale. 1998. "Being Different yet Feeling Similar: The Influence of Demographic Composition and Organizational Culture on Work Processes and Outcomes." *Administrative Science Quarterly*, 43:749–80.

Chatterjee, Arijit, and Timothy G. Pollock. 2017. "Master of Puppets: How Narcissistic CEOs Construct Their Professional Worlds." *Academy of Management Review*, 42:703–25.

Chen, John S., and Pranav Garg. 2018. "Dancing with the Stars: Benefits of a Star Employee's Temporary Absence For Organizational Performance." *Strategic Management Journal*, 39:1239–67.

Choudhury, Prithwiraj, Tarun Khanna, Christos A. Makridis, and Kyle Schirmann. 2022. "Intrafirm Communication and Novelty of Work Products in a Hybrid Remote Workplace: Evidence from a Field Experiment." Harvard Business School Working Paper, No. 22-063, March.

Chung, Chi-Nien, and Xiaowei Luo. 2008. "Institutional Logics or Agency Costs: The Influence of Corporate Governance Models on Business Group Restructuring in Emerging Economies." *Organization Science*, 19:766–84.

Clauset, Aaron. 2021. "Network Analysis and Modeling." *Working Paper - Syllabus*.

Clement, Julien, and Phanish Puranam. 2018. "Searching for Structure: Formal Organization Design as a Guide to Network Evolution." *Management Science*, 64:3879–95.

Clement, Julien, Andrew Shipilov, and Charles Galunic. 2018. "Brokerage as a Public Good: The Externalities of Network Hubs for Different Formal Roles in Creative Organizations." *Administrative Science Quarterly*, 63:251–86.

Clough, David R., Tommy Pan Fang, Balagopal Vissa, and Andy Wu. 2019. 'Turning Lead into Gold: How Do Entrepreneurs Mobilize Resources to Exploit Opportunities?." *Academy of Management Annals*, 13:240–71.

Clough, David R., and Henning Piezunka. 2020. "Tie Dissolution in Market Networks: A Theory of Vicarious Performance Feedback." *Administrative Science Quarterly*, 65:972–1017.

Coase, Ronald H. 1937. "The Nature of the Firm." *Economica*, 4:386–405.

———. 2000. "The Acquisition of Fisher Body by General Motors." *Journal of Law and Economics*, 43:15–32.

Coff, Russel W. 1997. "Human Assets and Management Dilemmas: Coping with Hazards on the Road to Resource-Based Theory." *Academy of Management Review*. 22:374–402.

Coleman, James S. 1988. "Social Capital in the Creation of Human Capital." *American Journal of Sociology*, 94: S95–120.

Colfer, Lyra J, and Carliss Y. Baldwin. 2016. "The Mirroring Hypothesis: Theory, Evidence, and Exceptions." *Indistrial and Corporate Change.* 25: 709–38.

Conner, Kathleen R., and C. K. Pralahad. 1996. "A Resource-Based Theory of the Firm: Knowledge vs. Opportunism." *Organization Science,* 7: 477–501.

Conti, Annamaria, and Christopher C. Liu. 2015. "Bringing the Lab Back in: Personnel Composition and Scientific Output at the MIT Department of Biology." *Research Policy,* 44: 1633–44.

Corritore, Matthew, Amir Goldberg, and Sameer B. Srivastava. 2020. "Duality in Diversity: How Intrapersonal and Interpersonal Cultural Heterogeneity Relate to Firm Performance." *Administrative Science Quarterly,* 65: 359–94.

Coutinho, James, Julia Brennecke, S. P. Borgatti, Travis J. Grosser, Adam M. Kleinbaum, Giuseppe Labianca, and Andrew Parker. 2019. "Towards a Theory of Organizational Network Effectiveness: Challenges and Opportunities." In *Academy of Management Proceedings* (Boston: Academy of Management).

Cross, Rob, and Inga Carboni. 2020. "When Collaboration Fails and How to Fix It." *Sloan Management Review.*

Cross, Rob, Reb Rebele, and Adam Grant. 2016. "Collaborative Overload." *Harvard Business Review,* January–February.

Csaszar, Felipe A. 2013. "An Efficient Frontier in Organization Design: Organizational Structure as a Determinant of Exploration and Exploitation,' *Organization Science.* 24: 1083–101.

Cyert, R. M., and James G. March. 1963. *A Behavioral Theory of the Firm* (Englewood Cliffs, NJ: Prentice Hall).

Dahlander, Linus, and Daniel A. McFarland. 2013. "Ties That Last:Tie Formation and Persistence in Research Collaborations over Time." *Administrative Science Quarterly,* 58: 69–110.

Dahlander, Linus, and Siobhan O'Mahony. 2011. "Progressing to the Center: Coordinating Project Work." *Organization Science.* 22: 961–79.

Dahlander, Linus, and Henning Piezunka. 2014. "Open to suggestions: How Organizations Elicit Suggestions through Proactive and Reactive Attention." *Research Policy,* 43: 812–27.

Dahlander, Linus, Martin Wallin, Gianluca Carnabuci, and Eric Quintane. 2021. "Forming New Collaborations in Remote Work." *California Management Review.*

Davis, James A. 1970. "Clustering and hierarchy in interpersonal relations." *American Sociological Review,* 35: 843–51.

Davis, Jason P, and Vikas A. Aggarwal. 2020. "Knowledge Mobilization in the Face of Imitation: Microfoundations of Knowledge Aggregation and Firm-Level Innovation." *Strategic Management Journal,* 41.

Davis, Jason P. 2007. "Collaborative Innovation, Organizational Symbiosis, and the Embeddedness of Strategy." Ph.D. diss., Stanford University.

———. 2008. "Network Plasticity and Collaborative Innovation: Pruning and Pairing Processes in Network Reorganization." In *Academy of Management Proceedings.* https://doi.org/10.5465/ambpp.2008.33650230.

———. 2014. "The Emergence and Coordination of Synchrony in Networked Industry Ecosystems." In *Collaboration and Competition in Business Ecosystems (Advances in Strategic Management, Vol. 30)* (Bingley, UK: Emerald Group Publishing Limited pp. 197-237.

———. 2016. "The Group Dynamics of Interorganizational Relationships: Collaborating with Multiple Partners in Innovation Ecosystems." *Administrative Science Quarterly*, 61: 621–61.

Davis, Jason P., and Kathleen M. Eisenhardt. 2011. "Rotating Leadership and Collaborative Innovation: Recombination Processes in Symbiotic Relationships." *Administrative Science Quarterly*, 56: 159–201.

Davis, Jason P., Kathleen M. Eisenhardt, and Christopher B. Bingham. 2007. "Developing Theory through Simulation Methods." *Academy of Management Review*, 32: 480–99.

———. 2009. "Optimal Structure, Market Dynamism, and the Strategy of Simple Rules." *Administrative Science Quarterly*, 54: 413–52.

Deal, Jennifer J., and Alec Levenson. 2021. "Figuring Out Social Capital Is Critical For the Future of Hybrid Work." *MIT Sloan Management Review*, July 2.

DeFilippis, Evan, Stephen Impink, Madison Singell, Jeffrey Polzer, and Raffaella Sadun. 2020. "Collaborating During Coronavirus: The Impact of COVID-19 on the Nature of Work." *Harvard Business School Organizational Behavior Unit Working Paper No. 21-006.*

DeJordy, Rich, Maureen Scully, Marc J. Ventresca, and W. E. Douglas Creed. 2020. "Inhabited Ecosystems: Propelling Transformative Social Change between and Through Organizations." *Administrative Science Quarterly*, 65: 931–71.

Di Stefano, Giada, and Maria Rita Micheli. 2022. "To Stem the Tide: Organizational Climate and the Locus of Knowledge Transfer." *Organization Science*. https://ssrn.com/abstract=3913891.

Diestre, Luis, and Nandini Rajagopalan. 2012. "Are all 'Sharks' Dangerous? New Biotechnology Ventures and Partner Selection in R&D Alliances." *Strategic Management Journal*, 33: 1115–34.

DiMaggio, Paul. 1988. "Interest and Agency in Institutional Theory." In *Institutional patterns and organizations*, ed. Lynne Zucker (Cambridge, MA: Ballinger:).

DiMaggio, Paul J., and Walter W. Powell. 1983. "The Iron Cage Revisited: Institutional Isomorphism and Collective Rationality in Organizational Fields." *American Sociological Review*, 48: 147–60.

Dodge, Sheila, Don Kieffer, and Nelson Repenning. 2018. "Breaking Logjams in Knowledge Work." *MIT Sloan Management Review*, September 6.

Dokko, G., and Lori Rosenkopf. 2010. "Social Capital for Hire? Mobility of Technical Professionals and Firm Influence in Wireless Standard Setting Committees." *Organization Science*. 21: 677–95.

Dunbar, R. I. M. 1992. "Neocortex Size as a Constraint on Group Size in Primates." *Journal of Human Evolution*. 22: 469–93.

Dushnitsky, Gary, and Michael J. Lenox. 2005. "When Do Firms Undertake R&D by Investing in New Ventures?." *Strategic Management Journal*. 26: 947–65.

Dyer, Jeff, David Kryscynski, Christopher Law, and Shad Morris. 2021. "Who Should Become a Business School Associate Dean? Individual Performance and Taking on Firm-Specific Roles." *Academy of Management Journal*, 64: 1605–24.

Dyer, Jeffrey H. 2004. "Using Supplier Networks to Learn Fastser." *Sloan Management Review*, Spring: 57–63.

Dyer, Jeffrey H., and Harbir Singh. 1998. "The Relational View: Cooperative Strategy and Sources of Interorganizational Competitive Advantage." *Academy of Management Review*. 23: 660–79.

Eesley, Charles, and Yanbo Wang. 2017. "Social Influence in Career Choice: Evidence from a Randomized Field Experiment on Entrepreneurial Mentorship." *Research Policy*, 46: 636–50.

Eggers, J. P., and Aseem Kaul. 2018. "Motivation and Ability? A Behavioral Perspective on the Pursuit of Radical Invention in Multi-Technology Incumbents." *Academy of Management Journal*, 61: 67–93.

Eisenhardt, Kathleen, Nathan R. Furr, and Christopher B. Bingham. 2010. "Microfoundations of Performance: Balancing Efficiency and Flexibility in Dynamic Environments." *Organization Science*. 21: 1263–73.

Eisenhardt, Kathleen, and Melissa Graebner. 2007. "Theory Building from Cases: Opportunities and Challenges." *Academy of Management Journal*, 50: 25–32.

Eisenhardt, Kathleen M. 1989. "Agency Theory: An Assessment and Review." *Academy of Management Review*, 14: 57–74.

Eisenhardt, Kathleen M., and L. J. Bourgeois III. 1988. "Politics of Strategic Decision Making in High-Velocity Environments." *Academy of Management Journal*, 31: 737–70.

Ellison, Nicole, Charles Steinfield, and Cliff Lampe. 2007. "The Benefits of Facebook "Friends:" Social Capital and College Students' Use of Online Social Network Sites." *J. Computer-Mediated Communication*, 12: 1143–68.

Emirbayer, Mustafa, and Jeff Goodwin. 1994. "Network Analysis, Culture, and the Problem of Agency." *American Journal of Sociology*, 6: 1411–54.

Ethiraj, Sendil K. 2007. "Allocation of Inventive Effort in Complex Product Systems." *Strategic Management Journal*. 28: 563–84.

Fama, Eugene. 1980. "Agency Problems and the Theory of the Firm." *Journal of Political Economy*, 88: 288–307.

Fama, Eugene, and Michel Jensen. 1983. "Separation of Ownership and Control." *Journal of Law and Economics*. 26: 301–25.

Felin, Teppo, Nicolai J. Foss, Koen H. Heimeriks, and Tammy L. Madsen. 2012. "Microfoundations of Routines and Capabilities: Individuals, Processes, and Structure." *Journal of Management Studies*, 49: 1351–74.

Felin, Teppo, Nicolai J. Foss, and Robert E. Ployhart. 2015. "The Microfoundations Movement in Strategy and Organization Theory." *Academy of Management Annals*, 9: 575–632.

Felin, Teppo, and Karim Lakhani. 2018. "What problems will you solve with blockchain?." *MIT Sloan Management Review*, 60: 32–38.

Felin, Teppo, and Todd R. Zenger. 2014. "Closed or Open Innovation? Problem Solving and the Governance Choice." *Research Policy*, 43: 914–25.

Fernandez, R. M., and R. V. Gould. 1994. "A Dilemma of State Power: Brokerage and Influence in the National Health Policy." *American Journal of Sociology*, 99: 1455–91.

Fernandez, Roberto M., Emilio J. Castilla, and Paul Moore. 2000. "Social Capital at Work: Networks and Employment at a Phone Center." *American Journal of Sociology*, 105: 1288–356.

Fernandez, Roberto M., and Isabel Fernandez-Mateo. 2006. "Networks, Race, and Hiring." *American Sociological Review*, 71: 42–71.

Fernandez, Roberto M., and Marie Louise Mors. 2008. "Competing for Jobs: Labor Queues and Gender Sorting in the Hiring Process." *Social Science Research*, 37: 1061–80.

Fernandez-Mateo, Isabel. 2007. "Who Pays the Price of Brokerage? Transferring Constraint through Price Setting in the Staffing Sector." *American Sociological Review*, 72: 291–317.

Fernandez-Mateo, Isabel, and Roberto M. Fernandez. 2016. "Bending the Pipeline? Executive Search and Gender Inequality in Hiring for Top Management Jobs." *Management Science*, 62: 3636–55.

Fernandez-Mateo, Isabel, and Sarah Kaplan. 2018. "Gender and Organization Science: Introduction to a Virtual Special Issue." *Organization Science*. 29: 1229–36.

Ferraro, Fabrizio, and Siobhan O'Mahony. 2012. "Managing the Boundaries of an "Open" Project." *The Emergence of Organizations and Markets*: 545–66.

Flammer, Caroline, and Aleksandra Kacperczyk. 2019. "Corporate Social Responsibility as a Defense against Knowledge Spillovers: Evidence from the Inevitable Disclosure Doctrine." *Strategic Management Journal*, 40: 1243–67.

Flammer, Caroline, and Jiao Luo. 2017. "Corporate Social Responsibility as an Employee Governance Tool: Evidence from a Quasi-Experiment." *Strategic Management Journal*, 38: 163–83.

Fleming, Lee, and Adam Juda. 2004. "A Network of Invention." *Harvard Business Review*, 82.

Fleming, Lee, Charles King III, and Adam I. Juda. 2007. "Small Worlds and Regional Innovation." *Organization Science*, 18: 938–54.

Fleming, Lee, and David M. Waguespack. 2006. "Brokerage, Boundary Spanning, and Leadership in Open Innovation Communities." *Organization Science*, 18: 165–80.

Flynn, Francis J., Ray Reagans, Emily T. Amanatullah, and Daniel R. Ames. 2006. 'Helping One's Way to the Top: Self-Monitors Achieve Status by Helping Others and Knowing Who Helps Whom." *Journal of Personality and Social Psychology*, 91: 1123–37.

Fonti, Fabio, and Massimo Maoret. 2016. "The Direct and Indirect Effects of Core and Peripheral Social Capital on Organizational Performance." *Strategic Management Journal*, 37: 1765–86.

Foss, Nicolai J., Henrik Lando, and Steen Thomsen. 2000. "The Theory of the Firm." In *Encyclopedia of Law and Economics*, ed. Boudewijn Bouckaert and Gerrit De Geest (Cheltenham, UK: Edward Elgar).

Francisco Polidoro Jr., Gautam Ahuja, and Will Mitchell. 2011. "When the Social Structure Overshadows Competitive Incentives: The Effects of Network Embeddedness on Joint Venture Dissolution." *Academy of Management Journal*, 54: 203–23.

Frank, K. A., and J. Y. Yasumoto. 1998. "Linking Action to Social Structure within a System: Social Capital Within and between Subgroups." *American Journal of Sociology*, 104: 642–86.

Freeland, Robert F. 2000. "Creating Holdup through Vertical Integration: Fisher Body Revisited." *Journal of Law and Economics*, 43: 33–66.

Freeman, John H., Glenn R. Carroll, and Michael T. Hannan. 1983. "The Liability of Newness: Age Dependence in Organizational Death Rates." *American Sociological Review*, 48: 692–710.

Gaba, Vibha, and Shantanu Bhattacharya. 2012. "Aspirations, Innovation, and Corporate Venture Capital: A Behavioral Perspective." *Strategic Entrepreneurship Journal*, 6: 178–99.

Galbraith, Jay. 1973. *Designing Complex Organizations* (Reading, MA: Addison-Wesley).

———. 1974. "Organization Design: An Information Processing View." *Interfaces*, 4: 28–36.

Galunic, Charles D., G Ertug, and Martin Gargiulo. 2012. "The Positive Externalities of Social Capital: Benefitting from Senior Brokers." *Academy of Management Journal*, 55: 1213–31.

Galunic, D. Charles, and Erin Anderson. 2000. "From Security to Mobility: Generalized Investments in Human Capital and Agent Commitment." *Organization Science*, 11: 1–20.

Galunic, D. Charles, and Kathleen M. Eisenhardt. 1996. "The Evolution of Intracorporate Domains: Divisional Charter Losses in High-Technology, Multidivisional Corporations." *Organization Science*, 7: 255–82.

Galunic, D. Charles, and Simon Rodan. 1998. "Resource Recombinations in the Firm: Knowledge Structures and the Potential For Schumpeterian Innovation." *Strategic Management Journal*, 19: 1193–201.

Garg, Sam. 2013. "Venture Boards: Distinctive Monitoring and Implications For Firm Performance." *Academy of Management Review*, 38: 90–108.

Gargiulo, Martin. 1993. "Two-Step Leverage: Managing Constraint in Organizational Politics." *Administrative Science Quarterly*, 38: 1–19.

Gargiulo, Martin, and M. Benassi. 1999. "The Dark Side of Social Capital." In *Social Capital and Liability*, ed. Shaul Gabbay and Roger Leenders (Norwell, MA: Kluwer).

Gargiulo, Martin, and G Ertug. 2015. "The Power of the Weak." In *Research in the Sociology of Organizations*, 40: 95–109.

Gatignon, Aline, and Hubert Gatignon. 2010. "Erin Anderson and the Path Breaking Work of TCE in New Areas of Business Research: Transaction Costs in Action." *Journal of Retailing*, 86: 232–47.

Gavetti, Giovanni. 2005. "Cognition and Hierarchy: Rethinking the Microfoundations of Capabilities Development." *Organization Science*, 16: 599–617.

Gawer, Annabelle, and Michael Cusumano. 2002. *Platform Leadership: How Intel, Microsoft, and Cisco Drive Industry Innovation* (Boston: Harvard Business School Press).

Gehman, Joel, Vern L. Glaser, Kathleen M. Eisenhardt, Denny Gioia, Ann Langley, and Kevin G. Corley. 2018. "Finding Theory–Method Fit: A Comparison of Three

Qualitative Approaches to Theory Building." *Journal of Management Inquiry.* 27: 284–300.

Gerber, Scott. 2018. "Why Your Inner Circle Should Stay Small, and How to Shrink It." *Harvard Business Review.* https://hbr.org/2018/03/why-your-inner-circle-should -stay-small-and-how-to-shrink-it.

Gibbons, R, and Rebbecca Henderson. 2012. "Relational Contracts and Organizational Capabilities." *Organization Science.* 23: 1350–64.

Gibbons, Robert. 2005. "Four formal(izable) theories of the firm?." *Journal of Economic Behavior & Organization,* 58: 200–45.

Gibbons, Robert, and Kevin J. Murphy. 1990. "Relative Performance Evaluation for Chief Executive officers." *ILR Review,* 43: S30–S51.

Gibbs, Michael, Friederike Mengel, and Christoph Siemroth. 2021. "Work from Home and Productivity: Evidence from Personnel and Analytics Data on IT Professionals." *University of Chicago Working Paper,* 2021–56.

Gibson, Cristina B., and Julian Birkinshaw. 2004. "The Antecedents, Consequences, and Mediating Role of Organizational Ambidexterity." *Academy of Management Journal,* 47: 209–26.

Gibson, Cristina, and Freek Vermeulen. 2003. "A Healthy Divide: Subgroups as a Stimulus for Team Learning Behavior." *Administrative Science Quarterly,* 48: 202–39.

Godart, Frédéric C., and Kim Claes. 2017. "Semantic Networks and the Market Interface: Lessons from Luxury Watchmaking." In *Structure, Content and Meaning of Organizational Networks (Research in the Sociology of Organizations, Vol. 53)* (Bingley, UK: Emerald Publishing.

Goldberg, Amir, Sameer B. Srivastava, V. Govind Manian, William Monroe, and Christopher Potts. 2016. "Fitting in or Standing Out? The Tradeoffs of Structural and Cultural Embeddedness." *American Sociological Review,* 81: 1190–222.

Golub, Benjamin, and Matthew Jackson. 2012a. "Does Homophily Predict Consensus Times? Testing a Model of Network Structure via a Dynamic Process." *Review of Network Economics,* 11: 9.

Golub, Benjamin, and Matthew O. Jackson. 2012b. "How Homophily Affects the Speed of Learning and Best-Response Dynamics." *Quarterly Journal of Economics,* 127: 1287–338.

———. 2012c. "Network Structure and the Speed of Learning Measuring Homophily Based on its Consequences." *Annals of Economics and Statistics.* https://ssrn.com/ abstract=1784542 or http://dx.doi.org/10.2139/ssrn.1784542.

Granovetter, Mark. 1995. *Getting a Job: A Study of Contacts and Careers* Chicago: University of Chicago Press.

———. 1983. "The Strength of Weak Ties: A Network Theory Revisited." *Sociological Theory,* 1: 201–33.

———. 1985. "Economic Action and Social Structure: The Problem of Embeddedness." *American Journal of Sociology,* 91: 481–510.

———. 2017. *Society and Economy: Framework and Principles* (Cambridge, MA: Harvard University Press).

Granovetter, Mark, and Richard Swedberg, eds. 2011. *The Sociology of Economic Life* (Boulder, CO: Westview Press).

Grant, Robert M. 1996. "Toward a Knowledge-Based Theory of the Firm." *Strategic Management Journal*, 17: 109–22.

Greenberg, Jason, and Ethan Mollick. 2017. "Activist Choice Homophily and the Crowdfunding of Female Founders." *Administrative Science Quarterly*, 62: 341–74.

Greve, Henrich, and Jay Kim. 2014. "Running for the Exit: Community Cohesion and Bank Panics." *Organization Science*. 25: 204–21.

Greve, Henrich R. 1998. "Performance, Aspirations, and Risky Organizational Change." *Administrative Science Quarterly*, 43: 58–86.

Grosser, Travis J., David Obstfeld, Giuseppe Labianca, and Stephen P. Borgatti. 2019. "Measuring Mediation and Separation Brokerage Orientations: A Further Step toward Studying the Social Network Brokerage Process." *Academy of Management Discoveries*, 5: 114–36.

Groysberg, Boris, Jeffrey T. Polzer, and Hillary Anger Elfenbein. 2011. "Too Many Cooks Spoil the Broth: How High-Status Individuals Decrease Group Effectiveness." *Organization Science*. 22: 722–37.

Gulati, R. 2007. "Silo Busting: How to Execute on the Promise of Customer Focus." *Harvard Business Review*, 85: 98–108.

Gulati, Ranjay, Dovev Lavie, and Harbir Singh. 2009. "The Nature of Partnering Experience and the Gains from Alliances." *Strategic Management Journal*, 30: 1213–33.

Gulati, Ranjay, Phanish Puranam, and Michael Tushman. 2012. "Meta-Organization Design: Rethinking Design in Interorganizational and Community Contexts." *Strategic Management Journal*, 33: 571–86.

Gulati, Ranjay, Maxim Sytch, and Adam Tatarynowicz. 2012. "The Rise and Fall of Small Worlds: Exploring the Dynamics of Social Structure." *Organization Science*. 23: 449–71.

Gupta, Abhinav, Sucheta Nadkarni, and Misha Mariam. 2019. "Dispositional Sources of Managerial Discretion: CEO Ideology, CEO Personality, and Firm Strategies." *Administrative Science Quarterly*, 64: 855–93.

Gupta, Anil K., Ken G. Smith, and Christina E. Shalley. 2006. "The Interplay between Exploration and Exploitation." *Academy of Management Journal*, 49: 693–706.

Hadley, Constance N, and Mark Mortensen. 2020. "Are Your Team Members Lonely?" *Sloan Management Review*, December 8.

Hahl, Oliver, Aleksandra "Olenka" Kacperczyk, and Jason P. Davis. 2016. "Knowledge Asymmetry and Brokerage: Linking Network Perception to Position in Structural Holes." *Strategic Organization*, 14: 118–43.

Hallen, Benjamin, Jason P. Davis, and Alex Murray. 2020. "Entrepreneurial Network Evolution: Explicating the Structural Localism and Agentic Network Change Distinction." *Academy of Management Annals*, 14: 1067–102.

Hallen, Benjamin L. 2008. "The Causes and Consequences of the Initial Network Positions of New Organizations: From Whom Do Entrepreneurs Receive Investments?." *Administrative Science Quarterly*, 53: 685–718.

Hallen, Benjamin L., and Kathleen M. Eisenhardt. 2012. "Catalyzing Strategies and Efficient Tie Formation: How Entrepreneurial Firms Obtain Investment Ties." *Academy of Management Journal*, 55: 35–70.

Hannah, Douglas P., and Kathleen M. Eisenhardt. 2019. "Bottlenecks, Cooperation, and Competition in Nascent Ecosystems." *Strategic Management Journal*, 40: 1333–35.

Hannah, Douglas P., Ron Tidhar, and Kathleen M. Eisenhardt. 2020. "Analytic Models in Strategy, Organizations, and Management Research: A Guide For Consumers." *Strategic Management Journal*, 42: 329–60.

Hannan, Michael T., and Glenn R. Carroll. 1995. "Theory Building and Cheap Talk About Legitimation: Reply to Baum and Powell." *American Sociological Review*, 60: 539–44.

Hannan, Michael T., and John Freeman. 1989. *Organizational Ecology* (Cambridge, MA: Harvard University Press).

Hansen, Morten T, Joel M. Podolny, and Jeffrey Pfeffer. 1999. "So Many Ties, So Little Time: A Task Contingency Perspective on the Value of Social Capital in Organization." *Administrative Science Quarterly*, 42: 1–50.

Hansen, Morten T., and Martine R. Haas. 2001. "Competing for Attention in Knowledge Markets: Electronic Document Dissemination in a Management Consulting Company." *Administrative Science Quarterly*, 46: 1–28.

Hargadon, Andrew B., and Beth A. Bechky. 2006. "When Collections of Creatives Become Creative Collectives: A Field Study of Problem Solving at Work." *Organization Science*, 17: 484–500.

Hargadon, Andrew, and Robert I. Sutton. 1997. "Technology Brokering and Innovation in a Product Development Firm." *Administrative Science Quarterly*, 42: 716–49.

Hart, Oliver. 1989. "An Economist's Perspective on the Theory of the Firm." *Columbia Law Review*, 89: 1757–74.

Hasan, Sharique, and Rembrand Koning. 2020. "Designing Social Networks: Joint Tasks and the Formation of Network Ties." *Journal of Organization Design*, 9:4.

Haveman, Heather A., Nan Jia, Jing Shi, and Yongxiang Wang. 2017. "The Dynamics of Political Embeddedness in China." *Administrative Science Quarterly*, 62: 67–104.

Haythornthwaite, Caroline. 2005. "Social Networks and Internet Connectivity Effects." *Information, Communication & Society*, 8: 125–47.

Hayward, Mathew L. A., Violina P. Rindova, and Timothy G. Pollock. 2004. "Believing One's Own Press: The Causes and Consequences of CEO Celebrity." *Strategic Management Journal*. 25: 637–53.

Helfat, Constance. 1994. "Firm-Specificity in Corporate Applied R&D." *Organization Science*, 5: 173–84.

Henderson, Rebbeca M., and Kim B. Clark. 1990. "Architectural Innovation: The Reconfiguration of Existing Product Technologies and the Failure of Established Firms." *Administrative Science Quarterly*, 35: 9–30.

Hernandez, Exequiel, and Anoop Menon. 2018. "Acquisitions, Node Collapse, and Network Revolution." *Management Science*, 64: 1652–71.

Hernandez, Exequiel, Wm. Gerard Sanders, and Anja Tuschke. 2015. "Network Defense: Pruning, Grafting, and Closing to Prevent Leakage of Strategic Knowledge to Rivals." *Academy of Management Journal*, 58: 1233–60.

Hernandez, Exequiel, and J. Myles Shaver. 2019. "Network Synergy." *Administrative Science Quarterly*, 64: 171–202.

Hill, Rachel A, and Robin I. M. Dunbar. 2003. "Social Network Size in Humans." *Human Nature*, 14: 53–72.

Hinds, Pamela J., and Diane E. Bailey. 2003. "Out of Sight, Out of Sync: Understanding Conflict in Distributed Teams." *Organization Science*, 14: 615–32.

Hinds, Pamela J., and Mark Mortensen. 2005. "Understanding Conflict in Geographically Distributed Teams: The Moderating Effects of Shared Identity, Shared Context, and Spontaneous Communication." *Organization Science*, 16: 290–307.

Hoang, Ha, and Frank T. Rothaermel. 2005. "The Effect of General and Partner-Specific Alliance Experience on Joint R&D Project Performance." *Academy of Management Journal*, 48: 332–45.

Hoffman, Mitchell, and Steven Tadelis. 2020. "People Management Skills, Employee Attrition, and Manager Rewards: An Empirical Analysis ." *Journal of Political Economy*, 129.

Hoffman, Chris. 2019. "How to Stop Slack from Taking Over Your Life." *New York Times*, August 28.

Holloway, Samuel S., and Anne Parmigiani. 2016. "Friends and Profits Don't Mix: The Performance Implications of Repeated Partnerships." *Academy of Management Journal*, 59: 460–78.

Huy, Quy H. 2016. "Distributed Attention and Shared Emotions in the Innovation Process: How Nokia Lost the Smartphone Battle." *Administrative Science Quarterly*, 61: 9–51.

Ibarra, Herminia. 1993. "Network Centrality, Power, and Innovation Involvement: Determinants of Technical and Administrative Roles." *Academy of Management Journal*, 36: 471–501.

———. 1995. "Race, Opportunity, and Diversity of Social Circles in Managerial Networks." *Academy of Management Journal*, 38: 673–703.

Ibarra, Herminia, and Roxana Barbulescu. 2010. "Identity as Narrative: Prevalence, Effectiveness, and Consequences of Narrative Identity Work in Macro Work Role Transitions." *Academy of Management Review*, 35: 135–54.

Ibarra, Herminia, and Mark Hunter. 2007. "How Leaders Create and Use Networks." *Harvard Business Review*, 85: 40–47.

Ibarra, Herminia, Martin Kilduff, and Wenpin Tsai. 2005. "Zooming in and Out: Connecting Individuals and Collectivities at the Frontiers of Organizational Network Research." *Organization Science*, 16: 359–71.

Ibarra, Herminia, and Jennifer L. Petriglieri. 2010. "Identity Work and Play." *Journal of Organizational Change Management*. 23: 10–25.

Ingram, Paul, and Lori Qingyuan Yue. 2008. "Structure, Affect and Identity as Bases of Organizational Competition and Cooperation." *Academy of Management Annals*. 2: 275–303.

Jackson, Matthew O. 2008. *Social and Economic Networks* (Princeton, NJ: Princeton University Press).

Jackson, Matthew, and Leeat Yariv. 2009. "Diffusion, Strategic Interaction, and Social Structure." In *Handbook of Social Economics*, ed. Bisin Benhabib, Jackson, (Boston: Elsevier).

Jacobides, M. G., C. Cennamo, and Annabelle Gawer. 2018. "Toward a Theory of Business Ecosystems." *Strategic Management Journal*, 39: 2255–76.

Jacobs, Abigail Z., and Duncan J. Watts. 2021. "A Large-Scale Comparative Study of Informal Social Networks in Firms." *Management Science*, 67: 5489–509.

Jensen, Michael, and William Meckling. 1976. "The Theory of the Firm: Managerial Behavior, Agency Costs, and Ownership Structure." *Journal of Financial Economics*, 3: 305–60.

Jeong, Hawoong, Z. Neda, and Albert-Laszlo Barabasi. 2001. "Measuring Preferential Attachment For Evolving Networks." Working Paper.

Jia, Nan. 2018. "The 'Make and/or Buy' Decisions of Corporate Political Lobbying: Integrating the Economic Efficiency and Legitimacy Perspectives." *Academy of Management Review*, 43: 307–26.

Jia, Nan, Kenneth G. Huang, and Cyndi Man Zhang. 2019. "Public Governance, Corporate Governance, and Firm Innovation: An Examination of State-Owned Enterprises." *Academy of Management Journal*, 62: 220–47.

Jonczyk, Claudia D., Yonghoon G. Lee, Charles D. Galunic, and Ben M. Bensaou. 2016. "Relational Changes During Role Transitions: The Interplay of Efficiency and Cohesion." *Academy of Management Journal*, 59: 956–82.

Jonsson, Stefan, Henrich R. Greve, and Takako Fujiwara-Greve. 2009. "Undeserved Loss: The Spread of Legitimacy Loss to Innocent Organizations in Response to Reported Corporate Deviance." *Administrative Science Quarterly*, 54: 195–228.

Joseph, John, Oliver Baumann, Richard M. Burton, and Kannan Srikanth. 2018a. *Organization Design* (Bingley, UK: Emerald Publishing Group).

Joseph, John, Oliver Baumann, Richard Burton, and Kannan Srikanth. 2018b. "Reviewing, Revisiting, and Renewing the Foundations of Organization Design." In *Organization Design* (Bingley, UK: Emerald Publishing).

Joseph, John, and Vibha Gaba. 2015. "The fog of feedback: Ambiguity and firm responses to multiple aspiration levels." *Strategic Management Journal*, 36: 1960–78.

Kacperczyk, Aleksandra, Christine M. Beckman, and Thomas P. Moliterno. 2015. "Disentangling Risk and Change: Internal and External Social Comparison in the Mutual Fund Industry." *Administrative Science Quarterly*, 60: 228–62.

Kahl, Steven, and Stine Grodal. 2016. "Discursive Strategies and Radical Technological Change: Multilevel Discourse Analysis of the Early Computer (1947–1958)." *Strategic Management Journal*, 37: 149–66.

Karim, Samina, and Aseem Kaul. 2015. "Structural Recombination and Innovation: Unlocking Intraorganizational Knowledge Synergy Through Structural Change." *Organization Science*. 26: 439–55.

Karunakaran, Arvind. 2021. "Status–Authority Asymmetry between Professions: The Case of 911 Dispatchers and Police officers." *Administrative Science Quarterly*, 67: 423–68.

Katila, Riitta, and Gautam Ahuja. 2002. "Something Old, Something New: A Longitudinal Study of Search Behavior and New Product Introduction." *Academy of Management Journal*, 45: 1183–94.

Katila, Riitta, Jeff Rosenberger, and Kathleen Eisenhardt. 2008. "Swimming with Sharks: Technology Ventures, Defense Mechanisms, and Corporate Relationships." *Administrative Science Quarterly*, 53: 295–332.

Katz, Daniel, and Michael Tushman. 1979. "Communication Patterns, Project Performance, and Task Characteristics: An Empirical Evaluation and Integration in an R&D Setting." *Organizational Behavior and Human Performance*. 23: 139–62.

Kauppila, Olli-Pekka, Lorenzo Bizzi, and David Obstfeld. 2018. "Connecting and Creating: Tertius Iungens, Individual Creativity, and Strategic Decision Processes." *Strategic Management Journal*, 39: 697–719.

Kellogg, Katherine C. 2012. "Making the Cut: Using Status-Based Countertactics to Block Social Movement Implementation and Microinstitutional Change in Surgery." *Organization Science*. 23: 1546–70.

Kellogg, Katherine C., Wanda J. Orlikowski, and JoAnne Yates. 2006. "Life in the Trading Zone: Structuring Coordination across Boundaries in Postbureaucratic Organizations." *Organization Science*, 17: 22–44.

Kellogg, Katherine C., Melissa A. Valentine, and Angèle Christin. 2020. "Algorithms at Work: The New Contested Terrain of Control." *Academy of Management Annals*, 14: 366–410.

Kennedy, Mark Thomas, and Peer Christian Fiss. 2009. "Institutionalization, Framing, and Diffusion: The Logic of TQM Adoption and Implementation Decisions among U.S. Hospitals." *Academy of Management Journal*, 52: 897–918.

Kilduff, M., and D. Krackhardt. 1994. "Bringing the Individual Back in: A Structural Anaysis of the Internal Market for Reptutation in Organizations." *Academy of Management Journal*, 37: 87–108.

Kilduff, Martin, and Wenpin Tsai. 2003. *Social Networks and Organizations* (London: Sage).

Kim, Jongwook, and Joseph T. Mahoney. 2005. "Property Rights Theory, Transaction Costs Theory, and Agency Theory: An Organizational Economics Approach to Strategic Management." *Managerial and Decision Economics*. 26: 223–42.

Kim, T., H. Oh, and A. Swaminathan. 2006. "Framing Interorganizational Network Change: A Network Inertia Perspective." *Academy of Management Review*, 31: 704–20.

Klein, Benjamin. 1988. "Vertical Integration as Organizational Ownership: The Fisher-Body–General Motors Relationship Revisited." *Journal of Law, Economics and Organization*, 4: 199–213.

Klein, Katherine J., Jonathan C. Ziegert, Andrew P. Knight, and Yan Xiao. 2006. "Dynamic Delegation: Shared, Hierarchical and Deindividualized Leadership in Extreme Action Teams." *Administrative Science Quarterly*, 51: 590–621.

Klein, Peter G. 2005. "The Make-or-Buy Decision: Lessons from Empirical Studies." In *Handbook of New Institutional Economics*, eds. Claude Menard and Mary M. Shirley (Boston: Springer).

Kleinbaum, Adam M. 2012. "Organizational Misfits and the Origins of Brokerage in Intrafirm Networks." *Administrative Science Quarterly*, 57: 407–52.

——. 2018. "Reorganization and Tie Decay Choices." *Management Science*, 64: 2219–37.

Kleinbaum, Adam M., Alexander H. Jordan, and Pino G. Audia. 2015. "An Altercentric Perspective on the Origins of Brokerage in Social Networks: How Perceived Empathy Moderates the Self-Monitoring Effect." *Organization Science*. 26: 1226–42.

Kleinbaum, Adam M., and Toby E. Stuart. 2014a. "Network Responsiveness: The Social Structural Microfoundations of Dynamic Capabilities." *Academy of Management Perspectives*. 28: 353–67.

Kleinbaum, Adam M., Toby E. Stuart, and Michael L. Tushman. 2013. "Discretion within Constraint: Homophily and Structure in a Formal Organization." *Organization Science*. 24: 1316–36.

Kleinbaum, Adam, and Toby E. Stuart. 2014b. "Network Responsiveness: The Social Structural Microfoundations of Dynamic Capabilities." *Academy of Management Perspectives*, 28: 353–67.

Kleinbaum, Adam, and Michael Tushman. 2007. "Building Bridges: The Social Structure of Interdependent Innovation." *Strategic Entrepreneurship Journal*, 1: 103–22.

Krackhardt, David. 1987. "Cognitive Social Structures." *Social Networks*, 9: 109–34.

——. 1990. "Assessing the Political Landscape: Structure, Cognition, and Power in Organizations." *Administrative Science Quarterly*, 35: 342–69.

——. 1992. "The Strength of Strong Ties: The Importance of Philos in Organizations." In *Networks and Organizations: Structure, Form, and Action*, eds. Nitin Nohria and Robert G. Eccles (Boston: Harvard Business School Press).

——. 1999. "The Ties That Torture: Simmelian Tie Analysis in Organizations." *Research in the Sociology of Organizations*, 16: 183–210.

Krackhardt, David, and Martin Kildruff. 1999. "Whether Close or Far: Perceptions of Balance in Friendship Networks in Organizations." *Journal of Personal and Social Psychology*, 76: 770–82.

Krems, Jaimie Arona, and Jason Wilkes. 2019. "Why are conversations limited to about four people? A theoretical exploration of the conversation size constraint." *Evolution and Human Behavior*, 40: 140–47.

Kuwabara, Ko, Claudius A. Hildebrand, and Xi Zou. 2018. "Lay Theories of Networking: How Laypeople's Belief's about Networking Affect Their Attitudes and Engagement towards Instrumental Networking." *Academy of Management Review*, 43: 50–64.

Kuwabara, Ko, Jiao Luo, and Oliver Sheldon. 2010. "Multiplex Exchange Relations." in *Advances in Group Processes*, eds. S. R. Thyre and E. J. Lawler (Bingley, UK: Emerald Group).

Kuwabara, Ko, X. Zou, Brandy Aven, C. Hildebrand, and S. Iyengar. 2020. "Lay Theories of Networking Ability: Beliefs That Inhibit Instrumental Networking." *Social Networks*, 62: 1–11.

Labianca, Giuseppe, and Daniel J. Brass. 2006. "Exploring the Social Ledger: Negative Relationships and Negative Asymmetry in Social Networks in Organizations." *Academy of Management Review*, 31: 596–614.

Labianca, Giuseppe, Daniel J. Brass, and Barbara Gray. 1998. "Social Networks and Perceptions of Intergroup Conflict: The Role of Negative Relationships and Third Parties." *Academy of Management Journal*, 41: 55–67.

Lahiri, Amrita, Emily C. Pahnke, Michael D. Howard, and Warren Boeker. 2019. "Collaboration and Informal Hierarchy in Innovation Teams: Product Introductions in Entrepreneurial Ventures." *Strategic Entrepreneurship Journal*, 13: 326–58.

Lakhani, Karim, and Eric von Hippel. 2003. "How Open Source Software Works: 'Free' User-to-User Assistance.." *Research Policy*, 32: 923–43.

Lampe, Cliff, Nicole Ellison, and Charles Steinfield. 2006. "A Face (Book) in the Crowd: Social Searching vs. Social Browsing. ACM Conference on Computer Supported Cooperative Work, Alberta Canada, November 4–8.

Lant, Theresa, and Stephen Mezias. 1990. "Managing Discontinuous Change: A Simulation Study of Organizational Learning and Entrepreneurship." *Strategic Management Journal*, 11: 147–79.

Laursen, Keld, and Ammon Salter. 2020. "Who Captures Value from Open Innovation —The Firm or Its Employees?." *Strategic Management Review*, 1: 255–76.

Lavie, Dovev, Jingoo Kang, and Lori Rosenkopf. 2011. "Balance within and across Domains: The Performance Implications of Exploration and Exploitation in Alliances." *Organization Science*. 22: 1517–38.

Lavie, Dovev, Uriel Stettner, and Michael L. Tushman. 2010. "Exploration and Exploitation Within and Across Organizations." *Academy of Management Annals*, 4: 109–55.

Lazer, David, and Allan Friedman. 2007. "Network Structure of Exploration and Exploitation." *Administrative Science Quarterly*, 52: 667–94.

Lazer, David, Brian Rubineau, Carol Chetkovich, Nancy Katz, and Michael Neblo. 2010. "The Coevolution of Networks and Political Attitudes." *Political Communication* 27: 248–74.

Lazzarini, Sergio G., Gary J. Miller, and Todd R. Zenger. 2006. "Dealing with the Paradox of Embeddedness: The Role of Contracts and Trust in Facilitating Movement out of Committed Relationships." *Organization Science*, 19: 709–28.

Leavitt, Harold J. 1989. "Suppose We Took Groups Seriously." In *Readings in managerial psychology*, ed. H. J. Leavitt, L. R. Pondy and D. M. Boje (Chicago: University of Chicago Press).

Lee, Jaemin, Joon Mahn Lee, and Ji-Yub (Jay) Kim. 2021. "The Role of Attribution in Learning from Performance Feedback: Behavioral Perspective on the Choice between Alliances and Acquisitions." *Academy of Management Journal*. https://doi.org/10.5465/amj.2019.1293.

Lee, Matthew, and Jason Jay. 2015. "Strategic Responses to Hybrid Social Ventures." *California Management Review*, 57: 126–47.

Lee, Sunkee, and Phanish Puranam. 2017. "Incentive Redesign and Collaboration in Organizations: Evidence from a Natural Experiment." *Strategic Management Journal*, 38: 2333–52.

Leonardi, Paul M. 2014. "Social Media, Knowledge Sharing, and Innovation: Toward a Theory of Communication Visibility." *Information Systems Research* 25: 796–816.

Leonardi, Paul M., Marleen Huysman, and Charles Steinfield. 2013. "Enterprise Social Media: Definition, History, and Prospects for the Study of Social Technologies in Organizations." *Journal of Computer-Mediated Communication*, 19: 1–19.

Lessard, Donald R., and Srilata Zaheer. 1996. "Breaking the Silos: Distributed Knowledge and Strategic Responses to Volatile Exchange Rates." *Strategic Management Journal*, 17: 513–33.

Levinthal, Dan. 1997. "Adaptation on Rugged Landscapes." *Management Science*, 43: 934–50.

Levinthal, Daniel A., and Maciej Workiewicz. 2018. "When Two Bosses Are Better Than One: Nearly Decomposable Systems and Organizational Adaptation." *Organization Science* 29: 207–24.

Levinthal, Daniel, and Hart E. Posen. 2007. "Myopia of Selection: Does Organizational Adaptation Limit the Efficacy of Population Selection?" *Administrative Science Quarterly*, 52: 586–620.

Li, Jian Bai. 2021. "On the Problem of Obligatory Relationships." Working Paper.

Li, Jian Bai, and Henning Piezunka. 2020. "The Uniplex Third: Enabling Single-domain Role Transitions in Multiplex Relationships." *Administrative Science Quarterly*, 65: 314–58.

Li, Stan Xiao, and Timothy J. Rowley. 2002. "Inertia and Evaluation Mechanisms in Interorganizational Partner Selection: Syndicate Formation among U.S. Investment Banks." *Academy of Management Journal*, 45: 1104–19.

Li, Yuan, Ning Li, Chuanjia Li, and Jingyu Li. 2020. "The Boon and Bane of Creative 'Stars': A Social Network Exploration of How and When Team Creativity Is (and Is Not) Driven by a Star Teammate." *Academy of Management Journal*, 63: 613–35.

Lingo, Elizabeth L., and Siobhan O'Mahony. 2009. "Nexus Work: Brokerage on Creative Projects." *Administrative Science Quarterly*, 55: 47–81.

Lomi, Alessandro, Tom A. B. Snijders, Christian E. G. Steglich, and Vanina Jasmine Torló. 2011. "Why Are Some More Peer Than Others? Evidence from a Longitudinal Study of Social Networks and Individual Academic Performance." *Social Science Research*, 40: 1506–20.

Luminaeu, Fabrice, Wenqian Wang, and Oliver Schilke. 2020. "Blockchain Governance—A New Way of Organizing Collaborations?" *Organization Science*, 32: 500–21.

Lungeanu, Alina, and Noshir S. Contractor. 2014. "The Effects of Diversity and Network Ties on Innovations: The Emergence of a New Scientific Field." *American Behavioral Scienctist*, 59: 548–64.

Luo, Xiaowei, and Chi-Nien Chung. 2005. "Keeping It All in the Family: The Role of Particularistic Relationships in Business Group Performance During Institutional Transition." *Administrative Science Quarterly*, 50: 404–39.

MacCormack, Alan, Carliss Y. Baldwin, and John Rusnak. 2012. "Exploring the Duality between Product and Organization Architectures: A Test of the Mirroring Hypothesis." *Research Policy*, 41: 1309–24.

Mahoney, Joseph T. 1992. "The Choice of Organizational Form: Vertical Financial Ownership Versus Other Methods of Vertical Integration." *Strategic Management Journal*, 13: 559–84.

Makadok, Richard, and Jay B. Barney. 2001. "Strategic Factor Market Intelligence: An Application of Information Economics to Strategy Formulation and Competitor Intelligence." *Management Science*, 47: 1621–38.

Malter, Daniel. 2014. "On the Causality and Cause of Returns to Organizational Status: Evidence from the Grand Crus Classes of the Medoc." *Administrative Science Quarterly*, 59: 271–300.

March, James G. 1992. "Learning and the Theory of the Firm." *Economia e Banca-Annali Scientifici*, 5–6: 15–35.

March, James G., and J. P. Olsen. 1984. "The new institutionalism: Organizational Factors in Political Life." *American Political Science Review*, 78: 734–47.

March, James G., and Herbert Simon. 1958. *Organizations* (New York: Wiley).

Marquis, Christopher, Marya Besharov, and Bobbi Thomason. 2011. "Whole Foods: Balancing Social Mission and Growth." *Harvard Business School Organizational Behavior Unit Case No. 410-023.* https://ssrn.com/abstract=2038034.

Marsden, P. V. 1982. "Brokerage Behavior in Restricted Exchange Networks." In *Social Structure and Network Analysis*, ed. P. V. Marsden and N. Lin (Beverly Hills, CA: Sage).

Mauskapf, M., E. Quintane, N. Askin, and J. Mol. 2017. "Embeddedness and the Production of Novelty in Music: A Multi-Dimensional Perspective." *Academy of Management Proceedings* (Briarcliff Manor, NY: Academy of Management).

Mayer, Kyle J., Deepak Somaya, and Ian O. Williamson. 2012. "Firm-Specific, Industry-Specific, and Occupational Human Capital and the Sourcing of Knowledge Work." *Organization Science* 23: 1311–29.

Mazmanian, Melissa, Wanda J. Orlikowski, and JoAnne Yates. 2013. "The Autonomy Paradox: The Implications of Mobile Email Devices for Knowledge Professionals." *Organization Science* 24: 1337–57.

McEvily, Bill, Giuseppe Soda, and Marco Tortoriello. 2014. "More Formally: Rediscovering the Missing Link between Formal Organization and Informal Social Structure." *Academy of Management Annals*, 8: 299–345.

McFadyen, M. Ann, and Albert A. Cannella Jr. 2004. "Social Capital and Knowledge Creation: Diminishing Returns of the Number and Strength of Exchange Relationships." *Academy of Management Journal*, 47: 735–46.

Mehra, Ajay, Martin Kilduff, and Daniel J. Brass. 2001. "The Social Networks of High and Low Self-Monitors: Implications for Workplace Performance." *Administrative Science Quarterly*, 46: 121–46.

Milgram, Stanley. 1967. "The Small World Problem." *Psychology Today* 2: 60–67.

Milward, H. Brinton, and K. G. Provan. 1998. "Principles for Controlling Agents: The Political Economy of Network Structure." *Journal of Administration Research and Theory*, 8: 203–21.

Miner, Anne S., P Bassoff, and C Moorman. 2001. "Organizational Improvisation and Learning: A Field Study." *Administrative Science Quarterly*, 46: 304–37.

Mintzberg, Henry. 2002. *The Strategy Process* (New York: Prentice Hall).

Mitsuhashi, Hitoshi, and Azusa Nakamura. 2022. "Pay and Networks in Organizations: Incentive Redesign as a Driver of Network Change." *Strategic Management Journal*, 43: 295–322.

Mizruchi, Mark S. 1989. "Similarity of Political Behavior among Large American Corporations." *American Journal of Sociology*, 95: 401–24.

Mizruchi, Mark S., Linda Brewster Stearns, and Anne Fleischer. 2011. "Getting a Bonus: Social Networks, Performance, and Reward among Commercial Bankers." *Organization Science* 22: 42–59.

Moldoveanu, Mihnea C., and Joel A. C Baum. 2014. *Epinets: The Epistemic Structure and Dynamics of Social Networks* (Stanford, CA: Stanford University Press).

Molla, Rani. 2019. "The Productivity Pit: How Slack Is Ruining Work." *Recode*. https://www.vox.com/recode/2019/5/1/18511575/productivity-slack-google-microsoft-facebook?ref=nodesk.

Monteiro, Felipe, and Julian Birkinshaw. 2017. "The External Knowledge Sourcing Process in Multinational Corporations." *Strategic Management Journal*, 38: 342–62.

Mors, Marie Louise, Susan Lynch, and Bjorn Lovas. 2008. "A Bridge Too Far: The Effect of Informal Ties Across Formal Boundaries on Individual Exploration Performance." Working Paper.

Mors, Marie Louise, Michelle Rogan, and Susan E. Lynch. 2018. "Boundary Spanning and Knowledge Exploration in a Professional Services Firm." *Journal of Professions and Organization*, 5: 184–205.

Nahapiet, Janine, and Sumantra Goshal. 1998. "Social Capital, Intellectual Capital and Organizational Advantage." *Academy of Management Review* 23: 242–66.

Naumovska, Ivana, Vibha Gaba, and Henrich Greve. 2021. "The Diffusion of Differences: A Review and Reorientation of 20 Years of Diffusion Research." *Academy of Management Annals*, 15: 377–405.

Neeley, Tsedal B. 2021. *Remote Work Revolution: Succeeding from Anywhere* (New York: Harper Business).

Neeley, Tsedal B., and Paul Leonardi. 2018. "Enacting Knowledge Strategy through Social Media: Passable Trust and the Paradox of Non-Work Interactions." *Strategic Management Journal*, 39: 922–46.

Nelson, Andrew. 2009. "Measuring Knowledge Spillovers: What Patents, Licenses and Publications Reveal about Innovation Diffusion." *Research Policy*, 38: 994–1005.

Newport, Calvin. 2016a. *Deep Work: Rules for Focused Success in a Distracted World* (New York: Little, Brown).

———. 2016b. *A World Without Email: Reimagining Work in an Age of Communication* (New York: Portfolio).

Nickerson, Jack A., and Brian R. Silverman. 2003. "Why Firms Want to Organize Efficiently and What Keeps Them from Doing So: Inappropriate Governance, Performance, and Adaptation in a Deregulated Industry." *Administrative Science Quarterly*, 48: 433–65.

O'Leary, Michael Boyer, and Mark Mortensen. 2010. "Go (Con)figure: Subgroups, Imbalance, and Isolates in Geographically Dispersed Teams." *Organization Science* 21: 115–31.

O'Mahony, Siobhán. 2003. "Guarding the Commons: How Community Managed Software Processes Protect Their Work." *Research Policy*, 32: 1179–98.

O'Mahony, Siobhán, and Beth A. Bechky. 2008. "Boundary Organizations: Enabling Collaboration among Unexpected Allies." *Administrative Science Quarterly*, 53: 422–59.

O'Mahony, Siobhán, and Fabrizio Ferraro. 2007. "The Emergence of Governance in an Open Source Community." *Academy of Management Journal*, 50: 1079–106.

O'Reilly, Charles A. III, and Jennifer A. Chatman. 1996. "Culture as Social Control: Corporations, Cults, and Commitment." *Research in Organizational Behavior*, 18: 157–200.

O'Leary, Michael, and Mark Mortensen. "Subgroups with Attitude: Imbalance and Isolation in Geographically Dispersed Teams."https://www.coursehero.com/file/p6gbbr3n/changes-based-on-expertise-or-other-individual-characteris-tics-Morgeson-et-al/.

Obstfeld, David. 2005. "Social Networks, the Tertius Iungens Orientation, and Involvement in Innovation." *Administrative Science Quarterly*, 50: 100–30.

———. 2012. "Creative Projects: A Less Routine Approach Toward Getting New Things Done." *Organization Science* 23: 1571–92.

———. 2013. *Getting New Things Done: Brokers, Knowledge, and Collective Action* (Stanford, CA: Stanford University Press).

Obstfeld, David, S. P. Borgatti, and Jason P. Davis. 2013. "Brokerage as a Process: Decoupling Third Party Action from Social Network Structure." In *Research in the Sociology of Organizations*, ed. Giuseppe (Joe) Labianca Daniel J. Brass, Ajay Mehra, Daniel S. Halgin, Stephen P. Borgatti (Bingley, UK: Emerald Insight Publishing.

Ocasio, William. 1997. "Towards an Attention-Based View of the Firm." *Strategic Management Journal*, 18: 187–206.

Ocasio, William, and John Joseph. 2005. "An Attention-Based Theory of Strategy Formulation: Linking Micro- and Macroperspectives in Strategy Processes." In *Strategy Process*, ed. Gabriel Szulanski, Joe Porac and Yves Doz (Bingley, UK: Emerald Group Publishing).

Ocasio, William, Jo-Ellen Pozner, and Daniel Milner. 2020. "Varieties of Political Capital and Power in Organizations: A Review and Integrative Framework." *Academy of Management Annals*, 14: 303–38.

Oh, Hongseok, Myung-Ho Chung, and Giuseppe Labianca. 2004. "Group Social Capital and Group Effectiveness: The Role of Informal Socializing Ties." *Academy of Management Journal*, 47: 860–75.

Orlikowski, Wanda J. 1992. "The Duality of Technology: Rethinking the Concept of Technology in Organizations." *Organization Science*, 3: 398–427.

Orlikowski, Wanda J., JoAnne Yates, Kazuo Okamura, and Masayo Fujimoto. 1995. "Shaping electronic communication: The metastructuring of technology in the context of use." *Organization Science*, 6: 423–44.

Owen-Smith, Jason, and Walter W. Powell. 2003. "Knowledge Networks as Channels and Conduits: The Effects of Spillovers in the Boston Biotechnology Community." *Organization Science*, 15: 5–21.

Ozcan, C. Pinar, and Kathleen M. Eisenhardt. 2008. "Origin of Alliance Portfolios: Entrepreneurs, Network Strategies, and Firm Performance." *Academy of Management Journal*, 52: 246–79.

Pachucki, Mark A., and Ronald L. Breiger. 2010. "Cultural Holes: Beyond Relationality in Social Networks and Culture." *American Review of Sociology*, 36: 205–24.

Pahnke, Emily A., Rory McDonald, Dan J. Wang, and Benjamin Hallen. 2015. "Exposed: Venture Capital, Competitors Ties, and Entrepreneurial Innovation." *Academy of Management Journal*, 58: 1334–60.

Pahnke, Emily Cox, Riitta Katila, and Kathleen M. Eisenhardt. 2015. "Who Takes You to the Dance? How Partners' Institutional Logics Influence Innovation in Young Firms." *Administrative Science Quarterly*, 60: 596–633.

Palmer, Donald. 1983. "Broken Ties: Interlocking Directorates, and Intercorporate Coordination." *Administrative Science Quarterly* 28: 40–55.

Parise, Salvatore, Eoin Whelan, and Steve Todd. 2015. "How Twitter Users Can Generate Better Ideas." *MIT Sloan Management Review*, 56: 21–25.

Perlow, Leslie A., Gerardo Andres Okhuysen, and Nelson Repenning. 2002. "The Speed Trap: Exploring the Relationship between Decision Making and Temporal Context." *Academy of Management Journal*, 45: 931–55.

Perrow, Charles. 1972. *Complex Organizations: A Critical Essay* (Glenview, IL: Scott, Foresman).

Pfarrer, Michael D., Timothy G. Pollock, and Violina P. Rindova. 2010. "A Tale of Two Assets: The Effects of Firm Reputation and Celebrity on Earnings Surprises and Investors' Reactions." *Academy of Management Journal*, 53: 1131–52.

Pfeffer, Jeffery. 1978. "The Micropolitics of Organizations." In *Environments and Organizations*, ed. M. W. Meyer (San Francisco: Jossey-Bass).

Pfeffer, Jeffrey. 1992. *Managing with Power: Politics and Influence in Organizations* (Boston: Harvard Business School Press).

Phelps, Corey, Ralph Heidl, and Anu Wadhwa. 2012. "Knowledge, Networks, and Knowledge Networks: A Review and Research Agenda." *Journal of Management*, 38: 1115–66.

Piezunka, Henning, and Thorsten Grohsjean. 2022. "Collaborations That Hurt Firm Performance but Help Employees' Careers." *Strategic Management Journal*. In press.

Piezunka, Henning, Wonjae Lee, Richard Haynes, and Matthew S. Bothner. 2018. "The Matthew Effect as an Unjust Competitive Advantage: Implications for Competition Near Status Boundaries." *Journal of Management Inquiry* 27: 378–81.

Piskorski, Mikolaj Jan. 2014. *A Social Strategy: How We Profit from Social Media* (Princeton, NJ: Princeton University Press).

Podolny, J, and James N. Baron. 1997. "Resources and Relationships: Social Networks and Mobility in the Workplace." *American Sociological Review*, 62: 673–93.

Podolny, J., and Morten T. Hansen. 2020. "How Apple Is Organized for Innovation." *Harvard Business Review* digital article (November–December), Product no. R2006F-PDF-ENG.

Pollock, Timothy G., Joseph F. Porac, and James B. Wade. 2004. "Constructing Deal Networks: Brokers as Network "Architects" in the U.S. IPO Market and Other Examples." *Academy of Management Review* 29: 50–72.

Polzer, Jeffrey T., C. Brad Crisp, Sirkka L. Jarvenpaa, and Jerry W. Kim. 2006. "Extending the Faultline Model to Geographically Dispersed Teams: How Colocated

Subgroups Can Impair Group Functioning." *Academy of Management Journal*, 49: 679–92.

Poppo, Laura, and Todd Zenger. 1998. "Testing Alternative Theories of the Firm: Transaction Cost, Knowledge-Based, and Measurement Explanations for Make-or-Buy Decisions in Information Services." *Strategic Management Journal*, 19: 853–77.

Posen, Hart E., and John S. Chen. 2013. "An Advantage of Newness: Vicarious Learning Despite Limited Absorptive Capacity." *Organization Science* 24: 1701–16.

Posen, Hart E., and Daniel A. Levinthal. 2012. "Chasing a Moving Target: Exploitation and Exploration in Dynamic Environments." *Management Science*, 58: 587–601.

Powell, Walter W., Keneth W. Koput, and Laurel Smith-Doerr. 1996. "Interorganizational Collaboration and the Locus of Innovation: Networks of Learning in Biotechnology." *Administrative Science Quarterly*, 41: 116–45.

Prato, Matteo, and Fabrizio Ferraro. 2018. "Starstruck: How Hiring High-Status Employees Affects Incumbents' Performance." *Organization Science* 29: 755–74.

Pratt, Michael. 1998. "To Be Or Not to Be: Central Questions in Organizational Identification." In *Identity in Organizations: Building Theory Through Conversations* (Thousand Oaks, CA: SAGE.

Pratt, Michael G. 2008. "Fitting Oval Pegs Into Round Holes:Tensions in Evaluating and Publishing Qualitative Research in Top-Tier North American Journals." *Organizational Research Methods*, 11: 481–509.

Provan, K. G., and Patrick Kenis. 2008. "Modes of Network Governance: Structure, Management, and Effectivenss." *Journal of Public Administration Research and Theory*, 18: 229–52.

Puranam, Phanish. 2018. *The Microstructure of Organizations* (Oxford, UK: Oxford University Press).

Puranam, Phanish, and Ranjay Gulati. 2008. "Renewal Through Reorganization: The Value of Inconsistencies between Formal and Informal Structure." *Organization Science* (forthcoming).

Puranam, Phanish, Marlo Raveendran, and Thorbjorn Knudsen. 2012. "Organization Design: The Epistemic Interdependence Perspective." *Academy of Management Review*, 37: 419–40.

Quintane, Eric, and Gianluca Carnabuci. 2016. "How Do Brokers Broker? Tertius Gaudens, Tertius Iungens, and the Temporality of Structural Holes." *Organization Science* 27: 1343–60.

Quintane, Eric, Guido Conaldi, Marco Tonellato, and Alessandro Lomi. 2014. "Modeling Relational Events: A Case Study on an Open Source Software Project." *Organizational Research Methods*, 17: 23–50.

Rahman, Hatim. 2021. "The Invisible Cage: Workers' Reactivity to Opaque Algorithmic Evaluations." *Administrative Science Quarterly*, 66: 945–88.

Ranganathan, Ram, and Lori Rosenkopf. 2014. "Do Ties Really Bind? The Effect of Technological and Relational Networks on Opposition to Standards." *Academy of Management Journal*, 57: 515–40.

Rauch, Madeleine, and Shahzad Ansari. 2022. "Waging War from Remote Cubicles: How Workers Cope with Technologies That Disrupt the Meaning and Morality of Their Work." *Organization Science*, 33: 83–104.

Reagans, Ray, Linda Argote, and Daria Brooks. 2005. "Individual Experience and Experience Working Together: Predicting Learning Rates from Knowing Who Knows What and Knowing How to Work Together." *Management Science*, 51: 869–81.

Reagans, Ray, Ezra Zuckerman, and Bill McEvily. 2004. "How to Make the Team: Social Networks vs. Demography as Criteria for Designing Effective Teams." *Administrative Science Quarterly*, 49: 101–33.

Reagans, Ray, and Ezra W. Zuckerman. 2001. "Networks, Diversity, and Productivity: The Social Capital of Corporate R&D Teams." *Organization Science*, 12: 502–17.

Reinecke, Juliane, and Shaz Ansari. 2015. "When Times Collide: Temporal Brokerage at the Intersection of Markets and Developments." *Academy of Management Journal*, 58: 618–48.

Ren, Yuqing, Kathleen M. Carley, and Linda Argote. 2006. "The Contingent Effects of Transactive Memory: When Is It More Beneficial to Know What Others Know?." *Management Science*, 52: 671–82.

Repenning, Nelson. 2001. "Understanding Fire Fighting in New Product Development." *Journal of Product Innovation Management*, 18: 285–300.

———. 2002. "A Simulation-Based Approach to Understanding the Dynamics of Innovation Implementation." *Organization Science*, 13: 109–27.

Repenning, Nelson, and John Sterman. 2002. "Capability Traps and Self-Confirming Attribution Errors in the Dynamics of Process Improvement." *Administrative Science Quarterly*, 47: 265–95.

Rider, Christopher I. 2009. "Constraints on the Control Benefits of Brokerage: A Study of Placement Agents in U.S. Venture Capital Fundraising." *Administrative Science Quarterly*, 54: 575–601.

———. 2012. "How Employees' Prior Affiliations Constrain Organizational Network Change: A Study of U.S. Venture Capital and Private Equity." *Administrative Science Quarterly*, 57: 453–83.

Rindova, Violina P., and Suresh Kotha. 2001. "Continuous "Morphing": Competing Through Dynamic Capabilities, Form, and Function." *Academy of Management Journal*, 44: 1263–80.

Rindova, Violina P., Timothy G. Pollock, and Mathew L. A. Hayward. 2006. "Celebrity Firms: The Social Construction of Market Popularity." *Academy of Management Review*, 31: 50–71.

Rogan, Michelle. 2014. "Too Close for Comfort? The Effect of Embeddedness and Competitive Overlap on Client Relationship Retention Following an Acquisition." *Organization Science* 25: 185–203.

Rogan, Michelle, and Henrich R. Greve. 2015. "Resource Dependence Dynamics: Partner Reactions to Mergers." *Organization Science* 26: 239–55.

Rogan, Michelle, and Marie Louise Mors. 2014. "A Network Perspective on Individual-Level Ambidexterity in Organizations." *Organization Science* 25: 1860–77.

———. 2017. "Managerial Networks and Exploration in a Professional Service Firm." *Organization Studies*, 38: 225–49.

Rothaermel, Frank T., and Maria Tereza Alexandre. 2009. "Ambidexterity in Technology Sourcing: The Moderating Role of Absorptive Capacity." *Organization Science* 20: 759–80.

Rowley, Tim J., Joel A. C. Baum, Andrew V. Shipilov, Henrich R. Greve, and Hayagreeva Rao. 2004. "Competing in Groups." *Managerial and Decision Economics* 25: 453–71.

Rowley, Timothy J., D. Behrens, and David Krackhardt. 2000. "Redundant Governance Structures: An Analysis of Structural and Relational Embeddedness in the Steel and Semiconductor Industries." *Strategic Management Journal* 21: 369–86.

Rowley, Timothy J., Henrich R. Greve, Hayagreeva Rao, Joel A. C. Baum, and Andrew V. Shipilov. 2005. "Time to Break Up: Social and Instrumental Antecedents of Firm Exits from Exchange Cliques." *Academy of Management Journal*, 48: 499–520.

Rubineau, Brian, and Roberto M. Fernandez. 2015. "Tipping Points: The Gender Segregating and Desegregating Effects of Network Recruitment." *Organization Science* 26: 1646–64.

Ruef, Martin. 2002. "Strong Ties, Weak Ties, and Islands: Structural and Culture Predictors of Organizational Innovation." *Industrial and Corporate Change*, 11: 427–49.

Ruef, Martin, Howard Aldrich, and N. Carter. 2003. "The Structure of Founding Teams: Homophily, Strong Ties, and Isolation among U.S. Entrepreneurs." *American Sociological Review*, 68: 195–222.

Sakhartov, Arkadiy V, and Timothy B. Folta. 2014. "Resource Relatedness, Redeployability, and Firm Value." *Strategic Management Journal*, 35: 1781–97.

Salancik, Gerald R. 1995. "Wanted: A Good Network Theory of Organization." *Administrative Science Quarterly*, 40: 345–49.

Sandvik, Jason J., Richard E. Saouma, Nathan T. Seegert, and Christopher T. Stanton. 2020. "Workplace Knowledge Flows." *Quarterly Journal of Economics*, 135: 1635–80.

Santos, Filipe M., and Kathleen M. Eisenhardt. 2005. "Organizational Boundaries and Theories of Organization." *Organization Science*, 16: 491–508.

Sasovova, Zuzana, Ajay Mehra, Stephen P. Borgatti, and Michaéla C. Schippers. 2010. "Network Churn: The Effects of Self-Monitoring Personality on Brokerage Dynamics." *Administrative Science Quarterly*, 55: 639–70.

Schilling, Melissa A., and Corey Phelps. 2007. "Interfirm Collaboration Networks: The Impact of Small World Connectivity on Firm Innovation." *Management Science*, 53: 1113–26.

Schilling, Melissa A., and H. Kevin Steensma. 2002. "Disentangling the Theories of Firm Boundaries: A Path Model and Empirical Test." *Organization Science*, 13: 387–401.

Seabright, Mark A., Dan Levinthal, and M. Fichman. 1992. "Role of Individual Attachments in the Dissolution of Interorganizational Relationships." *Academy of Management Journal*, 35: 122–60.

Seidel, Marc-David L. 2018. "Questioning Centralized Organizations in a Time of Distributed Trust." *Journal of Management Inquiry* 27: 40–44.

Selznick, Philip. 1949. *TVA and the Grass Roots: A Study in the Sociology of Formal Organization* (New York: Harper & Row).

Seong, Sorah, and Frédéric C. Godart. 2018. "Influencing the Influencers: Diversification, Semantic Strategies, and Creativity Evaluations." *Academy of Management Journal*, 61: 966–93.

Sharkey, Amanda J. 2018. "The Dark Side of Status." *Journal of Management Inquiry* 27: 368–70.

Shaw, Sonali K., and Frank Nagel. 2020. "Why Do User Communities Matter for Strategy?" *Strategic Management Review*, 1: 305–53.

Sherif, M., O. J. Harvey, J. B. White, W. R. Hood, and C. W. Sherif. 1961. *Intergroup Conflict and Cooperation: The Robbers Cave Experiment* (Norman, OK: University of Oklahoma, Institute of Group Relations).

Shi, Weilei, Livia Markoczy, and Gregory G. Dess. 2009. "The Role of Middle Management in the Strategy Process: Group Affiliation, Structural Holes, and Tertius Iungens." *Journal of Management*, 35: 1453–80.

Shipilov, A., and Annabelle Gawer. 2020. "Integrating Research on Interorganizational Networks and Ecosystems." *Academy of Management Annals*, 14: 92–121.

Shipilov, Andrew. 2012. "Strategic Multiplexity." *Strategic Organization*, 10: 215–22.

Shipilov, Andrew, Frédéric C. Godart, and Julien Clement. 2017. "Which Boundaries? How Mobility Networks Across Countries and Status Groups Affect the Creative Performance of Organizations." *Strategic Management Journal*, 38: 1232–52.

Shipilov, Andrew, Ranjay Gulati, Martin Kilduff, Stan Xiao Li, and Wenpin Tsai. 2014. "Relational Pluralism Within and between Organizations." *Academy of Management Journal*, 57: 449–59.

Shipilov, Andrew V., and Stan Xiao Li. 2012. "The Missing Link: The Effect of Customers on the Formation of Relationships among Producers in the Multiplex Triads." *Organization Science* 23: 472–91.

Shore, Jesse, Ethan Bernstein, and David Lazer. 2015. "Facts and Figuring: An Experimental Investigation of Network Structure and Performance in Information and Solution Spaces." *Organization Science* 26: 1432–46.

Siggelkow, Nicolaj, and Daniel Levinthal. 2003. "Temporarily Divide to Conquer: Centralized, Decentralized, and Reintegrated Organizational Approaches to Exploration and Adaptation." *Organization Science*, 14: 650–69.

Simmel, Georg. 1950. *The Sociology of Georg Simmel* (Glencoe, IL: Free Press).

Simon, Herbert. 1965. *Administrative Behavior* (New York: Free Press).

Sine, Wesley D., Hitoshi Mitsuhashi, and David A. Kirsch. 2006. "Revisiting Burns and Stalker: Formal Structure and New Venture Performance in Emerging Economic Sectors." *Academy of Management Journal*, 49: 121–32.

Singh, Jasjit, and Matt Marx. 2013. "Geographic Constraints on Knowledge Spillovers: Political Borders vs. Spatial Proximity." *Management Science*, 59: 2056–78.

Smith, Wendy K., and Marya L. Besharov. 2019. "Bowing before Dual Gods: How Structured Flexibility Sustains Organizational Hybridity." *Administrative Science Quarterly*, 64: 1–44.

Smith, Wendy K., Michael Gonin, and Marya L. Besharov. 2013. "Managing Social-Business Tensions: A Review and Research Agenda for Social Enterprise." *Business Ethics Quarterly* 23: 407–42.

Soda, Giuseppe, Marco Tortoriello, and Alessandro Iorio. 2018. "Harvesting Value from Brokerage: Individual Strategic Orientation, Structural Holes, and Performance." *Academy of Management Journal*, 61: 896–918.

Soderstrom, Sara, and Klaus Weber. 2020. "Organizational Structure from Interaction: Evidence from Organizational Sustainability Efforts." *Administrative Science Quarterly*, 65: 226–71.

Sorensen, Jesper B., and Toby E. Stuart. 2000. "Aging, Obsolescence and Organizational Innovation." *Administrative Science Quarterly*, 45: 81–112.

Sorenson, Olav. 2005. "Social Networks and the Persistence of Clusters: Evidence from the Computer Workstation Industry." In *Clusters, Networks and Innovation*, ed. S. Breschi and F. Malerba (New York: Oxford University Press).

Sorenson, Olav, and Michelle Rogan. 2014. "(When) Do Organizations Have Social Capital?." *Annual Review of Sociology*, 40: 261–80.

Sosa, Manuel E. 2011. "Where Do Creative Interactions Come from? The Role of Tie Content and Social Networks." *Organization Science* 22: 1–21.

Sosa, Manuel E., Martin Gargiulo, and Craig Rowles. 2015. "Can Informal Communication Networks Disrupt Coordination in New Product Development Projects?" *Organization Science* 26: 1059–78.

Stam, Wouter, Souren Arzlanian, and Tom Elfring. 2014. "Social capital of entrepreneurs and small firm performance: A meta-analysis of contextual and methodological moderators." *Journal of Business Venturing* 29: 152–73.

Stern, Ithai, and James D. Westphal. 2010. "Stealthy Footsteps to the Boardroom: Executives" Backgrounds, Sophisticated Interpersonal Influence Behavior, and Board Appointments." *Administrative Science Quarterly*, 55: 278–319.

Stettner, Uriel, and Dovev Lavie. 2014. "Ambidexterity under scrutiny: Exploration and exploitation via internal organization, alliances, and acquisitions." *Strategic Management Journal*, 35: 1903–29.

Stinchcombe, Arthur L. 1965. "Social Structure and Organizations." In *Handbook of Organizations*, eds. James G. March (Chicago: Rand McNally).

Stuart, Toby E., Ha Hoang, and Ralph C. Hybels. 1999. "Interorganizational Endorsements and the Performance of Entrepreneurial Ventures." *Administrative Science Quarterly*, 44: 315–49.

Stuart, Toby E., and Olav Sorenson. 2007. "Strategic Networks and Entrepreneurial Ventures." *Strategic Entrepreneurship Journal*, 1: 211–27.

Su, Jessica, Krishna Kamath, Johan Ugander, and Sharad Goel. 2019. "An Experimental Study of Structural Diversity in Social Networks." *In Proceedings of the 14th International AAAI Conference on Web and Social Media*. Burnaby, BC: PKP Publishing Services.

Sutton, Robert I. 2012. *Good Boss, Bad Boss: How to Be the Best . . . and Learn from the Worst* (New York: Business Plus).

Sytch, Maxim, and A. Tatarynowicz. 2014. "Friends and Foes: The Dynamics of Dual Social Structures." *Academy of Management Journal*, 57: 585–613.

Sytch, Maxim, Franz Wohlgezogen, and E. J. Zajac. 2018. "Collaborative by Design? How Matrix Organizations See/Do Alliances." *Organization Science*, 29: 1130–48.

Szulanski, Gabriel. 1996. "Exploring Internal Stickiness: Impediments to the Transfer of Best Practice within the Firm." *Strategic Management Journal*, 17: 27–43.

Tang, Yi, Cuili Qian, Guoli Chen, and Rui Shen. 2015. "How CEO Hubris Affects Corporate Social (Ir)Responsibility." *Strategic Management Journal*, 36: 1338–57.

Tatarynowicz, Adam. 2008. *On Firms in Networks: Strategies for Emergence, Evolution and Embeddedness* (na).

Teodoridis, Florenta, Michaël Bikard, and Keyvan Vakili. 2019. "Creativity at the Knowledge Frontier: The Impact of Specialization in Fast- and Slow-paced Domains." *Administrative Science Quarterly*, 64: 894–927.

Ter Wal, Anne L. J., Oliver Alexy, Jörn Block, and Philipp G. Sandner. 2016. "The Best of Both Worlds: The Benefits of Open-Specialized and Closed-Diverse Syndication Networks for New Ventures' Success." *Administrative Science Quarterly*, 61: 393–432.

Toh, Puay Khoon, and Francisco Polidoro. 2013. "A Competition-Based Explanation of Collaborative Invention Within the Firm." *Strategic Management Journal*, 34: 1186–208.

Tomaskovic-Devey, Donald, and Dustin Avent-Holt. 2019. *Relational Inequalities: An Organizational Approach* (Oxford, UK: Oxford University Press).

Treem, Jeffrey W., and Paul M. Leonardi. 2013. "Social Media Use in Organizations: Exploring the Affordances of Visibility, Editability, Persistence, and Association." *Annals of the International Communication Association*, 36: 143–89.

Tsai, Wenpin. 2001. "Knowledge Transfer in Intraorganizational Networks: Effects of Network Position and Absorptive Capacity on Business Unit Innovation and Performance." *Academy of Management Journal*, 44: 996–1004.

———. 2002. "Social Structure of "Coopetition" Within a Multiunit Organization: Coordination, Competition, and Intraorganizational Knowledge Sharing." *Organization Science*, 13: 179–90.

Tsai, Wenpin, and Sumantra Ghoshal. 1998. "Social Capital and Value Creation: The Role of Intrafirm Networks." *Academy of Management Journal*, 41: 464–76.

Tsui, Anne S., Terri D. Egan, and Charles A. O'Reilly III. 1992. "Being Different: Relational Demography and Organizational Attachment." *Administrative Science Quarterly*, 37: 549–79.

Tushman, M. L., and Thomas J. Scanlan. 1981. "Boundary Spanning Individuals: Their Role in Information Transfer and Their Antecedents." *Academy of Management Journal* 24: 289–305.

Tushman, Michael. 1977. "Special Boundary Roles in the Innovation Process." *Administrative Science Quarterly* 22: 587–605.

Tushman, Michael, and R. Katz. 1980. "External Communication and Project Performance: An Investigation into the Role of Gatekeepers." *Management Science* 26: 1071–85.

Tushman, Michael, Karim Lakhani, and Hila Lifshitz-Assaf. 2012. "Open Innovation and Organization Design." *Journal of Organization Design*. https://ssrn.com/abstract=2181927.

Tushman, Michael, and Charles A. O'Reilly III. 1996. "Ambidextrous Organizations: Managing Evolutionary and Revolutionary Change." *California Management Review*, 38: 8–30.

Uzzi, Brian. 1996. "The Sources and Consequences of Embeddedness for the Economic Performance of Organizations: The Network Effect." *American Sociological Review*, 61: 674–98.

———. 1999. "Embeddedness in the Making of Financial Capital: How Social Relations and Networks Benefit Firms Seeking Financing." *American Sociological Review*, 64: 481–505.

Uzzi, Brian, and Shannon Dunlap. 2006. "How to Build Your Network." *Harvard Business Review*, 83: 53–60, 151.

Uzzi, Brian, and Ryon Lancaster. 2003. "Relational Embeddedness and Learning: The Case of Bank Loan Managers and Their Clients." *Management Science*, 49: 383–99.

Uzzi, Brian, and Jarrett Spiro. 2005. "Collaboration and Creativity: The Small World Problem." *American Journal of Sociology*, 111: 447–504.

Vaara, Eero, Scott Sonenshein, and David Boje. 2016. "Narratives as Sources of Stability and Change in Organizations: Approaches and Directions For Future Research." *Academy of Management Annals*, 10: 495–560.

Vaisey, Stephen, and Omar Lizardo. 2010. "Can cultural worldviews influence network composition?" *Social Forces*, 88: 1595–618.

Van Zandt, Timothy. 2004. "Information Overload in a Network of Targeted Communication." *RAND Journal of Economics*, 35: 542–60.

Vasudeva, Gurneeta, Akbar Zaheer, and Exequiel Hernandez. 2013. "The Embeddedness of Networks: Institutions, Structural Holes, and Innovativeness in the Fuel Cell Industry." *Organization Science* 24: 645–63.

Vissa, Balagopal. 2011. "A Matching Theory of Entrepreneurs' Tie Formation Intentions and Initiation of Economic Exchange." *Academy of Management Journal*, 54: 137–58.

———. 2012. "Agency in Action: Entrepreneurs' Networking Style and Initiation of Economic Exchange." *Organization Science* 23: 492–510.

Vroom, Govert, and Javier Gimeno. 2007. "Ownership Form, Managerial Incentives, and the Intensity of Rivalry." *Academy of Management Journal*, 50: 901–22.

Watts, Duncan, and Steven Strogatz. 1998. "Collective Dynamics of 'Small World' Networks." *Nature*, 393: 440–42.

Weber, Libby, and Margarethe Wiersema. 2017. "Dismissing a Tarnished CEO? Psychological Mechanisms and Unconscious Biases in the Board's Evaluation." *California Management Review*, 59: 22–41.

Westphal, James D., and Ithai Stern. 2007. "Flattery Will Get You Everywhere (Especially If You Are a Male Caucasian): How Ingratiation, Boardroom Behavior, and Demographic Minority Status Affect Additional Board Appointments at U.S. Companies." *Academy of Management Journal*, 50: 267–88.

Westphal, James D., and Edward J. Zajac. 1994. "Substance and symbolism in CEO's long-term incentive plans." *Administrative Science Quarterly*, 39: 367–90.

———. 1997. "Defections from the Inner Circle: Social Exchange, Reciprocity, and the Diffusion of Board Independence in U.S. Corporations." *Administrative Science Quarterly*, 42: 161–83.

Williamson, Oliver. 1983. "Credible Commitments: Using Hostages to Support Exchange." *American Economic Review*, 73: 519–40.

———. 1996. *The Mechanisms of Governance* (New York: Free Press).

Williamson, Oliver E. 1975a. "The Economics of Governance: Framework and Implications." *Journal of Theoretical Economics*, 140: 195–223.

——. 1975b. *Markets and Hierarchies: Analysis and Antitrust Implications* (New York: Free Press).

——. 1991. "Comparative Economic Organization: The Analysis of Discrete Structural Alternatives." *Administrative Science Quarterly*, 36: 269–96.

Williamson, Oliver E., Sidney G. Winter, and R. H. Coase. 1991. *The Nature of the Firm: Origins, Evolution, and Development* (New York: Oxford University Press).

Xiao, Zhixing, and Anne S. Tsui. 2007. "When Brokers May Not Work: The Cultural Contingency of Social Capital in Chinese High-Tech Firms." *Administrative Science Quarterly*, 52: 1–31.

Yakubovich, Valery. 2005. "Weak Ties, Information, and Influence: How Workers Find Jobs in a Local Russian Labor Market." *American Sociological Review*, 70: 408–21.

——. 2013. "Getting a Job as a Favor in the Russian Post-Socialist Labor Market." *Asia Pacific Journal of Management*, 30: 351–72.

Yakubovich, Valery, and Ryan Burg. 2019. "Friendship by Assignment? From Formal Interdependence to Informal Relations in Organizations." *Human Relations*, 72: 1013–38.

Yakubovich, Valery, and Irina Kozina. 2000. "The Changing Significance of Ties: An Exploration of the Hiring Channels in the Russian Transitional Labor Market." *International Sociology*, 15: 479–500.

Yang, Longqi, David Holtz, and Sonia Jaffe, et al. 2022. "The effects of remote work on collaboration among information workers." *Nature Human Behaviour*, 6: 43–54.

Yenkey, Christopher B. 2018. "Fraud and Market Participation: Social Relations as a Moderator of Organizational Misconduct." *Administrative Science Quarterly*, 63: 43–84.

Yook, Soon-Hyung, Hawoong Jeong, and Albert-Laszlo Barabasi. 2002. "Modeling the Internet's large-scale topology." *Proceedings of the American Academy of Science*, 99: 13382–86.

Zaheer, Akbar, and Geoffrey G. Bell. 2005. "Benefiting from Network Position: Firm Capabilities, Structural Holes, and Performance." *Strategic Management Journal* 26: 809–25.

Zaheer, Akbar, and Giuseppe Soda. 2009. "Network Evolution: The Origins of Structural Holes." *Administrative Science Quarterly*, 54: 1–31.

Zammuto, Raymond F., Terri L. Griffith, Ann Majchrzak, Deborah J. Dougherty, and Samer Faraj. 2007. "Information Technology and the Changing Fabric of Organization." *Organization Science*, 18: 749–62.

Zhang, Victoria, and Marissa D. King. 2021. "Tie Decay and Dissolution: Contentious Prescribing Practices in the Prescription Drug Epidemic." *Organization Science*: 1–25.

Zhelyazkov, Pavel I., and Adam Tatarynowicz. 2021. "Marriage of Unequals? Investment Quality Heterogeneity, Market Heat, and the Formation of Status-Asymmetric Ties in the Venture Capital Industry." *Academy of Management Journal*, 64: 509–36.

Zollo, Maurizio, Jeffrey J. Reuer, and Harbir Singh. 2002. "Interorganizational Routines and Performance in Strategic Alliances." *Organization Science*, 13: 701–13.

Zott, Christoph. 2003. "Dynamic Capabilities and the Emergence of Intraindustry Differential Firm Performance: Insights from a Simulation Study." *Strategic Management Journal* 24: 97–125.

Zuboff, Shoshana. 2019. *The Age of Surveillance Capitalism: The Fight for a Human Future at the New Frontier of Power* (Hoboken, NJ: Wiley).

Zuzul, Tiona, Emily Pahnke, Jonathan Larson, et al. 2021. "Dynamic Silos: Modularity in Intra-Organizational Communication Networks Before and During the Covid-19 Pandemic." *Working Paper.*

Lightning Source UK Ltd.
Milton Keynes UK
UKHW010023040223
416451UK00003B/71